PAUL CLAUDEL'S

Le Soulier de satin:

A STYLISTIC,

STRUCTURALIST,

AND PSYCHOANALYTIC

INTERPRETATION

JOAN S. FREILICH   Paul Claudel's
Le Soulier de satin

A stylistic,
structuralist,
and psychoanalytic
interpretation

UNIVERSITY

OF TORONTO

PRESS

© University of Toronto Press 1973
Toronto and Buffalo
Printed in Canada
ISBN 0-8020-5279-7
LC 72-75739

University of Toronto Romance Series 23

TO SANDY

Contents

Tables and charts

Acknowledgments

I should like to express my gratitude to Professor Michael Riffaterre of Columbia University for his inspiration and support in the preparation of this study, and to Professor Leon S. Roudiez of Columbia University for his helpful suggestions. I also wish to thank Professor Norman N. Holland of the State University of New York at Buffalo, to whose work I am deeply indebted, and the late Dr Gustav Bychowski, Clinical Professor of Psychiatry at Downstate Medical Center, who read parts of the manuscript critically.

Éditions Gallimard has kindly granted permission to reprint passages from Claudel's *Théâtre, Œuvre poétique, Œuvres en prose,* and *Mémoires improvisés.* Permission to reprint a portion of Chapter 7 has been granted by *Claudel Studies,* where this material first appeared.

This book has been published with the help of a grant from the Humanities Research Council of Canada, using funds provided by the Canada Council, and with the help of the Publications Fund of the University of Toronto Press.   JSF

Introduction

New methods developed over the past two decades in three fields of literary analysis – stylistics, structuralism, and psychoanalytic interpretation – are based on an examination of the text from the reader's point of view, a radical break with conventional literary study, which focuses on the relationship of the text to other works written by the same or different authors, to the author's life and historical setting, or to various linguistic norms.

Recent stylistic studies have as their point of departure the reader's perception of certain elements of style as unpredictable, and thus 'marked,' in an otherwise unmarked context; such studies seek to determine which of these 'stylistic devices' are present within a given text and what their effect is on the reader's response to the work.[1]

Structuralist analyses involve the identification and description of the basic system of concepts around which the literary text is constructed. This fundamental system, or structure, is the source of the reader's sense that the text is a coherent whole, but it is itself an abstraction and can be perceived only through one or more of the variants through which it is actualized in the text.[2]

Finally, the psychoanalytic interpretation of a literary work attempts to elucidate the most fundamental affective concepts conveyed through the text, concepts which evoke corresponding emotional responses in the reader and which, although often unrecognized, are thus responsible for much of his interest in, and appreciation of, the work.[3]

Stylistic and structuralist methods have been used together in recent years, but this study of the *Soulier de satin* represents the first time that psychoanalytic interpretation has been included as part of a stylistic and structuralist analysis in which the focus throughout is on the relationship of the text to the reader and the point of departure is the reader's response to the work.[4]

Because the text is thus viewed in the same way in each case, these three approaches complement each other, and the insights gained from each method of analysis add to and enhance those obtained from the others. The convergence of stylistic devices, for example – the accumulation of several individual devices at a given point – functions both as a means of confirming the presence of stylistically effective elements in the text, and as an indication that an element of the basic structure is being expressed at this point. When this structure is itself described in psychoanalytic terms, the ideas involved are related in the form in which they have the greatest impact on the reader. Conversely, the stylistic and structuralist analyses add to the psychoanalytic interpretation because they make clear the specific ways in which the most fundamental emotional concepts expressed in the play and described here in psychoanalytic terms are repeatedly actualized in the text, and suggest how the linguistic and structural characteristics of these actualizations influence the reader's perception of this affective message.

Stylistic, structuralist, and psychoanalytic interpretations supplement each other especially well in an examination of imagery, because the co-action of form and content is clearly seen in the images of a work and because figurative expressions suggest several different ideas to the reader simultaneously and thus play a key role in enabling a single text to convey to the reader several different levels of meaning, including an affective message perceived for the most part only unconsciously.

A need has long existed for an intensive study of the *Soulier de satin*, for although it is widely recognized as Paul Claudel's most important work the play has often confused and puzzled readers at the same time as it has impressed them with its overall significance and poetic beauty.[5] Imagery was selected as the focal point of this study for the reasons noted above. In addition, previous considerations of Claudel's imagery concentrate on the relationship of this imagery to the author's philosophical and religious ideas.[6] The stylistic characteristics of Claudel's images have not yet been closely examined, nor have the specific ways in which these images convey different levels of meaning to the reader been sufficiently explored.

In Part I of this book, the imagery of the *Soulier de satin* is examined stylistically. In Chapter 1, the different stylistic factors that determine the effect of each image on the reader's apprehension of the text are reviewed; in Chapter 2, the various ways in which individual images are combined into long developments and the influence of these patterns of development on the reader's response to the text are studied. Other stylistic devices that contribute to the effectiveness of the images are examined in Chapter 3.

These first three chapters are organized around stylistic concepts; the resulting presentation does not directly reflect the frequency or pattern of occurrence in the *Soulier de satin* of the factors discussed. This method of organization was chosen because this is the first extensive analysis of the stylistic characteristics of imagery, and it therefore seemed preferable to explain the stylistic concepts involved in a systematic manner. Counts of the frequency of occurrence in the play of the factors examined are included in each chapter, however, and these will help to show the relative importance of the devices within the play. Patterns of occurrence of different types of images are explored in Parts II and III, and additional frequency counts are included there.

In Part II, three levels of meaning conveyed by the text are considered, and the role of imagery in expressing each level is examined – the narrative level or story line; the religious level, which deals with the theological significance of the situations depicted on the narrative level; and the emotional level, the most fundamental affective concepts conveyed by the text, discussed in psychoanalytic terms. The author's interventions in the text, which both suggest additional ideas to the reader and influence his response to the narrative, religious, and emotional levels, are also considered here.

In Part III, the emotional-level message is shown to be the basic system of concepts, or structure, around which the play as a whole is constructed, and the ways in which this structure is repeatedly actualized both synchronously and diachronically as the work continues are explored.

A glossary of stylistic and structuralist terms of importance in this study is included at the end of the book, as an aid to readers who may not be familiar with these types of literary analysis.

The passages cited in illustration throughout this book were selected as examples because in them the device or theme being examined is readily discernible and is responsible to a significant and evident degree for the effect of the image or images involved on the reader's response. In most cases there were many passages that fulfilled these criteria; the versets cited were then chosen at random from among them. One example was considered sufficient to illustrate each point discussed.

This book is limited as far as possible to an examination of the text of the *Soulier de satin* and of the response to it of a cultivated reader who may not be familiar with Paul Claudel's life or his other works. In order to isolate more accurately those factors in the text that determine the response of such a reader, material from other of Claudel's works or from the works of other authors or critics is not included unless it seems essential to the understanding of the study. References are made in the notes, however, to critical and literary works that may be of interest to those who wish to explore further some of the points raised.

The many actualizations of the emotional-level message, or structure, in the text of the *Soulier de satin* work together like the melodies of a musical counterpoint, appearing simultaneously and in alternation, each of interest in itself, and each – despite variations in texture and rhythm and the occasional introduction of a dissonant phrase – clearly subordinated to a single harmonic scheme. Like the listener who appreciates the beauty of a musical work but does not seek to identify the individual notes that are played and to understand how they produce the complex sounds he hears, the reader of the *Soulier de satin* who enjoys the poetic beauty of the play rarely attempts to isolate the elements of the text that evoke in him a many-sided response – at once aesthetic, intellectual, imaginative, spiritual, and emotional. The goal of this study of the *Soulier de satin* is to identify the specific linguistic elements that elicit such a manifold response in the reader and to show how these elements are combined in such a way as to create this complex impression in his mind.

PART ONE

STYLISTIC ANALYSIS

OF IMAGERY

1 Stylistic characteristics of images

All images involve two elements – the tenor, or the principal concept being expressed, and the vehicle, the terms through which it is conveyed to the reader and with which it is thereby identified.[1] The vehicle of the image presents the tenor in a concrete form; that is, in a form that can be perceived by the reader through one or more of his senses and which, when named, elicits specific sense impressions in his mind.[2] When the Guardian Angel, for example, refers to the American continents as. (III viii 257; 825)

> *Cette double bourse* de l'Amérique ... *cette double mamelle* ...

both vehicles evoke for the reader precise visual representations.[3] Because images elicit such definite sense impressions, their immediate impact tends to be strong and vivid.

Although the reader's response to an image is thus triggered by the concrete aspects of its vehicle, the meaning of the image as a whole is not the literal significance of the vehicle, but derives from the connection between tenor and vehicle. As a result, I.A. Richards notes, most images convey to the reader a whole complex of ideas:

> In the simplest formulation, when we use a metaphor we have two thoughts of different things active together and supported by a single word, or phrase, whose meaning is a resultant of their interaction ... Vehicle and tenor in cooperation give a meaning of more varied powers than can be ascribed to either.[4]

In the Angel's description of the Americas, the general shape of the 'double' objects named recalls the physical contours of the two joined American continents. The particular objects cited indicate that the newly discovered lands contain great wealth and are highly productive. In addition, the term *bourse* brings to mind the coveting of material goods; coming after *bourse*, *mamelle* evokes specifically an animal-like craving for physical comfort. Together these vehicles indicate that the interest of

Europeans in the Americas is based in great part on an inordinate desire for material gratification. This thought in itself then elicits an affective response on the part of the reader – a feeling of scorn for the greedy Europeans.

Some mental activity is required of the reader in order to comprehend the meaning of any image. In understanding poetic images, the reader is compelled to bring his imagination and emotions actively into play in making the connection between tenor and vehicle:

> Let us consider more closely what happens in the mind when we put together – in a sudden and striking fashion – two things belonging to very different orders of experience. The most important happenings ... are the mind's efforts to connect them ... In all interpretation we are filling in connections, and for poetry, of course, our freedom to fill in – the absence of explicitly stated intermediate steps – is a main source of its powers.[5]

In general, then, the greater the mental effort required of the reader in understanding an image, the more deeply involved he becomes with the text, and the greater the potential intellectual and affective impact of the image on him.[6]

The degree and kind of mental activity demanded of the reader in understanding a particular image and the specific impression that the image makes on his mind as a result are determined by several factors; notably, the relationship between tenor and vehicle, the nature of the vehicle itself, the ideas and feelings that the reader associates with the vehicle because of its previous use, and the context in which the vehicle is found.

RELATIONSHIP BETWEEN TENOR AND VEHICLE

The nature of the semantic connection between tenor and vehicle is one aspect of their relationship that has an effect on the reader's response. On the basis of this connection, images may be divided into the categories of metaphor, simile, metonymy, and concretization of an abstract concept.[7]

In both metaphors and similes, the tenor and vehicle are related through their semantic similarity. In the metaphor, the relationship between tenor and vehicle, often called the 'ground' of the image, is only implied: the vehicle takes the place of the literal expression of the tenor in the text, and this substitution

TABLE 1
Frequency count: stylistic characteristics of images

		Image elements
Categories of images, based on tenor-vehicle relationships		
Metaphor		4080
Simile		306
Metonymy		756
Concretization		361
Total images in play		5503
Nature of vehicle		
Hyperbole		644
Periphrase		73
Absolute image		185
Illogical vehicle, total		278
Personification	212	
Other illogical vehicles	66	
Ideas and feelings associated with vehicle		
Archetype		572
Cliché		384
Renewed cliché, total		83
Cliché renewed by grammatical change	6	
Cliché renewed by added word(s)	42	
Cliché used first in conventional way, then renewed	29	
Cliché renewed by other means	6	
Relationship of vehicle to context		
More than one meaning possible in context, total		329
Both meanings are figurative	194	
One meaning is figurative, one literal	135	
Metalinguistic comment follows image, total		134
Metalinguistic comment includes image(s)	106	
Metalinguistic comment does not include image	28	
Humorous statement, total		558
Comic	158	
Ironic	400	
Humour and poetry closely related, total		231
Conventional poetic techniques used to create humour	87	
Humour and poetry alternate in passage	76	
Humour and poetry coexist in expression	68	

indicates to the reader that the two terms are semantically alike. In the simile or comparison, on the other hand, the connection between tenor and vehicle is directly stated.

Because the nature of the connection between tenor and vehicle is the same in both types of images, a single analogy can be expressed in either a metaphor or a simile. The Actress likens Rodrigue to music in a simile and then immediately repeats almost the same analogy in a metaphor: (IV v 58–9; 903)

> ... vous êtes *comme la musique* qui ne vous demande rien mais qui, d'emblée, vous enlève et vous met d'accord avec elle.
>
> Dès que vous êtes là, *il y a de la musique,* je me livre avec ardeur, confiance et mesure ...

Both of these images express the Actress's feeling of being drawn into an emotional and spiritual communion with Rodrigue. What discrepancies there are in the meanings conveyed by the two vehicles derive not from the expression of the ground in the first image and not in the second, but from the difference in the precise tenors of the two images, that of the first analogy being Rodrigue himself and that of the second the general atmosphere when Rodrigue is present – in the second image, Rodrigue's power over the Actress seems to come from outside of himself and therefore to be greater than suggested by the initial simile.[8]

In metonymic images, tenor and vehicle only partially overlap in meaning; their semantic relationship is one of contiguity rather than of similarity. In most of the metonymies found in the *Soulier de satin,* a part of an object or situation is used to represent the whole. The vehicle chosen is usually a concrete detail which makes a more specific, and therefore more vivid, impression on the reader's mind than would a more generalized description of the tenor.

In telling how the European religious wars have been halted, Musique explains: (III i 43–4; 786)

> Par la volonté de mon époux et par *sa puissante épée*
> l'avalanche de l'Europe qui s'effondre
> A été arrêtée à moitié route ...

The expression *sa puissante épée* is a common metonymic image, but its effectiveness is renewed here by the sylleptic construction in which it is found – after the repetition of *par*, the reader expects to find a statement that is semantically similar to the abstract concept that followed the first *par*; the designation of a concrete situation in *sa puissante épée* is therefore particularly striking for him. The terms of the vehicle themselves designate a familiar object that can be readily visualized by the reader. These factors make the image a vivid means of evoking the Viceroy's prowess in battle.

A metonymic image may also have a poetic effect, stimulating the reader to consider and elaborate the implications of the tenor-vehicle relationship in his mind. The King describes what an explorer sees when he arrives in China as: (I vi 26; 687)

> ... cet immense remuement de *soies* et de *palmes* et de *corps nus*,
> ...

The reader can easily visualize the three objects named and can thus picture in his mind the scene that greets the traveller. In addition, each of these objects is associated by Westerners with Oriental countries and peoples; the three images, taken together, thus suggest to the reader an entire, exotic civilization and lead him to develop in his imagination a general picture of this distant land and strange way of life.[9]

In the concretization of an abstract concept – referred to hereafter simply as 'concretization' – the vehicle designates a tangible form of the tenor. An abstract concept is concretized when it is expressed in substantive form in a context that ordinarily requires a concrete term.

An abstract quality, for example, may be used in place of the concrete noun it would be expected to modify. The Angel tells how Rodrigue's earthly mission, after bringing him to and then beyond the New World, will eventually lead him to God: (III viii 219; 823)

> A travers *le nouveau* il est en marche pour retrouver *l'éternel*.

Because the objects to which these adjectives refer are not named in the text, the qualities of 'newness' and 'everlastingness' are stressed. The effect is to underscore for the reader a paradoxical aspect of Rodrigue's mission – although the Western Hemisphere has just been discovered and therefore seems to Europeans to be the epitome of 'newness,' what Rodrigue will actually come to know through his adventures in the Americas is something that has existed from the beginning of time.

A second aspect of the tenor-vehicle relationship that has an effect on the reader's response to the image is the 'distance' between tenor and vehicle. In order for an expression to function as an image, the difference between the literal significance of the tenor and that of the vehicle, sometimes referred to as the breadth of the ground or the 'angle' of the image, must be great enough so that the implication that the two concepts share a common area of meaning is surprising for the reader.[10] In general, a greater distance between tenor and vehicle will compel the reader to use his imagination more actively in linking the two concepts, and will therefore result in a more highly poetic image than will a lesser one.

In metaphors and similes, the distance between tenor and vehicle is determined by the degree of similarity between the two concepts. In the *Soulier de satin*, for example, a number of the vehicles of metaphors and similes designate sounds; the tenor is in some cases concrete and in others abstract, and the distance between tenor and vehicle varies accordingly.

Referring to the final notes of a cicada's song, Honoria remarks to Pélage: (II iii 1; 734)

> ... Elle se tait avec *cette longue tenue d'archet* que vous avez remarquée, *diminuendo,*
>
> ...

Although both tenor and vehicle are musical sounds, the distance between them is great enough to make this analogy function as an image for the reader. The metaphor both continues the personification of the insect begun earlier in the verset – which itself underscores Honoria's empathy with the forces of nature that surround her – and also suggests to the reader specific qualities of the sound the cicada is making.

Musique compares an abstract concept to a musical sound when she says to the Viceroy: (II x 101; 765)

> C'est moi *au fond de ton cœur cette note unique, si pure, si touchante.*

The reader is compelled to use his imagination much more actively here than in Honoria's image in order to conceive the common area of meaning between *moi au fond de ton cœur*, or the impression Musique makes on the thoughts and feelings of the Viceroy, and the *note unique*. In so doing, he understands that Musique expresses in this image her ability to bring the Viceroy into contact with the all-embracing 'harmony' of the spiritual plane of life.

In metonymic images, because the relationship between tenor and vehicle is one of overlapping or contiguous meaning, the distance between the two concepts is proportional in reverse to the extent of the semantic overlap. As a rule, the overlap will be less, and the distance between tenor and vehicle greater, when the tenor is a broad, generalized idea or situation.

Musique asks Prouhèze, in speaking of Rodrigue: (I x 73; 710)

> ... *votre visage* lui est pour toujours interdit?

Musique's use of the term *visage* as a metonymic reference to Prouhèze's physical presence reflects her expectation that, when with his beloved, Rodrigue would tend to focus his attention on her face. Later in the play, Camille warns Rodrigue: (II xi 66; 770)

> Car il y a tout de même cette Amérique au fond de vous, plus ancienne que *ce visage de femme* qui vous travaille ...

In this case, *visage* expresses metonymically not only Rodrigue's recollection of Prouhèze's physical appearance, but also his memory of the mutual love and understanding they were able to communicate to each other through such facial expressions as looks and smiles.[11] Because the image thus evokes a whole complex of abstract ideas and feelings, the distance between tenor and vehicle is greater, and the effect more highly poetic than in the first metonymy.

The tenor-vehicle distance in a concretization corresponds to the difference in the degree of concreteness between the abstract tenor concept and the concrete form in which it is stated in the vehicle. In general, if the concreteness of two vehicles is the same, the more abstract the tenor concept, the greater the distance involved. The Angel says of Rodrigue's mission, in the verset discussed above: (III viii 219; 823)

> A travers *le nouveau* il est en marche pour retrouver *l'éternel.*

The two qualities are concretized to the same degree here; but the tenor-vehicle distance is smaller in the first image than in the second, because the idea of 'newness' is more closely tied in the reader's mind to concrete objects than is the concept of 'eternity,' which cannot be associated with any tangible aspect of reality.

In some images, the reader is aware that a specific kind of distance separates tenor and vehicle. In the hyperbole, for example – a device used very often in the *Soulier de satin* – the reader recognizes that the vehicle is a deliberate overstatement of the tenor.

Prouhèze exaggerates Camille's cruel and dangerous nature when she refers to her task of restricting his activities at Mogador as: (III xiii 38; 850–1)

> ... la contrainte et commandement pendant dix ans de *cette bête féroce.*

The effect of such an exaggeration is to emphasize the area of common meaning between tenor and vehicle, and in many cases, to make it appear greater in intensity or degree than it actually is.

The distance between tenor and vehicle is especially great in two types of images in which the tenor cannot immediately be identified – the periphrase and the 'absolute' image. From the reader's point of view, one of the two interacting concepts from which the meaning of the expression derives is missing in such images; the distance between tenor and vehicle is limited only by the context and the specific terms of the vehicle.

In a periphrase, the tenor is designated through a description of one of its qualities, functions, or actions. The vehicle acts as a puzzle for the reader, who must actively use his imagination in order to determine first its tenor, and then the meaning of the image.

The Jesuit uses two periphrases in his prayer for Rodrigue's spiritual salvation: (I i 34–6; 668–9)

> ... Liez-le par le poids de *cet autre être sans lui si beau qui l'appelle à travers l'intervalle*!
> Faites de lui un homme blessé parce qu'une fois en cette vie il a vu *la figure d'un ange*!
> Remplissez ces amants d'un tel désir ...

Because Prouhèze has not previously been mentioned in the play, the reader at first has no idea of whom the Jesuit is speaking. The unusual grammatical structure of the first periphrase leaves the semantic relationship between the phrases *sans lui* and *si beau* unclear and thus adds to his difficulty in understanding the image. The added clause, *qui l'appelle à travers l'intervalle*, does not clarify the identity of *cet autre être*, but serves rather to reinforce the idea of *sans lui*, and to suggest that this unknown person is already seeking union with Rodrigue. The reader's curiosity is aroused by this periphrase; in the next verset, however, instead of finding the expected identification of *cet autre être*, he encounters another periphrase – *la figure d'un ange* – which heightens the tension created in his mind by the first enigmatic image. This second periphrase suggests two aspects of the unknown person's relationship with Rodrigue. First, since the Jesuit is now praying, the term *ange* reinforces the reader's impression that this person will help Rodrigue to attain spiritual redemption. Second, because this phrase is also a cliché commonly used in referring to a loved one, it indicates that the individual who will act to save Rodrigue's soul will be a beloved woman. In the next verset, the Jesuit's direct reference to *ces amants* confirms this second idea. At the same time, this literal phrase heightens the tension in the reader's mind, because although it resolves the enigma it also underscores the difference between the tenor of the periphrases – a beloved woman – and the ideas of separation and of holiness evoked by the two vehicles.

The tenors of other images cannot be precisely identified by the reader at any point in the text. The vehicles of such images do not express specific elements of reality, but correspond rather to feelings or concepts that can be described directly only in very general terms. These images seem to exist as independent linguistic units in the text, and can therefore be termed 'absolute.'[12] The distance between the unspecified abstract tenor and the concrete vehicle of an absolute image is necessarily relatively great, and such images are therefore always poetically effective.

Saint Denys describes Musique as she prays in the Church of Saint Nicholas as: (III i 61; 787)

> ... ce petit être qui prie de tout son cœur, les mains jointes et *les pieds de* son esprit *déchaussés*.

Because the phrases *les mains jointes* and *les pieds déchaussés* are grammatically and, if taken literally, semantically parallel, the shift from a literal description of Musique's physical appearance in the first phrase to a metaphoric indication of her emotional attitude (implied by the phrase *de son esprit*) in the second is surprising for the reader, and the vehicle is especially striking for him as a result. He cannot, however, identify any specific element of reality as the tenor of the image.

When the reader considers the terms of the vehicle in context, he recalls that removing one's shoes upon entering another person's house is in some societies a symbol of honour for the host and his property, and that this action is still performed as an indication of respect and submission by worshippers entering a Mohammedan mosque. Musique's 'taking off the shoes of her mind' when in church then suggests her reverence for God and the great humility she experiences in coming before him. Furthermore, because going without shoes is as a rule something done only by simple people, this image also recalls Musique's generally simple, childlike frame of mind.[13]

NATURE OF THE VEHICLE

A second determinant of the effect of an image on the reader is the nature of the vehicle itself.

Vehicle phrases that are illogical are always surprising for the reader.[14] With the exception of personifying expressions, such images are relatively rare in the *Soulier de satin* and are therefore especially striking for the reader when they do appear. Most illogical images are highly poetic, because the use of semantically incompatible terms within a single phrase implies that these words express one tenor concept; the reader must discover this idea through his own imaginative efforts.

When he describes to his court the newly discovered Americas, the King refers to these continents as: (I vi 31; 687)

   ... *ce calice de silence* ...

In the religiously oriented context of the *Soulier de satin*, this vehicle first evokes the use of the chalice during the ceremony of the Mass to hold the 'blood of Christ' as the individual worshipper partakes of it in receiving Communion and thus becomes one with God.[15] The word *silence* then brings to mind the pristine tranquillity of the Americas, which remain undisturbed by the turmoil of modern society. When the reader relates these two concepts to each other, he infers that the communion with God evoked by the chalice is attained in the Americas with the help of the prevailing silence and calm, which allow the individual to meditate without distraction on his relationship to the spiritual world and thus enable him to move closer to the heavenly realm.[16]

The personification of inanimate objects, parts of nature, or abstract qualities and feelings is a specific type of illogical phrase frequently found in the *Soulier de satin*. Personifying statements often give a dramatic quality to the descriptions in which they are used.

The King attributes a voluntary action to a natural feature when he says of the sun's reflection on the sea: (I vi 32; 687)

> ... je vois *le soleil m'inviter d'un long tapis déroulé* à ces régions qui me sont éternellement disjointes,
>
> ...

Since the King has just referred to parts of the natural world as 'ces choses qui sont l'œuvre d'un Dieu excellent' (17; 687), this personification implies that in bidding him send his explorers to the New World, the sun is carrying out the will of God himself.[17] The image then evokes the sun gods worshipped by many peoples – both gods of the New World Aztecs and Incas, and those of such other cultures as the Egyptian and the Greek. These associations add to the drama of the King's description, and help to stress the importance of the message sent to him. The phrase *d'un long tapis déroulé* evokes a familiar, concrete gesture of welcome, and thus makes the entire image more vivid for the reader.[18]

ASSOCIATIONS OF VEHICLE

The ideas and feelings that the reader associates with an image as a result of previous use of the vehicle terms generally suggest additional levels of meaning for the expression.

A vehicle that designates an archetypal object or situation has the potential ability to evoke in the reader's mind the thoughts and emotions that have commonly been associated with this object or situation in the past.[19] Whether or not the vehicle will in fact activate these associations depends on the specific context in which it is used – if this context presents a situation in some way similar to that in which the term was previously connected with these thoughts and feelings, the image will evoke these associations in the reader's mind.

In describing the attitude that the future conqueror of the

Americas must have towards the New World, the King declares: (I vi 65; 689)

> D'un seul éclair il a su que c'est à lui, et cette sierra toute bleue il y a longtemps qu'elle se dressait *à l'horizon de son âme* ...

The term *horizon* is often used to express a goal that is not an end in itself, but opens up new possibilities for the future. In context, the phrase *horizon de son âme* implies that ruling the Americas must have long represented for the conqueror in question just such a key to his own development.[20] Used in this sense, the word *horizon* is generally associated with feelings of hopeful anticipation, and the King's image thus also suggests that the conqueror must have been eagerly looking forward to the attainment of this goal.

If an image vehicle is a cliché, the stereotyped, familiar nature of the phrase can help to add new dimensions of meaning to the image in two ways. First, many clichés are used primarily in a specific social or literary context; such phrases will recall this original context wherever they are found. Second, as a cliché is used repeatedly over a period of time, it often acquires subtle, complex nuances of meaning, in addition to its most obvious significance. Because the image is commonly used, these nuances of meaning are familiar to the reader, and are immediately evoked in his mind by the vehicle.

When Prouhèze sees Rodrigue for the first time in ten years, she accuses him of having lost touch with her during their long separation: (III xiii 52–3; 851)

> ... si votre âme ... *n'avait pas bu aux eaux de l'Oubli,* Que de choses elle eût pu vous raconter!

Like most mythological citations, the cliché *boire aux eaux de l'Oubli* – a reference to the underworld river of Lethe, whose waters were reputed to cause loss of memory – is generally used only in noble or literary contexts. Because these *eaux* are associated with powerful spiritual forces, the phrase functions as a hyperbolic expression of forgetting.

By using this well-known hyperbole here, Prouhèze emphasizes the scope of Rodrigue's crime in her eyes, indicating that he had lost all spiritual and emotional, as well as physical, contact with her. At the same time, her use of a fixed, lofty expression suggests that she wishes to emphasize that the anxiety and resentment his 'forgetting' have caused her are not so great that they seriously trouble her refined, aristocratic bearing – for so long as she maintains this bearing, her own unhappiness will seem less overwhelming to her and she can feel that she is saving face in front of Rodrigue, despite his apparent rejection of her.

As clichés are repeatedly used, the reader ceases to be surprised by them when he encounters them in a text. In addition, he no longer needs to respond actively in order to understand their significance, but can accept as their meaning the stereotyped significance usually assigned to them. When a cliché thus fails to attract the reader's attention and to stimulate his imagination, an author may restore its original effectiveness by using the phrase in an unconventional way.

The expression of a cliché in an unusual manner automatically calls to mind the original phrase, and the contrast between the new use of the image and the original is striking for the reader. In addition, the reader is prompted to relate the meaning of the renewed cliché to the original significance of the expression; this comparison generally suggests additional levels of meaning for the new form of the image.

The Angel refers to the boundary that the Atlantic Ocean represented for the peoples of Western Europe before Columbus's voyage as: (III viii 214–5; 823)

> ... cet horizon mystique si longtemps
> Qui fut celui de *la vieille humanité* ...

The Angel's words may be interpreted as meaning that before Columbus's time Europeans' ideas were radically different from what they are at present; but the image also recalls the cliché *le vieil homme,* and its original use by Saint Paul in a reference to the spiritual status of the individual: 'Si toutes fois vous l'avez écouté, et si vous avez appris de lui [Jésus] ... / A dépouiller le vieil homme ...' (Eph. 4:21–2).[21] When the reader considers the meaning of the image as used by the Angel in relation to the statement by Saint Paul, the renewed cliché implies that the Europeans were 'old' in a religious sense as well, limiting themselves to conventional, and often erroneous, theological responses, and not opening themselves to the type of spiritual rejuvenation that would have helped them move within reach of a state of Grace.

Clichés are renewed in several different ways in the *Soulier de satin*. In the above example, the Angel changes the grammatical structure of the vehicle, making the singular noun into a collective term. In other cases, new words are added to the original expression. The Captain says of Camille: (III xii 2; 847)

> ... Il serait dommage qu'il finisse sa carrière autrement qu'*au bout d'une corde chrétienne*.

The idea expressed in *au bout d'une corde* – that of brutally ending the earthly life of a man – contrasts ironically with the concept suggested by *chrétienne* – compassionately saving his soul through religion. The disparity in tone between the popular, familiar cliché and the religious term *chrétienne* underscores this conflict in meaning. In addition, the alliteration of the /k/ sound in *corde* and *chrétienne* focuses the reader's attention on these two words in particular. This leads the reader to consider the term *corde* out of the context of the cliché and thus literally, and results in a second semantic contrast, this time between the literal, commonplace meaning of *corde* and the spiritual significance of *chrétienne*. These ironic elements make the image a particularly effective expression both of the Captain's thought and of his mocking attitude towards Camille.[22]

When a cliché is first used in a stereotyped manner and is then renewed, the contrast is even more striking for the reader. After Prouhèze has refused to leave Mogador with Rodrigue, Camille warns:

> Cela me chatouille ...
> Quand je pense que vous êtes *dans le creux de ma main*.

But Prouhèze replies that she has voluntarily accepted her mission at Mogador: (III xi 11; 758–9)

> *M'y suis-je pas mise moi-même?* ...

Camille's use of the original cliché fixes its stereotyped form more firmly in the reader's mind. Prouhèze's development of the same vehicle terms then unexpectedly breaks this reinforced pattern and is therefore particularly attention-getting. The alliteration of the /m/ sound and the grammatical error (omission of *ne*) help further to emphasize her point. At the same time, by answering Camille's taunt in his own terms, she indicates that she still refuses to submit to his domination.

CONTEXT

Still another determinant of the effect of an image on the reader's response is the context in which the expression is found.

Most words have several different potential meanings, both literal and figurative, but when they are spoken or written the context in which they are used imposes a specific interpretation on them. In some cases however – especially in poetic texts – the context allows the reader to assign simultaneously more than one meaning to a term.

If a word expresses figuratively two or more ideas, the image has more than one tenor and the reader must therefore consider simultaneously more than one tenor-vehicle relationship. This heightens his imaginative response to the image and thus increases its overall effectiveness.

The King refers to the path taken by ships between Spain and the American colonies as: (I vi 41; 688)

> ... *la large route d'or* qui relie l'une et l'autre Castille
> ...

The term *or* expresses two ideas in context. First, since the King has just said of America: 'C'est d'elle maintenant que mon Échiquier tire l'or vital qui anime ici toute la machine de l'État' (v. 39), this word evokes the gold and, metonymically, all the other raw materials sent to Spain by her explorers in the New World. Second, when the King spoke earlier of the sun's inviting him to the New World 'd'un long tapis déroulé'(32; 687), his words implied that by spreading this welcoming *tapis* the sun was carrying out the will of God himself;[23] in the above verset, the phrase *route d'or* recalls the earlier *tapis* and therefore also brings to mind the reflection of the sun on the water as it declines to the West, extending God's invitation to the Spaniards to follow.

As in other multiple-meaning images, because these two concepts are designated by a single term the reader considers them in relation to each other. In this case, the image suggests that the mineral wealth of the Americas is created by the same God who forms the tempting *route*. This interpretation is confirmed two versets later, when the King says that his boats '[lui] rapportent ces trésors païens enfantés par le soleil' (43; 688).

If only one of the meanings of a multiple-meaning image is figurative, the reader must also consider at least two areas of significance simultaneously, but in this case he has to use his imagination in understanding only one of these areas. The Jesuit says of his situation as he drifts on the sea: (I i 19; 667)

> ... et maintenant ... je puis me confier à *ces liens qui m'attachent*.

Because the Jesuit has just compared the mast of his boat to a Cross (v. 5), the term *liens* can be understood here both literally, as the ropes that tie him to the mast, and figuratively, as his bonds to God. The added *qui m'attachent* can similarly be taken in two ways – as a redundant, literal expression of the Jesuit's ties to the mast, or in the sense of 'showing fondness or affection,' a meaning which underscores the figurative significance of *liens*. Because one meaning of this statement refers to a concrete situation and the other to a spiritual state, the reader connects the two by assigning the spiritual significance to the earthly situation. He then understands that in submitting passively to his death on the mast of the ship, the Jesuit willingly puts himself completely under God's power.

In a metalinguistic development, the passage in which the image is found contains a direct comment on the vehicle. This remark may serve to clarify the meaning of the image. When the Cavaliers speak of their voyage to America, one says: (II i 46; 729)

> Il y a des gens à qui nous allons *porter la croix* de toutes les façons.

A second adds: (II i 47–8; 729)

> Ne l'avons-nous pas sur notre dos nous-mêmes ...
> Solidement fixée avec une sangle de cuir parmi le reste du fourniment?

The phrase *de toutes les façons* is metalinguistic in itself and suggests that the Cavaliers will use all possible means of converting the American natives to Christianity – brute force as well as less harsh forms of persuasion. The Second Cavalier's statement then implies that these men do not think of themselves as bringing their religion to the Americas only in the sense that they are Christians themselves and are in the service of a Christian King, but that each regards himself as a personal representative of Christ.

If an image is poetically evocative, the presence of a metalinguistic comment might be expected to reduce its suggestive power by limiting the extent to which the reader must actively use his own mind in understanding its meaning. In the *Soulier de satin*, however, when a poetic vehicle is followed by a metalinguistic development, the comment on the image itself usually contains one or more images which serve as additional springboards for the reader's imagination.

In describing her feelings as she swims towards the fleet of Juan of Austria, Sept-Épées explains: (IV x 63; 938)

> On avance *comme les anémones de mer, en respirant, par le seul épanouissement de son corps et la secousse de sa volonté.*

The two concretizations that follow Sept-Épées's comparison of her progress through the water to the way the sea anemone moves from place to place ostensibly explain this analogy – just as the anemone changes its location by inflating its body with water and shaking itself loose from the object to which it has been attached, so Sept-Épées advances by 'expanding her body' and 'shaking her will.' These two phrases, however, are absolute images, and the reader must actively use his imagination in order to grasp their meaning in context. Since Sept-Épées has just spoken of the water turning herself and la Bouchère into 'des êtres divins ... des corps glorieux' (v. 61), the phrase *épanouissement de son corps* first suggests the expansion of her human self beyond her usual earthly state, into a heavenly sphere of existence. *La secousse de sa volonté* then indicates that she herself provides the impulse for this movement, through her own freely made and strongly desired choice.

The context also plays a key role in determining the reader's response to humorous images, because humour is encoded in the text by the contrast of a term with its immediate context on one or more linguistic levels.[24]

When Rodrigue tells the ship's Captain that just hearing the name of Camille when he was near death was enough to revive him, the Captain replies: (ii viii 20; 755)

> Je vous comprends! Le nom de son rival, cela *vaut mieux qu'un moxa sur la plante des pieds.*

The contrast between the feelings of encouragement and inspiration evoked by Rodrigue's words and the crude form of physical stimulation cited by the Captain makes this statement humorous for the reader. In context, this comic remark underscores one factor heightening Rodrigue's suffering during the years he remains apart from Prouhèze – the lack of understanding by those among whom he lives.

Irony, a specific form of humour found extensively in the *Soulier de satin,* differs from other types of comedy in that it evokes in the reader's mind two distinct thoughts, which in many cases are in direct opposition with each other.[25] One of the King's Courtiers tells the men discussing the defeat of the Armada: (iv ix 19; 924)

> Tout cela est allé par le fond, *de profundis ...*

The words *de profundis* attract the reader's attention initially because as Latin terms they are printed in italics in the text. This phrase recalls the Catholic Service for the Dead, in which these words, the first of Psalm 124, are used to express metaphorically a state of deep despair; in the general context of the Courtier's speech the phrase suggests the grief of all who are present over the destruction of the Spanish fleet. In their immediate context, however, these words seem to refer to the 'death' of the boats rather than to that of the men, and this idea contrasts ironically with the religious meaning of the expression. At the same time, the preceding phrase, *par le fond*, recalls for the reader the literal meaning of the Latin terms, and the fact that the boats are, indeed, now located in 'the depths.' The contrast of the figurative meaning of the phrase with its literal significance in this passage is a second source of irony.

As a rule, humour reflects a mocking intent on the part of speaker or author – an intent that in the *Soulier de satin* may be directed at the subject being discussed, the person to whom the remarks are made, the speaker and his own situation, the author, or the reader himself.[26] Humour thus adds to the meaning of an image by suggesting to the reader the derisive feelings of the speaker, the author, or both. In the above description of the defeat of the Armada, because the Courtier is not intentionally being ironic, the reader understands that the author himself is ridiculing this character. More often, the character who is speaking is deliberately mocking a person, a situation, or an idea, and he thus reveals his own feelings.

In a discussion of religious concepts in which Prouhèze consistently expresses a reverent attitude towards God, Camille refers to the Supreme Being as: (III x 138; 839)

... *Le Vieillard dangereux* que nous racontent les prêtres ...

These words recall the way God is most often pictured – as an aged man with a long white beard who sits in judgment of mankind. The term *Vieillard*, however, has pejorative implications and indicates that this man is senile; the adjective *dangereux* underscores this impression by suggesting that his judgments and the punishments he subsequently meets out are erratic and uncontrollable. The implication that God is like an old man because he is mentally and physically enfeebled contrasts ironically with the commonly held belief that this resemblance is based on the Supreme Being's infinite wisdom and eternal life. The capitalization of *Vieillard* increases the irony by emphasizing that this disparaging phrase refers to God himself. Camille's words thus reveal his scoffing attitude towards traditional religious beliefs.

Humorous statements also elicit affective responses on the part of the reader: because these statements involve an element of mockery, they imply a value judgment on the part of speaker or author, and as a result they are likely to evoke in the reader his own feelings about the subject being ridiculed. In the case of irony, because two thoughts are brought forward in the reader's mind, two emotions are frequently evoked as well. Camille's reference to God as a *Vieillard dangereux* not only expresses his own derogatory thoughts about religion, but at the same time also recalls the reverent, often fearful, attitude he is deriding. Because they elicit such contradictory feelings, ironic images create tension in the reader's mind; the reader's response is thus further increased, and the effectiveness of the passage involved is heightened as a result.

Humour is present in varying degrees in almost every scene of the *Soulier de satin,* and is related to the poetic nature of the text in several different ways.

In some passages, the techniques of conventional poetry – the poetry of the 'classic' period of French literature – are used to create or to reinforce humorous effects. The Landlady in Panama says of Léopold's death: (III v 4–6; 806)

> ... A peine arrivé depuis deux jours à Panama et couic! le temps *d'en-lever son chapeau pour se torcher la tête,*
> *Un trait de l'archer Apollon,* comme disait Monsieur le Greffier de la Justice de paix,
> Vous l'a couché tout noir sur le pavé ...

The phrase *un trait de l'archer Apollon* conforms with traditional poetic conventions in that it avoids the direct designation of a prosaic occurrence – a case of sunstroke – by referring to it indirectly, through a periphrase, and by describing it in terms of a figure celebrated in ancient Greece. The lofty tone that these poetic devices give the phrase is humorous for the reader, because it contrasts with the commonplace event actually being described and the low social class of the speaker, with the preceding part of the sentence – which includes the popular expression *couic* and relates the inelegant action of wiping one's head (an action which seems particularly coarse here because the phrase *se torcher la tête* recalls the vulgar cliché *se torcher le cul*) – and with the following reference, in itself humorous, to a very minor local official, *Monsieur le Greffier de la Justice de paix.* The mocking tone of this linguistic humour is reinforced by the irony of the situation itself; that is, by the contrast between Léopold's extreme attitudes – as revealed in III ii by his excessive criticism of nature and his exaggerated praise of traditional language – and the fact that he is destroyed by his own fanatical views, for he is killed by the very nature he has scorned and in the traditional form he has praised. The derisive quality of this passage reveals Claudel's own contempt both for Léopold's ideas and for the overzealousness with which he adheres to them.[27]

In other cases in which mocking devices and poetry are present in a single passage, not only does the poetry reinforce the humorous effect, but at the same time the humour serves to heighten the poetic effectiveness of the text. This occurs in two types of developments in the *Soulier de satin.*

A humorous statement sometimes appears within an otherwise poetic passage.[28] Pélage tells Prouhèze of his past dedication to Africa: (II iv 27–8; 741)

> Oui, *je l'ai aimée. J'ai désiré sa face sans espoir.* C'est pour *elle,* dès que le Roi l'a permis, que j'ai quitté *mon cheval de Juge errant.*
> *Comme mes aïeux regardaient Grenade* ... (plus bas) *comme mes aïeux regardaient Grenade* ...

Pélage speaks of Africa here as if the continent were a cherished woman. The use of the past indefinite tense to express the feelings of 'loving' and 'wishing,' rather than the imperfect form in which the past tense of these emotions is usually stated, emphasizes that Pélage has completely given up hope of obtaining satisfaction through his relationship with Africa. Following his explanation in the previous scene of his failure to achieve a mutually rewarding relationship with a real woman, this comparison suggests that he originally turned to the continent as a kind of substitute wife, but that even 'she' has now disappointed him.

The last expression of this verset, *mon cheval de Juge errant,* is a metonymic reference to Pélage's position as a kind of circuit court judge. The term *cheval* is ironic here because riding around the countryside on a horse is the most insignificant and least glamorous aspect of being a judge, and contrasts with the important tasks such a person actually performs and the prestige usually accorded him by others.[29] In the context of this irony, the reader understands the term *errant* in two different ways, both of which are also ironic. First, when taken in the sense of 'continuously travelling' or 'wandering from place to place,' *errant* again stresses an unimportant aspect of Pélage's task as a judge. Second, in this mocking context, the reader recalls that *errant* also means 'mistaken.' This meaning of the term contrasts with the common assumption that a judge rules correctly and fairly. The capitalization of *Juge* heightens the effect of these ironic elements by emphasizing the significance of Pélage's occupation in the eyes of the public.

Pélage's ironic reference to his own role as a magistrate recalls the disparaging comments he made about his profession earlier in the play, in particular his remarks about the judge's emotional isolation from others.[30] Following the declaration of his strong attraction to Africa, this metonymic designation of his judgeship thus suggests that a second reason he sought a 'loving' relationship with Africa was to compensate for the loneliness imposed by his former occupation.

Pélage then begins to describe the religious mission he undertook in Africa, speaking again in poetic terms. The reference to Granada brings forward in the reader's mind the feelings of ardent dedication associated by Christians with such key battles as this victory of Catholic forces over the Arabs. In addition, because this evocation of Granada immediately follows the ironic reference to the unimportant aspects of Pélage's role as a judge, it suggests that still another reason for his participation in the struggle in Africa was his desire to use his life in a more vital, cogent way. The phrase *Juge errant* now evokes, through a flashback, the cliché *Juif errant*; like the Jews who wander because they have not yet accepted the rule of the Church, Pélage 'wanders' until, in Africa, he devotes himself completely to its cause.

The alternation of poetry and irony in this passage heightens the effectiveness of each part of the text, because each shift in tone, from poetic to mocking and back to poetic, is unexpected by the reader and therefore catches his attention. These shifts also serve to underscore the changes in subject matter within the passage – from Pélage's loving of Africa, to his earlier isolation as a judge, to the religious mission he undertook in Africa. Furthermore, the ironic statement serves as a transition between the two descriptions of Africa, setting apart and thus emphasizing the two different roles of the continent in Pélage's life – as a place where he sought emotional satisfaction, and as a place where he struggled for religious salvation, for others as well as himself.

Finally, a single image may be both humorous and poetic at the same time. The Clothmaker speaks to the Cavaliers of his attempt to dye a great quantity of cloth a red colour, in preparation for their expedition to the New World: (II i 26; 728)

> Mes ouvriers du matin jusqu'au soir *barbotent dans une lessive de feu et de massacre*! ils retirent de leurs cuves des drapeaux tout dégouttants *d'une sauce plus vermeille que la mer qui a englouti Pharaon*!

The words *de feu et de massacre* are poetically suggestive because they bring to mind two dramatic, violent forms of destruction, and elicit in response feelings of horror and repulsion. Since the Cavaliers have been speaking of their mission to a part of the world still inhabited by infidels, the phrase evokes in particular the devastating effects of the wars waged so fervently by the faithful in God's name. (The reference to Pharoah in the second part of the verset underscores this idea.)

This double vehicle, however, is also ironic in context, because the thoughts and feelings it evokes contrast sharply with the commonplace task of dyeing cloth described in the rest of the sentence – an activity which seems particularly unglamorous here because of the use of the terms *barbotent, lessive,* and *sauce* in this description. Through this irony, the Clothmaker mocks both the devastation inevitably caused by all wars, and that which will result specifically from the Cavaliers' religiously sanctified conquest of the New World. Two sets of opposing feelings are evoked in the reader in response. By mocking the ravages of war in general, the Clothmaker reveals the casual attitude of the Cavaliers towards the destruction they are about to cause, yet at the same time brings to mind the distress that most people feel at the thought of war. In addition, because the Clothmaker mocks specifically the Cavaliers' 'holy' conquest of the Americas, he indicates that these men have a similar off-hand attitude towards the religious purposes of their undertaking; this thought then recalls the ardent devotion Christians would be expected to feel while participating in such a sacred battle.[31]

The coexistence of irony and poetry in this figurative expression affects the reader's response in two ways. First, the contrast between the words *de feu et de massacre* and the preceding part of the sentence attracts the reader's attention and thus increases the general effectiveness of the expression, including its poetic suggestiveness. At the same time, the poetry sharpens the opposition between the two sets of conficting feelings that the ironic quality of the phrase brings to mind, as outlined above. In each case, the poetic power of the images reinforces that side of the conflict that is only indirectly evoked by the irony – fearful repulsion at the devastation of war, and avid dedication to a religious struggle. By intensifying these two affective conflicts, the poetry increases the tension they create in the reader's mind. Furthermore, the two feelings that are heightened by the poetry are themselves contradictory here, since the religious struggles that evoke such zealous responses involve in this case waging the battles that have such dismaying results. This conflict creates another area of tension for the reader, causing him to respond still more actively to the text and thus further heightening the overall effectiveness of this double vehicle.[32]

The four factors discussed in this chapter – the relationship between tenor and vehicle, the nature of the vehicle itself, the ideas and feelings that the reader associates with the vehicle because of its previous use, and the linguistic context in which the vehicle is found – affect the reader's response to all images; in the following chapter, image developments involving more than one vehicle element are discussed, and additional factors that influence the reader's response to these extended developments are examined.

Patterns of
image development

Image vehicles consisting of only one word or a brief phrase are relatively uncommon in the *Soulier de satin*. Such images are used primarily to relate the actions of the characters or to describe the setting in which these actions take place. The Actress, speaking to Rodrigue of his having made her his assistant, emphasizes the peremptory quality of his action: (IV vi 37; 902)

> Vous *m'avez annexée* sur-le-champ.

Rodrigue speaks in vivid terms of the scene he observed from the window of his Japanese prison: (IV ii 26; 869)

> D'un côté il y avait la campagne, c'était l'hiver, la campagne toute *craquelée* ...

Most images in the play are enlarged and embroidered upon, sometimes at great length. In general, the more intense a speaker's emotions or the more important the ideas he is expressing, the more lengthy and complex his image developments.[1]

SINGLE-THEME IMAGE DEVELOPMENTS

In most of the figurative developments of the play, the original analogy is expanded by the addition of vehicle elements that are derived from the same theme as the first vehicle; the meaning conveyed by the initial analogy is then gradually amplified as ideas closely related to the original tenor are compared to different aspects of the same vehicle theme. This type of development is often called an 'extended image.'

As in single-element images, the meaning conveyed by an extended image derives from the connection that the reader makes between tenor and vehicle. In this case, however, tenor and vehicle are not simple ideas, but groups or systems of closely interrelated concepts, and the meaning of the image as a whole therefore derives both from the relationship of each individual

TABLE 2
Frequency count: patterns of image development

			Image developments
Single-element images			371
Multiple-element developments			1893
Single-theme image developments, total		1270	
Tenor-vehicle relationship remains constant, total		655	
Tenor system is concrete	359		
Tenor system is abstract	296		
Tenor-vehicle relationship shifts, total		615	
Tenor system is part concrete, part abstract	226		
Autonomous element present in development	96		
Mixed metaphor present in vehicle system	113		
Metonymy present in vehicle system	180		
Multiple-theme image developments, total		469	
Image-sequence, total		363	
Logical	310		
Illogical	53		
Double image		106	
Single- and multiple-theme developments combined		154	

vehicle element to the part of the tenor system it expresses, and from the relationship of the complete vehicle system or 'code' development to the entire tenor system.[2]

The Actress uses an extended image in urging Rodrigue to accompany her to her home: (IV vi 128; 907)

> Venez avec moi *tout en haut de l'Europe, dans cette espèce de co-lombier tout entouré d'une palpitation d'ailes, d'où partent sans fin mes mouettes, mes colombes, à la picorée* vers toutes les mers du Monde!

The Actress has been praising England in this scene, citing the island nation's intimate connection with the sea as its most valuable resource. The words *tout en haut de l'Europe* recall the way geographic areas are pictured on maps, with the northernmost locations at the top of the page, and thus indicate that the Actress now speaks again of this country.[3]

The comparison of England to a *colombier* then recalls the use of doves as message carriers, and indicates that the activities of the British people help to establish lines of communication among different nations. Because in Christian tradition the dove frequently serves as a symbol of the Holy Ghost, this vehicle also suggests that by maintaining contact with many nations the British help to spread God's Word throughout the world.[4]

The reader next realizes that the phrase *une palpitation d'ailes* is related to the vehicle code metonymically, expressing through a specific detail the incessant movement of the birds around the dovecote. At this point, however, he can infer only that this movement corresponds to some kind of constant activity around England, and cannot be sure whether it is that of the whitecapped waves, or that of sailing ships.

The designation of the birds' movement through a reference to their beating wings makes the activity on the sea seem particularly frenzied; the substantivization of the verb *palpiter* reinforces this impression. Furthermore, since this verb is generally used in referring to human beings, it personifies the birds. Following both this personification and a word with religious connotations in context (*colombier*), the term *ailes* evokes the wings of heavenly creatures and therefore emphasizes that the English people help to bring other nations closer to God through their activities on the sea.[5]

Having recognized these personifications, the reader may now assume that the *ailes* are not waves, but the sails of British ships; this impression is confirmed when the Actress refers to the departing *mouettes* and *colombes*, which clearly represent the ships themselves. *Mouettes* are specifically sea-birds, and this vehicle thus stresses the location of the activity on the water; the word *colombes* both reinforces the implications of *colombier* and, because doves are domesticated birds, implies that despite their far-ranging activities on the sea the British sailors always remain closely tied to their homeland.[6]

Finally, the phrase *à la picorée* recalls the commercial aspects of the ventures being described and suggests that the travels of these ships *vers toutes les mers du Monde* also bring England material gains.

The meaning of an extended image is thus amplified gradually as each new vehicle element is added. In addition, when the reader comes to the end of the image, he has in mind – or can bring to mind by remembering and rereading – the entire group of ideas that constitute the tenor system and the complex of thematically similar vehicles through which these ideas are expressed, and can thus apprehend the image in a global, comprehensive manner.[7] When in so doing he relates these two systems of concepts to each other, additional nuances of meaning are usually suggested to him. In the Actress's comparison of England to a dovecote, the relationship of the two systems indicates that, as the centre of feverish activity which serves to link the country to all areas of the world, England is a place where life is exciting and stimulating, both intellectually, because the British seafarers come in contact with widely divergent cultures, and spiritually, because they play an active part in the progress of other peoples towards religious salvation.[8]

Because the reader must connect several individual vehicle elements with their respective tenors in understanding an extended image, his response to such a development depends in part on the consistency of the relationship between tenor and vehicle systems as the image progresses.

In many extended images of the *Soulier de satin*, the tenor and vehicle systems develop along parallel lines; each remains consistent in itself, and the relationship between successive elements of the vehicle system and the corresponding parts of the tenor system is approximately the same throughout the development.

Prouhèze explains why she remained at Mogador with Camille after the death of Pélage, describing the situation in Africa in terms of the well-known allegory of the shepherd-ruler and his flock: (III xiii 33–4; 850)

> Je dis que si *le royal berger* n'avait pas fait confiance à *ce chien* que je fus ici dix ans,
> *Le loup* lui *aurait dévoré* beaucoup plus de *moutons*.

The adjective *royal* indicates that the term *berger* is a metaphor for the Spanish King; the reader readily infers that the *loup* is Camille, and the *moutons* the innocent but weak Spaniards who live in Africa and on whom Camille preys through his unethical dealings with the Arabs.

Prouhèze expands this traditional allegorical framework by adding a fourth figure, the *chien*, to designate her own role. This vehicle evokes two very different views of her position, and thus creates tension in the reader's mind, which heightens the effectiveness of this part of the development. Applied to a human being, the term *chien* generally functions as a strong insult, and Prouhèze's use of this term here suggests that her task at Mogador was a degrading one. At the same time, following the statement that the King has *fait confiance* in his *chien*, the traditional view of the dog as a faithful and affectionate servant of man also comes to mind, and Prouhèze's comparison thus implies in addition that by remaining in Africa she acted out of loyalty to the King, fulfilling in an unassuming manner the duties assigned to her.

Each successive element of the tenor system of this image is a concrete factor in the situation at Mogador; the corresponding elements of the vehicle system are all related to the traditional shepherd-code allegory – for although the *chien* is not mentioned in the conventional allegory, the task performed by a shepherd's dog is familiar to the reader, and his role in relation to the other figures named is therefore immediately understood here. Each system thus remains consistent within itself as the image continues; and as a result, the relationship between the two systems does not change markedly as the development progresses; that is, it does not change to the extent that a shift in this relationship in itself affects the reader's response to the image.

In other extended images, the tenor system is entirely abstract, but again the relationship between tenor and vehicle systems remains approximately the same throughout the development.

In speaking with the Viceroy of their future relationship, Musique explains: (II xi 117–18; 766)

> ... *cette place que j'ai trouvée pour moi au-dessous de ton cœur,* tu la connais?
>
> *C'est la mienne* et si *tu m'y pouvais découvrir, je ne m'y sentirais pas aussi bien.*

This image development is absolute – the abstract concepts it expresses can be stated directly only in very general terms. As a result, the reader must actively use his imagination to determine the meaning of at least the initial element of the vehicle system. In this type of image, however, once the reader understands the initial analogy, if – as in Musique's image – the relationship between tenor and vehicle systems does not change as the development progresses, he can infer the remaining tenor elements and understand the rest of the development with relative ease.

In the above development, the phrase *au-dessous de ton cœur* indicates that the tenor of this initial analogy is the influence

Musique will have from now on over the Viceroy's 'deepest' feelings. By this point in the play, the reader knows that Musique and the Viceroy are linked to each other both emotionally and spiritually. When related to the tenor concept, the first vehicle therefore suggests that Musique will be an ever-present influence both on the Viceroy's responses to other people and on his relationship with God.

When Musique then presents the place that she can fill best (*c'est la mienne*) as being like a secret location, the reader understands that she is suggesting in her characteristic childlike manner that the exact source and character of her influence over the Viceroy must remain a mystery to all. This suggestion of mystery in itself then reinforces the reader's impression that her power over her lover is in part religious in origin.

The nature of the ground between tenor and vehicle systems may change markedly at one or more points in the development. The reader's attention is then drawn to the points where the shifts occur, and the specific ways in which the ground changes help to determine his response.

The vehicle system of an extended image may be entirely concrete, while the tenor system includes both abstract and concrete concepts. The distance between the tenor and vehicle systems is then greater when the abstract concepts are expressed, and the reader must use his imagination more actively in understanding these parts of the development.

The Angel says of China: (III viii 262; 825)

> ... la Chine éternellement dans *ce laboratoire intérieur* où *l'eau devient de la boue piétine ce limon mélangé à sa propre ordure.*

Following the reference to an 'interior' location, the reader infers that the tenors of the first dirt-code vehicles – *l'eau devient de la boue* and *limon* – relate to the vast areas of mud created in some inland areas of China by heavy seasonal rainfalls; these images thus indicate that the physical surroundings in this country are generally disagreeable. The words *sa propre*, however, indicate that the phrase *sa propre ordure* describes the nature of the Chinese people themselves; in the general religious context of the Angel's speech, the reader assumes that this vehicle refers to both the moral and the spiritual characteristics of these people. This tenor element is the first abstract concept to be expressed in dirt-code terms here and is more distant from the concrete vehicle system than are the previous concrete tenor elements. Both the attention-getting shift itself and the increased distance between tenor and vehicle heighten the effectiveness of this part of the development.

When the reader connects this last vehicle element with its tenor, he understands the expression to mean that the Chinese are particularly evil people. This impression is reinforced by flashback by the implications of the term *laboratoire* in context. Followed by a reference to the changing of one substance into another – *l'eau devient de la boue* – this word evokes the magical operations attempted by the alchemists, and suggests that the Chinese create this 'dirt' deliberately, under the influence of pagan spiritual powers.[9]

When the reader then relates the entire tenor and vehicle systems of this extended metaphor to each other, the fact that both the physical and the spiritual characteristics of the Chinese are described in one code suggests two additional thoughts to him. First, the comparison of both types of characteristics to various forms of dirt makes the lives of these people seem particularly wretched. Second, the expression of both the spiritual qualitites of a national group and their physical environment in one code indicates that these conditions are closely linked, perhaps by cause and effect; this implication is underscored here by the description of the two situations as *mélangés*.

Although the tenor system of the development just discussed includes both abstract and concrete concepts, all of these concepts can be readily inferred by the reader from the vehicle terms and their relationship to the parts of the tenor and vehicle systems previously expressed. In other extended images, one or more elements of the vehicle complex seem at first not to correspond to any aspect of the tenor system at all. The vehicle code then seems to have been enlarged upon without any connection to the group of ideas it originally expressed, and the tenor system itself seems to have 'disappeared.' Because such vehicles appear to exist independently in the text, they may be termed 'autonomous elements.'[10] In fact, these elements are not independent of the tenor system, but are absolute images expressing abstract concepts which, although not precisely identifiable by the reader, are part of the total system of ideas that the author is trying to convey.

Camille describes Africa in a long, fire-code development that begins: (I iii 109; 677–8)

> ... Les moucherons ne sont pas plus faits pour résister à cette extase de la lumière, quand elle pompe la nuit,
> Que les cœurs humains à cet appel *du feu capable de les consumer.* L'appel de l'Afrique!
> La terre ne serait point ce qu'elle est si elle n'avait *ce carreau de feu* sur le ventre, ce cancer rongeur, *ce rayon qui lui dévore le foie, ce trépied attisé* par le souffle des océans, cet antre *fumant, ce fourneau où vient se dégraisser l'ordure de toutes les respirations animales!*

The reader infers that the tenor of the first part of this fire-code development – *feu capable de les consumer* – is the intense heat of Africa and its power to debilitate those who live on the continent.[11] The expression *carreau de feu* recalls the phrase *carreaux de la foudre,* and thus suggests the divine origin of the African 'fire.' In this context, the words *rayon qui lui dévore le foie* bring to mind the story of Prometheus and the sacred fire that was the cause of his punishment; the term *trépied* recalls still another divine source of heat, the tripod of Sybil. The reader therefore concludes that the debilitating heat of Africa is an instrument of God's will.

In the last part of this development, however, only the term *fourneau* actually corresponds to this tenor system. The final clause – *où vient se dégraisser l'ordure de toutes les respirations animales* – cannot be related to any specific aspect of the African continent. This part of the vehicle complex therefore seems at first to exist independently in the text.[12]

When the reader tries to determine the tenor of this clause, the words *fourneau où vient se dégraisser,* followed by the reference to *respirations animales,* suggest that, just as minerals and other materials are often refined by fire, so this African 'furnace' is a place where living creatures come to be purified. Because this concept is both the first abstract element of the tenor system and also an idea which at first seems to the reader to be unidentifiable and eventually can be conceived by him only in very general terms, the distance between tenor and vehicle systems seems to increase very sharply here.[13]

In determining the meaning of this vehicle, the reader relates each part of the clause to the abstract tenor concept. The term *respirations* then indicates that what is being cleansed in Africa is something that derives from the innermost part of each individual and that at the same time gives life to him. The description of these *respirations* as *animales* and the references to *ordure* and *graisse* suggest that the people involved are very base individuals. The entire clause then recalls biblical descriptions of God's examination by fire of each human being, and his purification, again by fire, of those who are found to be lacking, as in Cor. 3: 13–15:

L'ouvrage de chacun sera mis en évidence, car le jour du Seigneur le fera connaître, parce qu'il sera révélé par le feu, et le feu mettra à l'épreuve l'ouvrage de chacun.
Si l'ouvrage de celui qui a bâti le fondement résiste, il en recevra la récompense.
Si, au contraire, l'ouvrage d'un autre est consumé, il en souffrira la perte; lui néanmoins sera sauvé, mais comme en passant par le feu.

This autonomous vehicle thus conveys the idea that Africa is a type of purgatory, a place where sinful creatures come to be tested and eventually purified by spiritual forces.

In the two types of extended images just discussed, the change in the relationship between tenor and vehicle systems results from a shift in the nature of the tenor system as the image develops. This relationship may also change as a result of variations in the vehicle system.

The vehicle systems of most extended images consist of words derived from a single thematic area. When terms derived from other themes are used along with the original code to express a single tenor system, the vehicles drawn from the new theme relate to the tenor system in a different way than did those taken from the original code.

Image developments whose vehicle systems include such aberrant elements are commonly termed 'mixed metaphors,' and are often considered to be stylistically faulty.[14] Such developments, however, may be highly effective, because the introduction of a new theme catches the reader's attention and because he must make a new connection between tenor and vehicle systems at this point. Claudel frequently 'mixes' his metaphors in such a way as to lead the reader to focus his attention on key vehicle terms.[15]

The Actress describes Rodrigue's influence over her in terms of music: (IV vi 58–60; 903–4)

> ... vous êtes *comme la musique qui ne vous demande rien mais qui, d'emblée, vous enlève et vous met d'accord avec elle.*
>
> Dès que vous êtes là, *il y a de la musique,* je me livre avec ardeur, confiance et *mesure* ... Vous êtes là et aussitôt je suis forte et gaie, je me sens toute brillante et toute *sonore*!
>
> C'est *comme un coup de trompette qui vous nettoie, comme une fanfare guerrière* qui ranime l'esprit abattu et le remplit de courage et de feu!

In two earlier scenes of the *Soulier de satin* – Musique's conversation with the Viceroy in II x and her prayer in the Church of Saint Nicholas in III i – the music code was used to describe a unity among individuals that involved both affective and spiritual ties.[16] When the Actress now expresses in music-code terms her feeling of being irresistibly drawn into an emotional communion with Rodrigue, the reader recalls the earlier uses of the theme and infers that Rodrigue's influence over her and the response he evokes in her in return are also partly religious in nature.

In the third verset, the phrase *coup de trompette* continues to develop the original music code, but the word *nettoie* is derived from a different thematic area. As in most mixed metaphors, the illogical statement that results startles the reader and becomes the focus of his attention.

In this case, the phrase *coup de trompette* evokes a call to battle and thus suggests that as part of her sense of communion with Rodrigue the Actress feels inspired to join him in a mutual struggle. The cleansing-code term *nettoie* then indicates that this struggle is specifically Rodrigue's attempt to spread the beliefs of the Catholic Church throughout the world, an endeavour through which he and the Actress can be spiritually purified. (The Actress then returns to the music code in the clause, *c'est une fanfare guerrière*, reaffirming here the importance of these common efforts and going on to describe the emotions that the thought of this mission evokes in her.)

The relationship between tenor and vehicle systems also changes as a result of a shift in the vehicle system when one or more vehicle elements function as metonymies within an otherwise metaphoric development.

If only one code is used in an extended image, all vehicles

drawn from this code must be related in the same way, either through similarity or through contiguity, to the tenor system being expressed. Within such a development, however, part of the vehicle system may itself be designated metonymically. The resulting vehicle element is then related through contiguity to the rest of the vehicle system, and the part of this system it expresses is itself related through similarity or contiguity to the tenor system. Since there are thus two grounds between the vehicle and its tenor, the reader must perform two mental processes in determining its meaning, and the effectiveness of the words involved is heightened as a result.

Prouhèze uses an extended Cross-code development in describing the suffering Rodrigue will undergo as a result of his sinful love for her: (ii xiv 41–2; 779)

'Oui, je sais qu'il ne m'épousera que sur la croix ...

'Si je ne puis être son paradis, du moins je puis être sa croix! Pour que son âme avec son corps y soit écartelée je vaux bien ces deux morceaux de bois qui se traversent!

In the first verset, Prouhèze suggests that Rodrigue's love can never lead to an earthly union with her, but only to a painful personal sacrifice, which will serve as the means through which he will atone for his sins. When she goes on to declare that she herself will be his Cross the reader understands that she will be the instrument through which this penitential act is brought about.

Prouhèze then repeats these ideas in more specific terms. The words son âme avec son corps y soit écartelée indicate that Rodrigue will suffer both spiritually and physically. The Cross is then evoked again, but this time through a metonymy, ces deux morceaux de bois qui se traversent. The increased effort demanded of the reader in understanding this part of the development helps to stress for him the idea that the metonymy expresses – the significance of these pieces of wood derives entirely from the sacrifice performed in relation to them and, Prouhèze implies, she has as much power as they to bring about a similar act on the part of Rodrigue.[17]

When a code is enlarged upon and developed in any type of extended image, it is likely to assume a certain importance in the reader's mind. If a vehicle derived from the same thematic material appears in a subsequent passage of the play, it will in most cases recall for the reader the earlier use of the theme and the concepts it then expressed; at the same time, it may also suggest an entirely new complex of ideas.

If the tenor system expressed by the theme when it reappears is within, or closely connected with, the tenor system it originally conveyed, the relationship between tenor and vehicle in the new image will be similar to that in the earlier development. The reader will then understand the new use of the code by relating the vehicle to the group of meanings he remembers the initial development of the theme to have expressed.[18]

When Camille first describes Africa in terms of fire, in the passage discussed above, the tenor system includes both the intense heat of Africa and the way in which men who live there are purified through the gradual destruction of their evil selves; the meaning of the image is that Africa is a place where sinful human beings come to be tested, and eventually cleansed, by God.

Camille again speaks in fire-code terms in II ix. As Prouhèze looks out a window of the Mogador fortress, Camille warns: (II ix 36; 760)

... On ne peut regarder longtemps sans danger *ce gouffre de feu.*

From the context, it is clear that the dangerous object to which Camille refers is the African desert surrounding Mogador. Since this tenor is closely connected to the tenor system of the previous fire-code development, the reader can understand the new vehicle by relating it to the concepts conveyed through the earlier image. He then recalls references in biblical descriptions of the Day of Judgment to the bottomless pit from which smoke rises 'comme la fumée d'une grande fournaise' (Apoc. 9:2), and into which those judged by God to be excessively sinful will be thrown (Apoc. 14:15); and he understands that the specific danger to which Camille refers here is the possibility that a person will be found by God to be so evil that he is condemned to remain for ever in this endlessly burning hell.

Other fire-code vehicles are used in the *Soulier de satin* to express ideas that are not related to the tenor system of Camille's original development. The Sergeant, for example, refers to Musique as: (I viii 30–1; 704)

Cette mouche à feu que j'ai attrapée avec la main ...

The tenor of this image is Musique's nature, as seen through the Sergeant's eyes, and the reader must therefore make an entirely new connection between tenor and vehicle systems here. In so doing, he understands that this statement expresses the Sergeant's feeling that Musique is like something of great value which most men glimpse from a distance and long to acquire for themselves, but which always manages to remain just beyond reach and therefore seems all the more tantalizing.

The Sergeant, however, indicates that he himself has been able to seize this elusive object. Furthermore, by using concrete, commonplace terms to describe Musique and his relationship to her – *mouche à feu* rather than the more elegant *luciole*, and *avec la main* – he underscores both his familiarity with this tempting girl and his disdainful attitude towards her. This passage thus reinforces the impression the Sergeant attempts to give of himself throughout the scene, that he is a cunning seducer of women, especially attracted to those of whose *naïveté* he can take advantage.

When a thematic code is used to express the same tenor system at several different points in the text, the specific ideas conveyed at each reappearance of the theme add to its general significance. The vehicles derived from such a code at any one point in the text bring forward in the reader's mind all of the nuances of meaning that it has expressed up to that point. The complex of meanings evoked by the theme thus expands gradually as the play continues.

Rodrigue first refers to Prouhèze as a star in I vii: (91–4; 695–6)

> ... c'est elle-même tout entière qui est *une étoile* pour moi!
> Jadis sur la mer des Caraïbes, quand à la première heure du matin je sortais de ma caisse étouffante pour prendre la veille,
> Et qu'une seconde on me montrait cet astre *réginal*, cette splendide étoile toute seule *au bandeau du ciel transparent*,
> Ah! c'était *le même saisissement au cœur une seconde, la même joie immense et folle*!

In this passage, Rodrigue first compares Prouhèze to a star and then describes the morning star he saw as he sailed near the New World. The term *splendide* emphasizes the beauty of this star, and the words *réginal* and *toute seule* indicate the uniqueness of its beauty. *Réginal* – a neologism apparently derived from the Latin *regina* – also suggests the power of the star for Rodrigue, and because of its phonetic similarity to *virginale* evokes the idea of purity. Finally, *réginal* recalls in context two Latin appellations for the Virgin Mary used in Catholic ritual, *Regina Coeli* and *Stella Maris*; these associations both stress the purity of this celestial body and reveal its spiritual importance. The religious significance of the star is then underscored by the phrase *au bandeau du ciel transparent*, which suggests that it serves as a link between the earthly world and a heavenly realm. When Rodrigue finally declares that Prouhèze and the star evoke in him the same exalting joy, he implies that Prouhèze, too, inspires and encourages him through her unique physical beauty, leading him to a pure spiritual existence beyond earthly life.

Later in this scene, Rodrigue again uses star-code imagery in referring to Prouhèze's ability to bring him nearer to the spiritual plane of life, but he still does not indicate exactly how she fulfils this religious role: (i vii 149–50; 698–9)

> Si je lui apprends qu'elle n'est pas née pour mourir, si je lui demande son immortalité, *cette étoile* sans le savoir *au fond d'elle-même qu'elle est,*
>
> Ah! comment pourrait-elle me refuser?

In III viii, Prouhèze and her Guardian Angel also discuss her relationship with Rodrigue in terms of her being a 'star' for him: (III viii 170–81; 820)

> L'ANGE GARDIEN: Et moi je ferai de toi *une étoile.*
> DONA PROUHÈZE: *Une étoile!* c'est *le nom dont il m'appelle* toujours dans la nuit.
> Et mon cœur tressaillait profondément de *l'entendre.*
> L'ANGE GARDIEN: N'as-tu donc pas toujours été *comme une étoile* pour lui?
> DONA PROUHÈZE: *Séparée!*
> L'ANGE GARDIEN: *Conductrice.*
> DONA PROUHÈZE: *La voici qui s'éteint* sur terre.
> L'ANGE GARDIEN: Je *la rallumerai* dans le ciel.
> ...
> ... je ferai de toi *une étoile flamboyante dans le souffle* du Saint-Esprit.

Prouhèze's confession that *étoile* is the name by which Rodrigue 'calls' her at night and the Angel's declaration that she has always been a 'star' for her lover indicate that the tenor of this development is again Prouhèze's role as an inspiration for Rodrigue. Now, however, this task is described in more specific terms –

after her earthly death, Prouhèze will live on in heaven; her alluring 'brilliance' will derive directly from the Holy Spirit, and when she encourages Rodrigue, it will be to follow her to God.

Later in Day 3, in her final meeting with Rodrigue, Prouhèze again describes herself as being a star for him, saying in answer to his accusations that she has betrayed him: (III xiii 166–9; 857)

> Eh quoi, noble Rodrigue, aurais-tu donc voulu que je remette entre tes bras une adultère?
> Et plus tard quand Don Pélage est mort et que j'ai jeté cet appel à toi,
> Oui, peut-être il vaut mieux qu'il ne t'ait pas atteint.
> Je n'aurais été qu'une femme bientôt mourante sur ton cœur et non pas *cette étoile éternelle* dont tu *as soif*!

The words *dont tu as soif* indicate that this star-code vehicle expresses once more the inspiration and encouragement that Prouhèze has provided Rodrigue; the vehicle therefore evokes for the reader the various aspects of this role that have been suggested by the previous developments of the code. In this case, Prouhèze adds the idea that it is specifically because their love has remained unsullied by sinful physical contact that she will be able to continue to guide Rodrigue after her death, leading him ultimately to God. (This final religious goal is emphasized here by the alliterative adjective *éternelle*.)

MULTIPLE-THEME IMAGE DEVELOPMENTS

In two other types of image developments found in the *Soulier de satin* – the 'image-sequence' and the 'double image' – vehicles derived from different areas of subject matter are used to express a single, limited tenor concept.

In the image-sequence, a series of vehicles drawn from different thematic areas expresses a single thought.[19]

Don Gil says of the Cavaliers' mission to the New World: (II i 31, 728)

> Car c'est nous en rouge qui portons la foi ... à *ces vers humains, à toutes ces gueules de lézards, à ces simulacres décolorés qui grouillent dans l'ombre humide* ou *qui errent sur les tables désolées de l'altitude.*

The syntactic structure of this development – the parallel structure of the three noun phrases, reinforced by the anaphoric repetition of *à ces* – indicates that these vehicles express one tenor concept, which is itself revealed by the context – Gil speaks here of the individuals to whom the Cavaliers will bring Christianity during their expedition to the Americas.

Because each vehicle of an image-sequence designates a different object or situation, each conveys a somewhat different idea to the reader. Since these vehicles all express one basic thought, as the reader progresses through the development he brings the ideas they convey together in his mind and relates them to each other. To the extent that these ideas differ from each other, the significance of the development as a whole expands as each new vehicle is added; to the extent that they are similar, their common area of significance is emphasized.

In the first vehicle of Gil's sequence, *ces vers humains,* the term *vers* evokes a creature commonly considered to be ugly and repulsive, and thus makes the American natives seem to be very lowly people. The pejorative implications of the term are underscored here by its contrast with *humains.*

The natives are then compared not merely to a second distasteful animal, the *lézard,* but to its *gueule,* a part of the body considered particularly ignoble. Because the word *gueules* evokes specifically the idea of gluttony, it suggests that one of the lowliest qualities of these people is their craving for immediate material gratification.

The first words of the third vehicle, *simulacres décolorés,* in themselves suggest the lack of real substance of the creatures being described. Following the reference to *lézards,* these words also recall that some species of lizard can change their colours, a thought which then underscores these people's lack of meaningful identity.

The two clauses that follow this phrase are themselves images, and may be considered to be part of the third vehicle of the series. In the first of these clauses, the term *grouillent* adds detail, and thus vividness, to the reader's mental representation of the *vers* and *lézards.* Because dark, humid areas are such unpleasant places in which to live, the phrase *dans l'ombre humide* – apparently an allusion to swamps or to the underside of rocks, where these reptiles often crawl – stresses once more their despicable nature.

In the second clause, the term *errent* underscores the idea expressed by *simulacres*, by implying that the natives have no purpose for their actions, but simply wander about aimlessly; the adjective *désolés* then points up their isolation from other people. The phrase *de l'altitude* is also an image here, because the term *altitude*, when used by itself, expresses literally only the concept of relative elevation and not, as here, a particularly high degree of elevation. The use of the word in this unusual manner emphasizes the great height of the plateaus on which some of these people live and thus indirectly stresses their separation from most other human beings.

Because all of these vehicles convey a very disparaging view of the American indigenes, this idea is strongly emphasized for the reader by the development as a whole. The emotional responses evoked by the vehicles are also very similar, since at least one term in each element elicits feelings of repulsion and disgust. This affective response both underscores the meaning conveyed most intensely by the development and, by increasing the reader's active involvement with the text, intensifies its overall impact on him.

Furthermore, this particular image-sequence also conveys a second level of meaning. Several terms of the sequence are associated with specific religious contexts, which are recalled now because at the beginning of the verset Gil clearly evokes the sacred nature of the Cavaliers' mission (*nous ... portons la foi*). In the first two vehicles, because the worm and the lizard move with their bodies directly on the ground, and because their elongated shape is like that of the snake, these animals are associated by the reader with the snake who tempts Eve, and to whom God says, 'Parce que tu as fait cela, tu es maudit entre tous les animaux et les bêtes de la terre. Tu ramperas sur le ventre, et tu mangeras la terre tous les jours de ta vie' (Gen. 3:14).[20] In addition, the lizard is specifically mentioned in Lev. 11:28–30 as one of the animals to be shunned by the Children of Israel because it is *impur*. The two vehicles thus suggest that the natives are spiritually as well as physically repugnant. This thought is then reinforced by the reader's recollection that the term *simulacres* was used in the past to designate pagan idols. Finally, in this context, the word *errent* calls to mind the cliché *Juif errant*, and implies that like the Jews, these people live meaningless, solitary lives because they have not yet chosen Jesus as their Saviour.

Taken together, the religious associations of these terms thus suggest that the primary reason the natives are so lowly and remain so isolated from others is that they have not yet accepted the rule of God and the Church. In addition, these religious thoughts in themselves evoke feelings of aversion towards the heathen Americans and thus reinforce the sense of repugnance elicited by the other associations of the vehicle terms, thereby further heightening the overall impact of the development on the reader.

In Gil's image-sequence, each object or situation named is related to one of two similar animals; the three vehicles are thus clearly interconnected, and the image-sequence seems consistent and logical to the reader. In other image-sequences found in the play, the vehicle elements are drawn from completely different areas of reality, and the objects or situations they designate bear no such obvious relationship to each other; these developments seem illogical to the reader.

Most illogical image-sequences in the *Soulier de satin* are absolute; in each case, the reader must therefore first stretch his imagination in order to conceive the abstract tenor concept being expressed. When the dissimilar vehicles of such a sequence are then related by the reader to this tenor, the ground between the tenor and each vehicle element is different and the ideas conveyed are often widely divergent as a result. In bringing these ideas together in order to understand the significance of the development as a whole, the reader must again actively use his imagination. For these reasons, illogical image-sequences are usually highly effective.

Prouhèze relates her feelings as the Angel introduces her to a new spiritual state: (III viii 199; 821)

> ... c'est *un rayon qui me perce*, c'est *un glaive qui me divise*, c'est *le fer rouge effroyablement appliqué sur le nerf même de la vie*, c'est *l'effervescence de la source qui s'empare de tous mes éléments pour les dissoudre et les recomposer*, c'est *le néant à chaque moment où je sombre* et Dieu *sur ma bouche qui me ressuscite*, et supérieure à toutes les délices, ah! c'est *la traction impitoyable de la soif, l'abomination de cette soif affreuse qui m'ouvre et me crucifie!*

The parallel structure of these clauses, reinforced by the anaphoric repetition of *c'est*, indicates that these very different vehicles express a single tenor concept. In the versets immediately preceding this development, the Angel tells Prouhèze that he is bringing her into a spiritually purifying situation ('DONA PROUHÈZE: ... Rends-la-moi donc enfin, cette eau où je fus baptisée! / L'ANGE GARDIEN: La voici de toutes parts qui te baigne et te pénètre'). The reader therefore infers that the tenor being expressed here is the way in which Prouhèze experiences this religious purification.

The first two vehicles indicate that Prouhèze now feels herself to be assaulted and, in the process, 'opened' by her attacker (*me perce, me divise*); her defences are thus destroyed. The third vehicle then reveals that the very source of her life is struck in this assault (*appliqué sur le nerf même de la vie*). The next two elements put less stress on the painful aspects of the purifying experience, but add the idea that Prouhèze, although destroyed (*les dissoudre, néant ou je sombre*), is restored to life (*les recomposer, me ressuscite*), and indicate the role of God in this process of rebirth.

Prouhèze then relates a directly contradictory feeling: the disjunctive phrase *supérieure à toutes les délices* implies that the sensations she has been describing have been joyful as well as painful. Immediately afterwards, she stresses once more the torturous quality of her experience (*traction impitoyable, l'abomination de cette soif affreuse*); but here the references to her great 'thirst' and to the *traction* with which it pulls her onward underscore her conflicting feelings – Prouhèze longs intensely for these purifying 'waters' despite both the agony of this longing itself, and the suffering involved in actually undergoing the cleansing process.

Prouhèze states once more that her defences are being penetrated (*m'ouvre*); and in the final – and therefore particularly attention-getting – statement of this long verset, declares that she is being 'crucified.' The term *crucifie* often functions as a cliché expressing extreme pain; in this context, however, the word also implies that through this torturous experience Prouhèze is being cleansed of past sins and is thus moving closer to salvation.

When the ideas conveyed by the individual vehicle elements of this sequence are brought together by the reader, they indicate that the spiritual purification Prouhèze is now experiencing involves intense suffering, yet causes her to feel extremely joyful at the same time, and that it entails first the destruction of her human, earthly nature, and then her spiritual rebirth. The effectiveness of the development is heightened markedly by the tension that this description of directly conflicting feelings creates in the reader's mind.

This image-sequence, too, has a second level of meaning, conveyed to the reader through the erotic connotations of several of the vehicle terms, including the repetitive references to opening actions, the description of the *source,* the mention of God's activity directly on Prouhèze's mouth, and the relation of the simultaneous experiencing of pleasure and pain. Taken together, these connotations indicate that Prouhèze's purifying experience involves a relationship with a spiritual force that is equivalent to a human erotic experience. In the general context of this scene, the image-sequence thus suggests that Prouhèze achieves in this moment a sinless form of satisfaction which in effect compensates her for her sacrifice of carnal gratification during her life on earth.

The double image is a multiple-theme development in which a tenor is compared to a vehicle, and the meaning of this first image is then itself compared to a second vehicle.[21] Because the meaning of the first image serves as the tenor of the second, the ideas expressed by the two images are very closely related. In fact, most double images actually convey only one concept to the reader, the second analogy clarifying or enlarging upon the idea suggested by the first. (In this sense, the second image functions as a metalinguistic comment on the initial analogy.)

Rodrigue uses a double image when he refers to America as: (I vii 56; 694)

> Celle-là qui depuis l'éternité était inconnue de tous jusqu'à moi,
> *ensevelie comme un enfant dans ses langes,*
>
> ...

The term *ensevelie* is generally used in describing the burial of the dead, and therefore suggests in itself that the American continents have been as far removed from the attention of Europeans as are the dead from the minds of the living. The added simile is then especially striking for the reader, because instead of a vehicle such as 'un mort dans son linceul,' which might be expected after *ensevelie,* Rodrigue speaks of the opposite situation, the newborn infant in swaddling-clothes. This comparison indicates that although the Americas previously went unnoticed by Europeans, they are not so much like those whose life is over as they are like the very young, whose eventual development is not perceived, but whose potentialities remain unlimited.

The term *ensevelie* is often used in speaking of past situations as well as of people, but the added *comme un enfant* clearly personifies the Americas here; this personification both stresses the dynamic quality of the development of the New World and underscores Rodrigue's feelings of concern for the burgeoning region.

SINGLE- AND MULTIPLE-THEME IMAGE DEVELOPMENTS COMBINED

Extended images, image-sequences, and double images are sometimes used in combination to express a group of inter-related ideas.

Rodrigue tells Daibutsu that he could never learn to meditate on nature as the Japanese do: (iv ii 31–2; 869)

> Je n'aurais pas pu *offrir* mon esprit à la nature *comme une feuille de papier parfaitement blanc, une chose à jeun,*
> Sur laquelle les ombres peu à peu se présentent, se dessinent et se teignent de diverses couleurs,
>
> ...

Rodrigue's first words evoke the total passivity that the Japanese try to achieve while meditating, as part of which the mind is cleared of all thoughts of its own and is turned towards nature, which can then act upon it. The metaphor *offrir* and the following painting-code simile form a double image; the simile is then developed by the phrase *une chose à jeun,* with which it forms a two-part image-sequence. When applied to a person, the expression *à jeun* implies that the individual is usually not in this 'empty' state and that he expects eventually to be 'filled'; here the phrase suggests that when the meditator achieves the desired passivity, his mind is not simply cleared, but is ready to receive new ideas.

The first metaphor of the next verset, *ombres,* is drawn from still another vehicle code and evokes the vagueness with which the ideas that nature communicates to man first appear and the aura of mystery that surrounds them. The disjunctive *peu à peu* then suspends the development of the sentence; the rhythm of this clause corresponds to – and therefore stresses – the idea being expressed: the slowness with which these thoughts gradu-ally take shape in the contemplator's mind.

The second and third of the verbs that follow enlarge upon the painting-code image, forming an extended development. These three verbs continue to emphasize the gradual formation of

nature's message in the meditator's mind, because they designate successively more distinct appearances of his thoughts. The
reflexive form of the verbs suggests that these thoughts come forward and take shape under their own power, and thus underscores their activity and independence relative to the contemplator's quiescence.

An image-sequence, a double image, and an extended image
are thus combined in this passage in order to describe to the
reader in vivid terms a specific type of mental activity unfamiliar
to most Westerners but especially characteristic of the Far East.

In all image developments, the reader connects a series of vehicle
elements with one or more tenor concepts in order to ascertain
the meaning of each part of the image and of the development
as a whole; as in single-element images, the relative effectiveness of the development depends primarily on the degree of
attention the reader focuses on the figurative terms, the amount
of mental activity he expends in determining their significance,
and the affective responses they evoke in his mind.

Any factor disturbing the consistency of the tenor or vehicle
systems as a development progresses – and thus altering the
tenor-vehicle relationship – heightens the effectiveness of the
passage for the reader by drawing his attention to the words
most directly involved and by compelling him to make new con-
nections between the two systems. The poetic power of the
Soulier de satin derives to a great extent from the presence of
image developments that involve such shifts, and that thus star-
tle the reader, engaging his attention and stimulating him to use
his imagination and emotions more actively in relation to the
text.

3   Convergent stylistic devices

Each image that catches the reader's attention and evokes a mental response on his part constitutes in itself a stylistic device. Stylistic devices, however, are not usually found singly in a literary text, but are located in groups or clusters. The nature and degree of the reader's response to any particular passage depends on the combined effects of all of the devices that come together, or converge, at that point.[1]

Stylistic devices that converge with images help to attract more of the reader's attention to the figurative terms, and thus heighten their effectiveness for him. Many of these devices also orient the reader's reaction in more specific ways. Convergent devices were discussed in relation to the images cited as examples in Chapters 1 and 2; in this chapter, the types of devices that most frequently converge with images in the *Soulier de satin* are studied systematically, and the particular effects of each on the reader's response to the text are shown. First, stylistic devices that relate to four different aspects of the text – syntax, rhythm, phonology, and the appearance of the printed text – are considered. Then, stylistic devices created by repetition are examined.[2]

STYLISTIC DEVICES RELATED TO SYNTAX

In the *Soulier de satin,* as in other plays, the text represents for the most part impromptu spoken language, and some syntactic patterns that would be startling to the reader in most formal texts – some types of incomplete sentences, for example – are therefore not unexpected here. As a rule, only those constructions that are not usually found in informal speech will be striking for the reader, and will thus function as stylistic devices, within the framework of the play.[3]

Stylistic devices relating to syntax frequently involve changes in the usual word order of the sentence. The unexpected inversion of a substantive and its modifying adjective, for example, makes both terms more attention-getting for the reader, and usually

TABLE 3
Frequency count: convergent stylistic devices

		Image elements affected
Devices related to syntax, total		820
Inversion of substantive and adjective		95
Anteposition of phrase or clause, total		180
At beginning of sentence or clause	128	
Within sentence or clause (converges with disjunctive)	52	
Disjunctive, total		485
Ellipsis		31
Syllepsis		29
Devices related to rhythm, total		236
Prose rhythm, total		71
Irregular rhythmic development of sentence or clause	16	
Pattern of sentence length broken	55	
Metrical rhythm, total		103
Irregular rhythmic development of verset	32	
Pattern of verset length broken	71	
Prose and metrical rhythm conflict, total		62
Grammatical unit broken by metrical rhythm	49	
Stress-group broken by metrical rhythm	13	
Devices related to phonology, total		35
Unusual sound pattern	35	
Devices related to appearance of printed text, total		153
Unexpected capitalization	112	
Unusual punctuation	41	
Devices created by repetition, total		1660
Semantic repetition, total		760
Repetition of image vehicle	319	
Repetition in different words, total	441	
Figuratively only (image-sequence)	310	
First literally, then figuratively	76	
First figuratively, then literally	55	
Grammatical repetition, total		372
Converges with semantic repetition	332	
Converges with semantic opposition	40	
Rhythmic repetition or apparent equivalence, total		317
Asyndeton and anaphora present	29	
Polysyndeton and anaphora present	35	
Anaphora only present	246	
Phonological repetition, total		211
Within single phrase	153	
Converges with semantic repetition	58	

suggests that the adjective should be understood figuratively or impressionistically.

In speaking of the Protestant peoples of Northern Europe, the Viceroy asks his band of followers: (II v 44; 748)

> Qu'ont voulu ces *tristes* réformateurs sinon faire la part de Dieu ...

The position of the adjective before the noun it modifies indicates that the word *tristes* should be taken metaphorically. In this context, two figurative meanings may come to mind: first, this word recalls the tendency of Protestant churches to call for simplicity and austerity in religious ceremonies and in the daily lives of clergy and laymen; and second, the reader familiar with Claudel's writings is reminded of his belief that those who reject the Catholic Church can never experience the great joy that is, for him, a vital part of all true religious experience.[4]

When the usual positions of noun and adjective are inverted, the adjective may be considered to be anteposed, or put before that element of the sentence on which it depends grammatically and semantically. Other grammatical elements, including phrases and clauses, may also be placed in anteposition within their respective sentences.

The anteposed words are usually placed at the beginning of a sentence or independent clause. Saint Denys begins his description of the Europeans' search for happiness with the exclamation: (III i 79; 788)

> *A l'orient de tout* voilà *le véritable niveau humain!* ...

Since the metaphoric prepositional phrase, *à l'orient de tout* depends semantically on both the noun phrase *niveau humain,* and the preposition *voilà,* and also depends grammatically on *voilà,* the reader would not expect this image to be expressed before the later terms; the phrase is therefore particularly attention-getting for him.

In addition, the meaning of the anteposed words is not clear at first. A brief period of suspense is created, and the reader must use his own imagination to relate by flashback the words following the anteposition to the anteposed terms themselves and in this way determine the meaning of the statement as a whole. In this case, he infers that the tenor being expressed is the *véritable niveau humain,* the situation that is most fitting for human beings. Because Saint Denys has been speaking of the human condition in religious terms, the reader now recalls the special significance of the *orient* in Catholic tradition, and in particular, the belief that the Saviour will arrive from the East (cf. Isa. 41:2, 25 – 'Qui a fait sortir le juste de l'orient, et qui l'a appelé en lui ordonnant de le suivre? ... Je l'appellerai du septentrion, et il viendra de l'orient'). He then concludes that for Saint Denys the situation that is most suitable for humans is that which they will find through Christ and his Church.

The addition of the phrase *de tout* reinforces this impression by suggesting that the term *orient* refers here not to a relative direction, but to a specific, ultimate 'easterly' situation. Furthermore, the French term *orient* has been used in the past to express the idea of a beginning; taken in this sense, the entire anteposition *à l'orient de tout* designates a situation that is 'the beginning of all' – again, a description appropriate to the Church, which leads man back to God, the origin of the universe and of all life within it.

Anteposed terms may be located within a sentence or clause, rather than at the beginning. The anteposition then constitutes a disjunctive – a word or group of words that come between, and thus separate, two terms that would ordinarily follow each other. A disjunctive expression interrupts both the syntactic and the semantic developments of the sentence in which it is found.

As the Jesuit comes to the concluding words of his prayer, he explains: (I i 22; 668)

> Et maintenant voici *la dernière oraison de cette messe que mêlé déjà à* la mort *je célèbre par le moyen de moi-même* ...

The first, Mass-code vehicles of this sentence indicate only that the Jesuit considers the words he now speaks to constitute a formal prayer offering to God. When the relative pronoun *que* then modifies the term *messe,* the reader expects a clause to follow in which the significance of this particular 'Mass' is more fully explained; instead, the disjunctive *mêlé déjà à la mort* interrupts the sentence. The reader's attention is first drawn to this unexpected, interfering image, which expresses in concrete terms the imminence of the Jesuit's death. Because this phrase is also an anteposition, however, its significance in context – the specific

relation of the Jesuit's impending death to his prayer offering –
is not yet fully clear.

The reader then pays still closer attention to the final part of
the sentence, which he expects will contain the conclusion of the
clause introduced by *que* and will also amplify the significance
of the anteposed disjunctive. Here, the terms *je célèbre par le
moyen de moi-même* continue to develop the Mass-code image,
indicating that just as Jesus is symbolically sacrificed during each
Mass, so, through this particular prayer, the Jesuit offers himself
in sacrifice to God. When the reader relates this concept by
flashback to the disjunctive image, he understands that this is
an ultimate sacrifice on the part of the Jesuit, a personal Crucifixion, and thus the means through which he can attain salvation. (The alliteration of the /m/ sound in both the Mass-code
development and the disjunctive underscores the link in the significance of these two parts of the sentence.)

The verset as a whole now evokes conflicting feelings in the
reader. The implication that the Jesuit approaches religious salvation elicits feelings of relief and joy, which are opposed to the
grief and apprehension evoked by the reference in the disjunctive to his approaching death. The tension created by this conflict of emotions intensifies the reader's response to the sentence
as a whole. The presence of the anteposed disjunctive heightens
this tension, and thus further increases the reader's response, by
compelling him to consider the two parts of the sentence directly
in relation to each other, thereby causing him to bring together
in his mind the antithetical groups of feelings.

Most disjunctive expressions found in the *Soulier de satin* do
not constitute antepositions, but depend rather on previously
expressed terms or do not depend on any specific element of the
sentence at all.

The Viceroy of Naples refers to his country as: (II v 13; 746)

... cette Italie *où toutes les routes à travers la couronne des Alpes abou-
tissent* ...

Following the reference to Italy, the words *où toutes les routes* in
themselves recall the saying 'Tous les chemins mènent à Rome';
the disjunctive, separating subject from verb, then acts as a
teaser, leaving the reader wondering for a moment just how this
renewed proverb will be completed.

Because it is a renewed expression, the interrupted clause is especially striking for the reader; furthermore, like the original proverb, it is doubly metaphoric – it indicates that Italy is located at the geographic centre of Europe, but this suggestion is itself a figurative expression of the social, political, and religious importance of the country.

The disjunctive phrase has no specific grammatical connection with any part of the sentence and depends semantically on *routes*. This comparison of the Alps to a crown expresses the same idea as did the interrupted clause, and thus stresses this thought for the reader – for the Viceroy, Italy is the leader of all Europe. The disjunctive structure of the sentence in itself helps to emphasize the idea still further by drawing the reader's attention, first, to the interrupting phrase and, then, to the verb that completes the renewed proverb.

Stylistic devices may also involve syntactic factors other than the order of words; two devices found in the *Soulier de satin* that relate to different aspects of syntax are the ellipsis and the syllepsis.[5]

In the ellipsis, a word or phrase that the reader expects to find within a statement is omitted.[6] Many constructions that would be considered elliptical according to traditional grammatical rules are not surprising to the reader in the ostensibly spoken text of the *Soulier de satin*. Even in spoken contexts, however, the reader expects to be able readily to understand every statement. When the omission of part of a sentence interferes with his ability to comprehend a remark, the ellipsis is startling to him, and thus functions as a stylistic device.

After he learns of the defeat of the Armada, the King speaks of the role of this ill-fated venture in the struggle against heretical forces in England, and concludes: (I iv 19; 885)

J'ai fait ma tâche, *j'ai bouché ce trou par où l'Accusateur contre moi eût pu passer*, j'adore Dieu maintenant *de toutes parts autour de ma foi une parfaite enceinte.*

From the context, the reader infers that the *tâche* to which the King refers first is his duty to join wholeheartedly in the battle against heresy, giving selflessly of his personal power and wealth. The extended protection-code image that follows then discloses his belief that by fulfilling this obligation to the Church through the Armada he has made certain that the *Accusateur*, the devil's advocate, will have no charges to bring against him on the Day of Judgment.

In the last part of the verset, the phrases *de toutes parts* and *autour de ma foi* are anteposed, and their significance is therefore not at first understood by the reader. When he seeks the expected clarification in the final part of the verset, however, he finds that the verbal expression that would make this statement grammatically complete is omitted, leaving the meaning of the clause as a whole unclear. The reader must use his imagination, first to infer the general nature of the missing words, and then to determine the exact interrelationship of the phrases that make up this clause.

In this case, he concludes that if the missing terms were added these phrases would be part of a relative clause expressing the idea that the *parfaite enceinte* 'exists' or 'is situated' *de toutes parts autour de ma foi*. The statement as a whole then implies that through his attempt to destroy a major threat to the Catholic Church the King has definitively reaffirmed and secured his spiritual relationship with God.

In a syllepsis, two or more semantically unrelated expressions are grammatically dependent on a single term. Isabel describes Mexico as: (III vi 3; 807)

> Un royaume dix fois plus grand et plus beau que l'Espagne, *avec ses mines et ses plantations et le pétrole, et cette ouverture au Nord sur l'Infini*,
> ...

The four noun phrases that follow *avec* all function as objects of this preposition. Taken together, the first three phrases express metonymically the abundant natural resources discovered in Mexico by the Europeans and already being exploited by them. In the final phrase, however, the concretizations *ouverture* and *Infini* evoke the as yet uninvestigated – and therefore still unlimited – prospects offered by the vast region lying to the North. Furthermore, the capitalization of *Infini* indicates that this final statement refers not only to the physical wealth of the new territory, but also to the possibility, alluded to earlier in the play, that the exploration of this area by the Spaniards will lead the world as a whole closer to an ultimate religious 'Infinity' – an eternal, heaven-like state – because it will bring God's Word to the heathens of North America and will thereby unite them spiritually with all other Catholics.

The last statement of this series thus differs in meaning from the preceding three phrases, although it is grammatically dependent on the same preposition. This shift in semantic content, without a corresponding change in grammatical function, is surprising for the reader and helps to increase the effectiveness of the images found in the last segment of the development. (Within the final statement, the term *Infini* is especially attention-getting, both because it is unexpectedly capitalized and because it follows the disjunctive *au Nord.*)

STYLISTIC DEVICES RELATED TO RHYTHM

As in other poetic texts, two distinct rhythmic structures coexist in the *Soulier de satin* – the 'prose rhythm,' which derives from the grammatical organization of the words, and the metrical pattern, which is superimposed on the prose rhythm.[7] The combination of these two structures determines the overall rhythm of each passage of the text.

In French prose statements, the alternation of stressed and unstressed syllables creates an iambic rhythmic pattern. Each iambic unit – each unit of one or more unstressed syllables followed by a stressed syllable – is known as a 'stress-group'; as a rule, each corresponds to a single grammatical unit.[8] Any disruption in the anticipated pattern of these groups within a sentence will function as a stylistic device.[9]

Most declarative sentences, for example, can be divided into two parts: first the protasis, in which the stress-groups are marked by generally rising pitch, and then the apodosis, in which the pitch falls. The final syllables of the protasis and the apodosis are accented more strongly than are the other stressed syllables of the sentence. As a rule, the two parts of the sentence are approximately equal in length, or the protasis is somewhat longer than the apodosis; the strongest accent within the sentence thus falls either in the middle of the statement or slightly past the middle. If the two parts of a sentence or an independent clause differ significantly in length, this intonational and stress pattern is unexpectedly broken, and the unusual rhythm that results is stylistically effective.

In speaking of his relationship with Rodrigue, Isidore exclaims: (I vii 38; 693)

> Pauvre Isidore! Ah! *quel maître as-tu tiré au sort! en quelles mains par le désagrément des éléments lourds et subtils de la matière as-tu chu?*

Isidore first expresses his bewilderment at finding himself Rodrigue's servant through a cliché: *quel maître as-tu tiré au sort!* He then repeats this idea in metaphoric terms, beginning with part of the cliché, *tomber entre les mains de quelqu'un – en quelles mains.* A long disjunctive, however, interrupts the sentence and delays the conclusion of this second cliché. The words of the disjunctive are learned in tone – the phrase *désagrément des éléments* evokes the chemical process by which the various components of a complex substance are separated from each other; and the terms *éléments lourds et subtils* recall philosophical theories concerning the basic substances of which all matter is composed. The scientific and philosophical associations of these terms contrast ironically with the subject matter being discussed, the prosaic tone of the preceding statement, and the relatively low social status of the speaker. The first part of the disjunctive also contains a comic rhyme: *désagrément – des éléments.*

The final verb of the statement, *as-tu chu,* is again ironic, and contrasts with the microcontext in several ways. First, following the words *en quelles mains,* the reader expects Isidore to complete the sentence using the verb *tomber;* when the disjunctive interrupts the development of the sentence, the reader's anticipation of this completion of the cliché grows. The unexpected renewal of the expression through the use of the verb *choir* then clashes with the reader's recollection of the original phrase. Second, *choir* is rarely used except in poetic and comic texts; both the lofty – but in context ironic – and the comic tones of the preceding statement are thus continued here. Furthermore, the form of the verb used here, the past indefinite, is archaic; the phrase *as-tu chu* therefore seems learned as well as poetic, and the elevated tone is thus intensified. Finally, Isidore uses the auxiliary verb *avoir* here instead of the correct auxiliary, *être;* this grammatical error in itself points up the contrast between his noble, learned language and his actual social situation. (The repetition of the /y/ sound in *as-tu chu* helps to focus the reader's attention on these words and thus further heightens their overall effectiveness.)

The protasis of this statement, which begins with the phrase *en quelles mains,* is extended by the long disjunctive, and does not end until the word *matière.* [10] The reader is then surprised when the apodosis is far shorter, consisting of only the verbal phrase, *as-tu chu.* The ironic and comic effects of the sentence are increased by this rhythmic device, not only because it draws the reader's attention to the final words of the statement, but also because the difference in the lengths of the protasis and the apodosis adds still another element of contrast to the sentence and thus underscores those points of opposition that make the passage humorous.

In a prose statement, sentences themselves constitute rhythmic units that are generally larger and more clearly marked than stress-groups. In the *Soulier de satin,* these units vary considerably in length. If, however, several successive sentences are of approximately the same length, they form a rhythmic pattern for the reader. The appearance of an unusually long or short sentence then breaks this pattern, and the aberrant length of the new statement functions as a stylistic device.

Rodrigue evokes a part of the world that lies beyond the area familiar to Western man: (IV viii 133; 919)

> Et derrière ces pays d'autres pays et d'autres pays encore et finale- ment l'inconnu. Personne, il y a cinquante ans, ne savait ce qu'il y a. *Un mur.*

The first two sentences of this verset are of approximately the same length. The third, however, is very much shorter and therefore surprises the reader. [11] In context, the reader infers that this elliptical statement is a concrete expression of the intellectual and spiritual barriers that completely separated Europeans from distant areas of the world only fifty years before Rodrigue's time.

In the *Soulier de satin,* as in most of Claudel's poetry, the metrical organization of the text involves the division of the words into versets, which are marked for the reader by the typographical arrangement of the printed page.

The internal rhythmic structure of these versets parallels the two-part intonation and stress pattern of most French sentences – as a rule, each contains two primary accents, one within the verset and the other at its end. Although the location of both primary and secondary accents shows considerable variation, the first primary accent falls near the middle of the verset often enough so that when it does not the resulting rhythmic unbalance is surprising for the reader and functions as a stylistic device.

In explaining how he is himself related to Rodrigue, Fernand says to Léopold Auguste: (II ii 92; 797)

> Nul n'ignore qu'en effet il fit jadis au fiancé de ma sœur, cavalier
> plein de promesses, Don Luis, *un trou,*
> ...

The first rhythmic segment of this verset continues through the two expressions placed in apposition to the phrase *fiancé de ma sœur*; the first primary accent thus falls on *Luis*. The second segment is then markedly shorter, consisting of only the final two words, *un trou.*

This image refers to the wound that Rodrigue inflicted on Luis with his sword as the latter attempted to elope with Fernand's sister. The phrase is humorous for the reader, because the common, insignificant nature of a *trou* contrasts sharply with the noble, important-sounding description of Luis that precedes. The long disjunctive placed between the verb *fit* and its direct object heightens the effectiveness of the image; the unexpected brevity of the second segment of the verset further intensifies its impact – in particular its comic effect, because the difference in the lengths of the two parts of the verset underscores their semantic contrast.

Like the sentences of the play, the versets of the *Soulier de satin* constitute in themselves rhythmic units that may vary considerably in length.[12] As is the case with sentences, however, several successive versets are often similar in length and thus form a pattern for the reader. If an unusually long or short one follows, the resulting change functions as a stylistic device.

Most often, an extremely short verset breaks the pattern created by several longer ones. At their final meeting off the coast of Mogador, Rodrigue and Prouhèze talk of her intention to return to the fortress, where she faces certain death. In several versets of moderate length, Rodrigue speaks of the promise Prouhèze will be breaking if she allows herself to be killed and thus separates herself from him irrevocably: (III xiii 92– · 853)

> Cette promesse que tu m'as faite, cet engagement que tu as pris,
> ce devoir envers moi que tu as assumé,
> Elle est telle que la mort aucunement
> Envers moi n'est pas propre à t'en libérer
> Et que si tu ne la tiens pas mon âme au fond de l'Enfer pour l'éter-
> nité t'accusera devant le trône de Dieu.

He then declares: (III xiii 96–7; 853)

> Meurs puisque tu le veux, je te le permets! Va en paix, *retire* pour
> toujours de moi *le pied de ta présence adorée*!
> *Consomme l'absence*!

In the last two versets cited, Rodrigue repeats the same idea – his acceptance of Prouhèze's departure from the ship – three times. He first expresses this concept in a 'dead' cliché, *va en paix*, and then repeats it in the clause beginning, *retire pour toujours de moi*. The words *retire le pied* are a metonymic reference to Prouhèze's departure; the expression *ta présence adorée* is a second cliché, renewed here because it functions as a development of the preceding figurative statement. The presence of the disjunctive *pour toujours de moi* heightens the effectiveness of both of these images.

The third expression of Rodrigue's agreement – *consomme l'absence* – attracts the reader's attention immediately, because the two words constitute a verset that is markedly shorter than the preceding few lines of verse. In context, the term *consomme* not only conveys the idea of an ending or termination, but also evokes two specific contexts in which this verb is commonly used. First, because Rodrigue has just said that if Prouhèze breaks her promise to him he will accuse her *devant le trône de Dieu*, the reader recalls the frequent use of the verb *consommer* in references to the 'end of time,' when God will make his final judgment of mankind – as, for example, in the biblical expression *la consommation du siècle* (Matt. 13:49), or in the popular phrases *la consommation du monde* and *la consommation du temps*. Although Rodrigue has not yet openly acknowledged the religious reasons for his separation from Prouhèze, his use of the term *consomme* here suggests that he at least senses that this separation has been ordained by God and has been decreed by him to be irreversible. Second, because Rodrigue is still deeply in love with Prouhèze and continues to desire her physical presence, the reader recalls that this verb is also used in the expression *con-sommer le mariage*. The contrast of the words *consomme l'absence* with this remembered expression emphasizes that Rodrigue must now suffer the loss of Prouhèze, instead of attaining the union with her that he has so long desired.

The term *absence* is itself concretized here, because it functions as the object of *consomme;* expressed in this tangible form, Prouhèze's departure seems an even harsher blow for Rodrigue to bear. The idea of his bereavement is further stressed by the contrast of *absence* with the preceding evocation of his beloved's *'présence' adorée*.

By drawing the reader's attention to the words *consomme l'ab-sence,* the unexpected brevity of this phrase helps to emphasize still further the ideas so strongly conveyed by these terms in context – the great loss that Rodrigue will suffer if Prouhèze returns to Mogador, and the finality of this separation.

As stated above, the overall rhythm of any passage of the text is determined by a combination of the prose rhythm of the words and the metrical pattern that is superimposed upon it.

These two rhythmic systems may or may not correspond with each other. In the *Soulier de satin*, the two systems usually coincide – the end of a verset, for example, generally converges with the end of a major grammatical unit. For this reason, when the two systems are not in accord, the resulting rhythmic clash is especially striking for the reader.

After Rodrigue has urged the Spanish King to share the wealth of the Americas with other European peoples, the *Ministre de l'Oltramar* exclaims: (IV ix 157–8; 933)

> Nous ne pouvons pourtant pas faire de l'Amérique que le génie et la vertu de votre inoubliable grand-père ont fait *sortir du sein* des Indes
> *La pâture banale* de toute l'Europe!

In the first of these versets, the long disjunctive beginning *que le génie* separates the verbal expression *faire de l'Amérique* from its object and thus leaves the reader wondering just what the Spaniards 'cannot do to America.' The unexpected verset break that follows the disjunctive heightens the suspense.

The reader then pays particular attention to the first words of the following verset, which he expects will satisfy his curiosity.

These terms are ironic in context. Earlier in this scene, Rodrigue described America in terms of food, saying of the natural wealth of the country: 'Il y a dedans de quoi faire pour tout le monde pendant des siècles un repas énorme' (IV x 141; 931) and going on to explain that this 'food' has been offered by God to all men as a means through which they might become united with each other and with himself: 'Je veux que tous les peuples célèbrent la Pâque à cette table énorme entre les deux Océans qu'Il nous avait préparée' (v 144). When the Minister now describes the Americas as a kind of animal fodder, his words suggest that what the Europeans seek in the New World is immediate, self-indulgent, physical gratification; this use of food imagery contrasts ironically with Rodrigue's description of the continents in terms of a religiously sanctified repast and the resulting implication that the Americas should be a source of spiritual satisfaction for all men. (The contrast in tone between the commonly used terms *la pâture banale* and the preceding poetic cliché *sortir du sein* heightens this ironic effect.)

Because the disjunctive and the rhythmic clash lead the reader to focus his attention on the phrase *la pâture banale*, these devices help to emphasize for him the idea conveyed by the irony here – the Minister's contempt for Rodrigue and for his generous, far-sighted views on the disposition of the resources of the New World.

In the passage just discussed, the first verset ends within a major grammatical unit (an infinitive clause), but not within a stress-group. When a verset break interrupts not only a grammatical unit but a single stress-group as well, the disaccord between rhythmic patterns is even more striking.

Saint Denys describes Musique as she prays in the Church of Saint Nicholas: (III i 62–4, 787)

> ... pour elle *la cavité* de ce lieu est aussi redoutable
>> Que si, *l'obscure fumée de ce monde entr'ouverte*, elle
>> Envisageait *le buisson ardent*, ou *le propitiatoire dans le tonnerre*,
> ou *l'Agneau sur son livre scellé*.

In the first verset, the substantive *la cavité* makes the empty, hollow quality of the church seem to be a tangible substance. This impression in itself evokes a feeling of uneasiness in the reader, which is intensified by the adjective *redoutable*.

The verset break following *redoutable* then interrupts the

development of the sentence, separating the word *aussi* from the second term of the compound conjunction, *que*. Prose and metrical rhythm thus conflict at this point, but a stress-group is not interrupted. In this case, the disruption of the sentence serves to heighten the reader's suspense over the unknown situation in the church.

In the following verset, the disjunctive, *l'obscure fumée de ce monde entr'ouverte*, again interrupts the semantic development of the sentence, leaving the reader still in suspense. This phrase expresses metaphorically Musique's ability to transcend the usual limits of human understanding – the expression *l'obscure fumée* is commonly used in traditional Church writings in referring to these limits, and is itself redundant; the effect of the tautology is to emphasize the completeness of man's blindness to the spiritual world.

This second verset ends not only within a clause, but also within a single stress-group – *elle envisageait*. According to the metrical pattern of the text, since *elle* is the last syllable of the verset it should receive the second primary accent; the prose rhythm, however, requires that the pronoun be unaccented. The tension between the two rhythmic systems is thus especially great at this point. Because this verset break delays the semantic development of the sentence once again, it serves first to intensify still further the reader's expectant yet apprehensive feelings, and then to direct his attention towards the final verset of the development, which he expects will relieve his suspense.

Saint Denys now names several concrete objects through which, according to biblical accounts, the Divine Presence has been revealed to human beings in the past; these objects function as metaphoric expressions of the spiritual phenomena that Musique observes. The references to familiar biblical events evoke in the reader the feelings of awe with which the appearances of God are associated in scriptural narratives, and suggest that Musique, too, is filled with fearful wonder as the spiritual world is now revealed to her. The reader's feelings are especially strong at this point because they are reinforced by the anxiety that has been growing in him throughout the passage.

In both of the above examples, the conflict between grammatical and metrical rhythmic patterns occurs at the end of the verset. These two rhythmic systems may also come in conflict within the verset – as, for example, when a clause or a sentence ends within the verset. Rhythmic conflicts of this kind, however, occur very frequently in the *Soulier de satin,* and therefore do not usually function in themselves as stylistic devices.

The 'sound' of a statement is determined for the reader not only by the rhythm of the passage, but also by the phonological structure of the words. If the pattern of phonemes within a word or phrase differs markedly from that of most words of the text, it functions as a stylistic device.

When such an unusual sound pattern converges with an image vehicle in the *Soulier de satin,* it generally adds an element of humour to the expression.[13] After Léopold has praised Pedro de las Vegas, Fernand exclaims: (III ii 78; 796)

> O sublime *Guipuzcoan!* ...

In this periphrase, Pedro is designated by the name of the Spanish Basque province where he was born.[14] Fernand's use of a place name in referring to this scholar reflects the importance of one's birthplace in the eyes of traditionalists such as Léopold and Fernand, for whom a person's character is determined in great part by the cultural heritage he receives from the region in which he is raised.

The sound of the word *Guipuzcoan* seems comic to the reader in a French context, and the contrast between the grandeur evoked by the term *sublime* and this ridiculous name makes the image ironic in context: from the reader's point of view, Fernand's words serve to mock the scholar he is ostensibly praising. Since Fernand believes himself to be in agreement with las Vegas, he would not deliberately refer to him in a disparaging way; the reader therefore understands that Claudel is expressing his own derisive attitude through this image, not only towards the narrow-minded Pedro, but also towards Fernand and Léopold, who blindly accept this pedant's intolerant views.

The appearance of the text in print is still another aspect of the literary work to which the reader responds. Since this appearance is determined primarily by the typography of the printed work, any typographical feature that is surprising to the reader in context will be stylistically effective.

The typographical device that most often converges with images in the *Soulier de satin* is the unexpected capitalization of the vehicle terms. In most cases, such capital letters not only catch the reader's attention, but also suggest that the object or action designated has unusual significance.

In speaking of Rodrigue's mission to the Far East, the Angel says of the people he will encounter there: (III viii 264; 825)

> Tels sont ces peuples qui gémissent et attendent, le visage tourné vers *le Soleil levant.*

Following the words *gémissent et attendent,* this reference to the rising sun functions as an archetype, evoking in the reader the feelings of optimistic anticipation with which this event is often associated, and thus underscoring the longing of these peoples for relief from their suffering. In addition, this image indicates that the Orientals look specifically to the East as the source of their salvation; since Rodrigue will be approaching the area from this direction, the Angel's words imply that he will play an important role in bringing help to these tormented peoples.

The unexpected capitalization of *Soleil,* however, indicates that this particular 'sun' also signifies something more exceptional. Because the Angel has been speaking in this scene of the religious purposes of Rodrigue's mission, the image recalls Isaiah's prophecy that the Saviour of mankind will arrive from the East, from the direction of the rising sun;[15] the words *Soleil levant* then suggest that the salvation awaited by the Orientals is specifically that offered by the Catholic Church, in the name of Jesus.

Punctuation marks used in unexpected positions may serve to heighten the effectiveness of images by visually setting apart the terms of the vehicle from the other words of the passage.

As Camille and Prouhèze await the final Arab attack on Mogador, Camille tells Prouhèze: (III x 75; 836)

> Une ride nous est communiquée sur la mer qui bientôt va *me guérir de ce 'toi, ma rose!' pour toujours.*

The first part of this verset expresses metaphorically Rodrigue's approach by sea. The quotation marks that separate the words *toi, ma rose* from the rest of the sentence are unexpected; the exclamation point that precedes the second quote reinforces their effect.

The phrase *ce 'toi, ma rose!'* is a metaphor designating Prouhèze, and is ironic here, contrasting with the microcontext in several ways. First, the term *rose* is a common poetic epithet for a beloved person, and is thus semantically incompatible with the preceding *guérir*. Second, the words *toi, ma rose* function as an apostrophe and thus contrast both semantically and syntactically with the preceding demonstrative, *ce*.

Finally, the punctuation marks that set this image off from the rest of the sentence not only draw the reader's attention to the ironic terms themselves, but also underscore still another element of contrast: the quotes indicate that the entire phrase is used here as a linguistic formula, and thus point up the opposition that exists between the common use of the expression as a heartfelt, intimate appeal to a beloved person, and the conventional – and thus impersonal and dispassionate – manner in which Camille uses these words here.

In referring to Prouhèze and Rodrigue ironically, Camille ostensibly reveals his scorn for these lovers. In context, however, this irony reinforces the reader's impression that although Camille would like to feel that he detests Prouhèze he in fact desires her both physically and spiritually, and is intensely jealous of Rodrigue as a result.

STYLISTIC DEVICES CREATED BY REPETITION

The repetition of a linguistic element may catch the reader's attention and thus function as a stylistic device, even though there is no specific point of contrast between the repeated element and the reader's expectations. Such devices are found with particular frequency in poetry, because repetition on all linguistic levels – semantic, phonetic, grammatical, rhythmic, etc. – is an essential characteristic of this literary form.[16]

Semantic repetition is found to an unusually great degree in all of Claudel's writing, especially in his poetic works.[17] Since the *Soulier de satin* is a play, the frequency with which ideas are repeated in this particular text undoubtedly results not only from a tendency Claudel apparently had to express his thoughts in a repetitive manner and from the poetic nature of the work, but also from an attempt on his part to suggest spoken language, for people tend to repeat themselves far more often when they are talking spontaneously than when they are writing. In addition, because spectators cannot linger over or reread pages of a dramatic work when it is performed, repetition is necessary in an acted play if the ideas expressed are to be successfully conveyed to the audience.

In the simplest form of semantic repetition, a word or group of words is restated without change; the chief effect is to emphasize the idea that the reiterated terms express. When image vehicles are repeated in this way in the *Soulier de satin*, however, the microcontext of the image is usually altered; the new microcontext then helps to clarify or to amplify the meaning of the vehicle.

As Sept-Épées swims towards Don Juan's fleet, Rodrigue expresses his fervent hopes for her success: (IV xi 74–5; 944)

> Va à ta destinée, mon enfant! va combattre pour Jésus-Christ, *mon agneau*, à côté de Juan d'Autriche,
> *L'agneau que l'on voit sur les peintures avec sa petite bannière sur l'épaule.*

In the first verset, Rodrigue uses the term *agneau* as part of a common expression of endearment; the image conveys his deep affection for his young daughter. When he repeats this vehicle in the next verset, the metalinguistic statement that follows suggests additional thoughts: since Rodrigue refers specifically here to the *agneau* that symbolizes Jesus in his role as the innocent victim offered in sacrifice to God, the term now implies that Sept-Épées is like Christ in that she, too, is about to sacrifice her own life in order to save the souls of other, more sinful people. (The mention of the *petite bannière* recalls the specific idea symbolized by this emblem – the victory of Jesus over sin and death – and thus underscores the impression that Sept-Épées, also, will now attempt to conquer these evils.)[18]

The meaning of the second image is further expanded by the shift in modifiers from the possessive pronoun *mon* to a direct article. As a result of this shift, the second verset could also be interpreted as referring either to *Jésus Christ* or *Juan d'Autriche*. This ambiguity suggests that the second image in fact refers to all three individuals mentioned in the previous verset, and thus implies that by sacrificing their own earthly happiness in order to lead others to redemption both Sept-Épées and Don Juan become like Christ. (This impression is reinforced by the similarity of sounds in the names *Juan d'Autriche* and *Jésus Christ.*)

A second form of semantic repetition is the expression of a concept two or more times in different words. If all expressions of the repeated concept are figurative, the development constitutes an image-sequence; this particular type of semantic reiteration was discussed in Chapter 2.[19] If the concept is first stated literally and then repeated in figurative terms, the repetition serves both to emphasize the idea and to suggest additional thoughts to the reader.

In speaking of the relationship of Africa to Spain, Prouhèze refers to the continent as: (III xiii 28; 850)

> Cette Afrique à la porte du Royaume, *cet immense grenier à sauterelles qui trois fois nous a recouverts du temps de Tarif et de Yousouf et des Almohades,*
>
> ...

In the first part of the metaphoric statement, the word *sauterelles* recalls the roles of these insects in the Bible, as one of the ten plagues to strike Egypt (Ex. 10:4–6, 12–15), and as creatures who will rise from the bottomless pit on the Day of Judgment to torture those who have led evil lives (Apoc. 9:3–10). The term *grenier* indicates that these repulsive, frightening beings are being kept in reserve on the continent. These first vehicles thus reinforce the impression given the reader earlier in the play that Africa is a spiritual hell-on-earth, and suggest that its evil inhabitants pose a serious threat to the Spanish Catholics who live such a short distance away.

The remainder of the figurative development describes the contamination of Spain in the past by this concentration of spiritual evil. In the clause beginning *qui trois fois,* Prouhèze refers to Arab leaders who led invasions of Spain: the polysyndetical repetition of *et* in this trinary group stresses each name individually, and thus emphasizes that the Africans have overrun the country on several different occasions.[20] In addition, the phonemic structure of the second and third names cited is different from that of most French terms; in context, these unfamiliar sounds make the Arab leaders seem even more terrifying.

By referring to Africa both literally and figuratively here, Prouhèze thus not only indicates the general importance of the continent, but also stresses the danger that the barbarous African forces represent to the future of Catholic Spain.

When a concept is expressed first figuratively and then literally, the literal statement usually serves both to clarify and to emphasize the meaning of the image.

Pélage tells Balthazar that before he returns to Africa he must respond to an appeal that he has just received: (I ii 8; 669)

> Cette lettre de *la veuve dans la montagne*, cette lettre de ma cousine dans ma main.

In the periphrase through which the writer of the letter is first designated, only her sex, marital status, and general physical surroundings are indicated; these facts evoke an affective response on the part of the reader – compassion for this woman who has been left alone in a harsh, desolate region – and also arouse his curiosity.

The restatement of the tenor concept in literal terms then clarifies at least the general relationship of the *veuve* to Pélage. The reiteration in both phrases of the idea that a woman has made this appeal stresses the helplessness of the person who needs aid; the repetition of the terms *cette lettre* emphasizes the imperativeness of this request. Together, these repetitions indicate that Pélage has no choice but to respond to his cousin, despite the resulting inconvenience to his own plans.

In the *Soulier de satin*, as in most poetic texts, grammatical repetition often coincides with semantic reiteration and reinforces its effects.[21]

The Double Shadow speaks of the consequences of the meeting of Prouhèze and Rodrigue at Mogador: (II xiii 12; 777)

> Maintenant je porte accusation contre cet homme et cette femme par qui *j'ai existé une seconde seule pour ne plus finir* et par qui *j'ai été imprimée sur la page de l'éternité*!

In the first dependent clause, the phrases *une seconde seule* and *pour ne plus finir* describe this forbidden meeting, which lasted only a moment but whose consequences will remain forever, in the form of the Shadow. The irrevocability of these consequences is then restated in concrete, book-code terms. This image development (continued in the following verset) recalls references in biblical and liturgical texts to the 'book' in which each person's past is recorded and on the basis of which his ultimate spiritual fate is determined by God, and indicates that the eternal repercussions of this meeting relate specifically to the spiritual destiny of the two lovers.[22]

The semantic repetition in this sentence thus serves both to emphasize the reiterated idea and to suggest an additional thought to the reader. The anaphora *par qui j'ai* and the syntactic similarity of the two clauses – in both, *j'ai* is followed by a past participle and modifying phrases – help to stress further the repeated concept.

Semantic and grammatical repetition coincide so frequently in most poetic works that when two statements whose semantic relationship is unclear are syntactically similar the reader usually concludes that the two statements are similar in meaning as well. If the parallel terms are images, the reader infers that they express a single tenor concept. In an illogical image-sequence, for example, the similar syntactic structure of the vehicles is often a key factor in indicating that the different vehicles express the same tenor. This is the case in the illogical image-sequence discussed in Chapter 2, Prouhèze's description of her feelings as she enters a spiritually purifying state: (III viii 199; 821)

> ... c'est *un rayon qui me perce,* c'est *un glaive qui me divise,* c'est *le fer rouge effroyablement appliqué sur le nerf même de la vie,* c'est *l'ef-fervescence de la source qui s'empare de tous mes éléments pour les dis-soudre et les recomposer,* c'est *le néant à chaque moment où je sombre* et Dieu *sur ma bouche qui me ressuscite,* et supérieure à toutes les délices, ah! c'est *la traction impitoyable de la soif, l'abomination de cette soif affreuse qui m'ouvre et me crucifie!*

The close semantic relationship of grammatically parallel state-ments may involve a contrast, as well as a similarity, of meaning. Opposing aspects of a single situation, for example, are some-times expressed in syntactically parallel phrases; the grammati-cal similarity of the statements then helps to underscore their antonymic relationship.

Recalling Columbus's voyage to America, the King describes the New World as: (I vi 30; 687)

> ... un monde *de feu* et *de neige* à la rencontre de nos enseignes détachant *une escadre de volcans!*

The syntactically similar phrases *de feu* and *de neige* are semantically related in that both express metonymically the geographical conditions of the Americas, but they suggest opposite types of situations.

Taken together, these two expressions first evoke the wide range of climatic conditions found in the New World. When the King then mentions the *escadre de volcans*, the reader understands by flashback that these phrases may also designate this particular physical formation, in which 'fire' is produced from a 'snowy' peak. The semantic contrast of the two images, heightened by their grammatical similarity, thus underscores the astonishing character of this land, where such opposing physical conditions exist side by side, not only within one territory, but within a single geographic feature.

Because the rhythmic pattern of a French sentence is determined primarily by the syntax of the statement, rhythmic repetition generally converges with grammatical similarity. Since in poetry syntactically parallel statements are usually semantically similar, semantic, grammatical, and rhythmic repetition frequently coincide. Except for brief phrases, however – the King's reference to *un monde de feu et de neige*, for example – the repetitive statements are not as a rule rhythmically identical; the reader is given the impression that their rhythm is the same by convergent stylistic devices, such as the anaphora, sometimes used in conjunction with the asyndeton or the polysyndeton.

The repetition of the same word or group of words at the beginning of each of a series of phrases constitutes an anaphora. In telling Prouhèze how he has attempted to communicate with her in the past, the Guardian Angel asks: (III viii 48; 814)

> Et toi-même, dis-moi s'il est bien vrai que tu ne l'aies jamais ressenti au fond de toi-même ... *ce coup sourd, cet arrêt net, cette touchée urgente?*

Each successive adjective in this image-sequence – *sourd, net, urgente* – presents the Angel's approach to Prouhèze as more distinct and more pressing. The final phrase is particularly striking for the reader because the concretization *touchée* – which indicates that the Angel now contacts Prouhèze in person, rather than from a distance – is a neologism. The three images are asyndetically juxtaposed – that is, the conjunction that would ordinarily link the last two is omitted; this construction in itself gives an impression of rapidity, which underscores the general urgency of these appeals.

These three phrases are semantically and grammatically similar; and although the form of the initial demonstrative differs in each case, the repetition of this adjective is perceived by the reader as an anaphora. The asyndeton adds to the reader's impression that the phrases are rhythmically equivalent by creating attention-getting breaks between them, thus separating them into clearly defined rhythmic units. Even though the phrases are not rhythmically identical, the repetitive syntactic pattern, together with the anaphora and the asyndeton, give the reader the impression that they are rhythmically equivalent. The grammatical and apparent rhythmic repetition help to under-score for the reader the semantic similarity of the three phrases and to stress the idea that this repetition suggests – the persever-ance of the Angel in his attempts to guide Prouhèze.

In the polysyndeton, a conjunction is used more often than is necessary; when a series of phrases is polysyndetically joined, the conjunction is usually repeated before each addition to the series.

The Actress begs Rodrigue to accept the command of England, but he expresses his reluctance to relinquish the freedom he has been able to enjoy while living on the sea, and asks her in return: (IV vi 112; 906)

> Et de nouveau vous allez me rendre *aux murs*, et *aux meubles*, et *aux papiers?* ...

Each of the vehicles of this image-sequence expresses metonym-ically the restrictive situation in which Rodrigue would find himself if he accepted this administrative position: the words *murs* and *meubles* evoke the tangible curbs that would be imposed on his physical activities by his role as governor, and the term *papiers* calls to mind the intellectual limitations that would result from his constant involvement with petty daily affairs. The repetition of the same idea in the three images emphasizes the stringency of these restraints.

The polysyndeton created by the repetition of *et* before each addition to this series functions like the asyndeton in separating the parts of the series into distinct units; together with the anaphoric repetition of *aux,* it gives the reader the impression that the phrases are rhythmically equivalent. The grammatical similarity of the phrases and this rhythmic resemblance reinforce the effect of the semantic repetition. In addition, because the term *et* expresses an adding or cumulative process, the repetition of this particular conjunction in itself stresses the accumulation of restrictive controls and in this way further underscores the constraining nature of this position.[23]

As a rule, when the repetition of phonological elements functions as a stylistic device in the *Soulier de satin,* this repetition occurs in words that are closely related in meaning, although they may not be semantically repetitive, and serves to underscore this link.

Phonological repetition may stress the connection between the component terms of a single expression. In thinking aloud of the defeat of the Armada, the King asks himself critically: (iv iv 15; 885)

   Comment appeler le Roi qui *bâtit sur la mer mouvante* ...

This image is especially striking for the reader because it is a renewal of the cliché, *bâtir sur un sol mouvant.* The reader recalls that the original cliché is used to express the undertaking of a hazardous or doubtful enterprise, and thus understands the King to be admitting here that he has invested his country's resources in an unsound venture. The contrast between the substitute term *mer* and the original *sol* also underscores the nautical character of the ill-fated project.

The repetition of the /m/ sound in the phrase *mer mouvante* draws the reader's attention to these two words in particular, and thus underscores the semantic connection between them. Since the word *mer* is not part of the original cliché, but the term *mouvante* is, the alliteration reinforces the reader's awareness that the image is a cliché renewal, and in this way emphasizes both the idea expressed by the original expression and the different nuance of meaning conveyed in contrast by the renewal.

In addition, the adjective *mouvante* is redundant when applied to *mer,* since the waters of all seas are constantly shifting in position; this redundancy in itself emphasizes the precariousness of the King's venture.[24] By stressing the interrelationship of these two terms, the alliteration also underscores this tautology for the reader, and thus further accentuates the riskiness of the undertaking.

If the terms that are characterized by similar sounds are semantically repetitive, the phonological repetition serves to heighten the effectiveness of the semantic reiteration. Such phonological repetition often converges with grammatical and rhythmic repetition as well.

In describing Rodrigue's mission to the Far East, the Angel explains that he will free the Oriental peoples from their confining, isolated state: (III viii 259; 825)

> Il va reconnaître ... ces portions *cloisonnées et comprimées* qui recherchent non pas une issue mais leur centre.

The terms *cloisonnées* and *comprimées* both express the restrictive conditions under which the Orientals live; in context, the reader understands that these limitations are intellectual and spiritual as well as physical.

These semantically similar words are characterized by both alliteration (repetition of the initial /k/ sound) and assonance (repetition of the final /e/), and are morphologically and rhythmically alike as well. The convergence of repetition on four linguistic levels – semantic, grammatical, rhythmic, and phonological – puts great emphasis on the concept that the images express.[25]

The reader's response to each individual image of the *Soulier de satin* is thus determined not only by the stylistic characteristics of the image itself and its relationship to other figurative expressions employing the same or related vehicle codes or found in the same passage, but also by additional stylistic devices that converge with the vehicle terms and that contribute significantly to the overall impact of the image on the reader's mind.

PART TWO

LEVELS OF MEANING

AS EXPRESSED

THROUGH IMAGERY

The narrative level

The text of the *Soulier de satin* conveys three levels of meaning to the reader as the play progresses: the story line or narrative level; the religious level, which reveals the theological significance of the situations depicted on the story line; and the emotional level, the most fundamental affective concepts expressed by the text.

The narrative level of the play consists of the earthly situations and actions in which the characters of the play take part as the work progresses.[1] This story line involves two closely related groups of ideas – the psychological nature of the characters, including their basic personality traits and their emotional reactions to specific situations, and the concrete events in which they participate. Imagery plays a different role in the expression of each of these areas.

PSYCHOLOGICAL MAKE-UP OF CHARACTERS

As will be shown in Chapters 5 and 6, the development of the *Soulier de satin* clearly reflects a specific, religiously determined view of human life. Critics have sometimes charged that because the work reflects this theological view the individual characters are not 'true to life,' but function rather as one-dimensional representatives of particular religious or ethical attitudes. Two aspects of the play's development seem to support this opinion. First, the position of each character with regard to Catholicism is clearly indicated and many speakers are also shown to play particular spiritual roles in relation to other individuals. Second, several characters who appear in the play are clearly unlike human beings in a number of significant ways; in most cases, the nonhuman qualities of these characters evoke specific spiritual or moral attitudes, which the speakers then come to represent for the reader.[2]

Most characters of the *Soulier de satin*, however, also exhibit personality traits and emotional reactions similar to those of human beings. As a result, even though the religious or moral positions they exemplify may seem more important to the reader than their human characteristics, they do not remain entirely one-dimensional for him. These human traits are conveyed to the reader in two different ways – they are suggested indirectly, by the stylistic qualities that predominate in the character's speech, and they are described directly, either by the character in question or by one of the other speakers.

The psychological make-up of any person determines to a great extent the stylistic qualities of his speech, including the types of images he uses in expressing himself. Similarly, in a literary work the stylistic qualities of a character's speech reflect his basic personality traits and serve as an indirect means of conveying these traits to the reader. Because a play is composed almost entirely of direct statements by the characters, their speech is an especially important means of revealing their personalities to the reader.

In the *Soulier de satin,* the speech of many characters conforms with the reader's preconceived notions of the way members of three social groups – upper class, lower class, and children – usually talk. This conformity with popular stereotypes of speech gives the reader the impression that the attitudes of these characters are similar to those commonly believed to be held by members of the social groups in question.[3]

Most of the principal characters of the *Soulier de satin* – including Prouhèze, Rodrigue, Pélage, and Camille – belong to the upper levels of Spanish Renaissance society.[4] The thematic content of the images used by these characters points up their social standing when the vehicles they employ include terms usually found only in learned or literary works or references to historical or literary events, because at the time at which the *Soulier de satin* ostensibly takes place only individuals of noble origins could receive a formal education.

Rodrigue employs both literary and historical references in describing the passageway he created across the mountainous Isthmus of Panama: (III xi 20; 844)

> Que parle-t-on dans les classes *d'Annibal et de ses éléphants?* Moi,
> à la tête de douze vaisseaux, j'ai gravi les monts ...

Rodrigue's comparison of his accomplishment to that of Hannibal reveals his great pride in his own ingenuity and his belief that his achievements, too, will help determine the future course of events in the civilized world. The poetic term *monts* (which is literal in context), together with the preceding reference to a historical event, give Rodrigue's statement a learned, serious tone which itself underscores both the importance of the actions being described and the noble upbringing of the speaker.

According to a popular stereotype, upper-class individuals tend to avoid the direct expression of disagreeable, offensive, or very intense thoughts and feelings, in order to maintain a consistently reserved, genteel demeanour in the presence of others. The noble characters of the *Soulier de satin* often keep from stating such objectionable thoughts directly by using images that enable them to convey their ideas in a covert or extenuated manner; these include archetypal terms, clichés, and ironic expressions.

Speaking of the power that women exercise over the men who love them, Rodrigue asks: (III xiii, 104–6; 854)

> Et tout de même d'où serait venue pour César et pour Marc-Antoine ...
>
> ...
>
> Le pouvoir tout à coup *de ces yeux* et *de ce sourire* et *de cette bouche* comme si jamais auparavant ils n'avaient baisé le visage d'une femme,
>
> ...

In this metonymic description of the woman who was so influential in the life of each of these great men, the words *cette bouche* function as an archetype, evoking the erotic sensations with which this part of the body is often associated. By including this image here, Rodrigue suggests in a veiled, and thus socially acceptable, way that sensual appeal was one determinant of the power of these women over the men who were so captivated by them.[5]

When an upper-class speaker expresses an objectionable thought through a stereotyped expression commonly used by the members of his own social group, he can assume both that his listeners will readily grasp his meaning, and that his words will not be considered distasteful. Musique, praying in the Church of Saint Nicholas, uses such a cliché to describe her own pregnant state, referring to herself as: (III i 58; 787)

> ... moi, la Musique, lourde du *fruit que je porte.*

Ironic statements can serve to reveal, yet mask, offensive thoughts and feelings because they evoke two opposing thoughts in the reader's mind.

When Rodrigue stops at Mogador on his way to America and tries to convince Prouhèze to come away with him, he and Camille meet and discuss her refusal to leave Africa. At one point, Camille explains: (II xi 18–20; 767–8)

> Quand *votre ombre gentille aura passé, fantôme désormais d'une autre rive,*
>
> *Celle du Maure* habitera encore ce château,
>
> Familière d'une autre, *couvrant, protégeant de sa noirceur une autre;*
>
> ...

By referring to Rodrigue as a shadow, Camille makes him seem totally insignificant in relation to the situation at Mogador; the term *gentille,* understood in the sense of pagan or unbeliever, underscores his position as an outsider.[6] Camille's scorn for his rival is emphasized by the mocking tone of his words. The phrase *votre ombre gentille* is ironic, because two other possible meanings of *gentille* in context – noble by birth and gracious or agreeable – contrast with the idea of paganism. *Gentille* also conflicts with the word *ombre* – taken in any of the three senses, it cannot logically modify this noun. Finally, the idea of graciousness contrasts with the concept of death, which the first statement as a whole evokes.

The words *aura passé* reinforce the ironic effect because the two possible meanings of the verb here also conflict with each other – these words may be understood literally, since Rodrigue is in fact 'passing by' Mogador on his way to America; but following the term *ombre* they also function as a euphemistic expression of dying. Similarly, in the second part of the verset irony is created by a term that evokes both Rodrigue's departure from Mogador and his death – coming after the first reference to death and the word *fantôme,* the term *rive* brings to mind the rivers of Hell; this thought then conflicts with the reader's knowledge that Rodrigue is in fact leaving Mogador for the *autre rive* of the New World. Because they evoke Rodrigue's death, both of these ironic references to his departure further emphasize his total exclusion from future events at Mogador.

Camille continues to develop the shadow-code image in the second and third versets, referring to his own presence as *celle du Maure,* and speaking of Prouhèze as *une autre.* In the third verset, the description of the two shadows' activity contains an additional element of contrast – here, irony results from the opposition between Camille's professed desire to shelter

Prouhèze (*couvrant, protégeant une autre*), and the fact that the instrument of this safekeeping will be *noirceur*, a quality associated with evil intentions and deeds.

This shadow-code development creates in the reader's mind two conflicting impressions of Camille's attitude towards Rodrigue and Prouhèze. On the surface, Camille maintains his gentlemanly demeanour. His words are a polite, respectful – and thus most acceptable – description of what will soon occur at Mogador; taken in this sense, the passage suggests that an amiable, if reserved, relationship exists between the two rivals. The elements of ironic contrast, however, also evoke feelings that directly oppose this highly refined surface – in particular a deep animosity, which reveals Camille's continuing hostility towards both his competitor in love and the woman who resists him.[7]

The speech of the lowborn characters of the *Soulier de satin* – the Negress, Isidore, Daibutsu, the Italian Sergeant, the fishermen, the Captain, and the soldiers – conforms with commonly accepted stereotypes of lower-class conversation in two ways: it reflects the speakers' primitive or simple-minded views of the world around them, and it displays an almost total lack of subtlety and discretion.

These characters' simple-minded outlook apparently results from their lack of formal education and the limited nature of their contacts with areas of life outside of their own immediate surroundings, and is reflected in their tendency to compare all types of situations to objects and events closely related to their everyday lives.

Thus, when the fishermen discuss the mysterious object they believe lies under the water, they use several images directly related to their seafaring pursuits. In telling Mangiacavallo that his hands are not sensitive enough to hold the line with which they are searching, Alcochete asks rhetorically: (iv i 12; 861)

> Et toi, quoi est-ce que tu sentirais un peu avec tes pattes qui sont *plus épaisses que de la peau de requin*? ...

(In this case, the social class of the speaker is also underscored by his use of the grammatically incorrect, but typically lower-class expression, *quoi est-ce que*.)

The lower-class characters reveal their lack of both subtlety and tactfulness by stating all kinds of ideas in very strong terms, frequently through hyperbolic images.

The ideas so forcefully expressed may be relatively innocuous.

In explaining why a child has been asked to hold the rope with which he hopes to locate a treasure lying under the sea, Bogotillos compares the delicate, sensitive person needed for this task to an object generally considered to be the epitome of tenderness: (IV i 13; 862)

> ... Mais pour s'en servir il faut un petit corps tendre, des mains fraîches *comme une feuille de rose* ...

Even when they express disagreeable or offensive thoughts, these characters tend to stress their ideas by stating them in hyperbolic terms. Alcochete's comparison of Mangiacavallo's hands to *la peau de requin*, cited above, is one example. In another passage, as three soldiers standing guard at Mogador speak of what has occurred at the fortress since Prouhèze's arrival, one uses the phrase: (III iv 13; 805)

> ... Du moment où *c'te foutue chienne* de Prouhèze ...

This particular hyperbole reflects the speaker's lower-class background not only because it is openly insulting to Prouhèze, but also because it includes an adjective with vulgar associations. In context, the image serves to express the soldier's contempt for the woman he feels is to blame for the precarious situation in which the defenders of Mogador now find themselves.[8]

The only speaking characters in the *Soulier de satin* who are children are Sept-Épées and la Bouchère. When they talk, these two young girls repeatedly display the primitive outlook, lack of subtlety, and egoism generally considered typical of children.

Two other characters, Musique and Rodrigue, also speak in a childlike manner at certain points in the play.[9] Their speech then serves to remind the reader that their attitudes, at least for the moment, are dominated by the same uncritical frankness and the same simple-minded conception of the world around them as are exhibited consistently by Sept-Épées and la Bouchère.[10]

As in the case of the lower-class adults, the simple-minded outlook of the children results primarily from their limited exposure to areas of life beyond their own immediate surroundings, and is reflected in the restricted thematic content of the vehicles they employ. These images are drawn primarily from the children's routine daily activities or from those few areas of the natural world with which they have managed to come in contact.

Sept-Épées says of Rodrigue's desire to bring happiness into the lives of recently conquered Englishmen: (IV x 23; 936)

Il va *peindre* toute l'Angleterre *bleu ciel*.

This image may be understood as a reference to Rodrigue's painting of religious pictures at this time. Painting, however, is also a favourite activity of children, and the phrase *bleu ciel* recalls specifically the child's tendency to paint simple scenes in flat colours – blue sky, green grass, yellow sun.

When the children discuss religious ideas, several of the images they use in presenting their thoughts underscore the way their undeveloped mentality facilitates their belief in irrational theological concepts, and in this way contributes to their strong religious faith.[11]

Musique refers to the heavenly realm as: (III i 55; 787)

... *cette république enchantée* où les âmes *se rendent visite sur ces nacelles qu'une seule larme suffit à lester*.

The description of this realm as *enchantée*, together with the personification of the *âmes* who live there, makes the Christian heaven seem very much like the fabulous countries described in children's fairy stories. These images thus reveal that for Musique fairy-tale magic and traditional religious forces need not be contradictory, and may in fact complement each other. (The phrase *cette république enchantée* is particularly striking for the reader because the adjective *enchantée* contrasts sharply with the political ideas commonly associated with the term *république*.)[12]

Like the lower-class characters, the children exhibit a lack of discretion in expressing their thoughts, and tend to state all kinds of ideas in terms of extremes. When Sept-Épées brags to la Bouchère of her father's past exploits, she emphasizes his ability as a warrior through a hyperbolic simile: (IV iii 33; 881)

... Tu verras mon père! Il sait tout. Il n'y a rien qu'il ne puisse faire s'il veut. Qu'est-ce que c'est, à côté de lui, que *Dragut et Barberousse*?[13]

This boastful statement seems particularly childlike to the reader because it conveys Sept-Épée's unquestioning faith in her father's ability and power, a form of egoism typical of children.

Although the children of the play do not express themselves as crudely as the lower-class characters occasionally do, they, too, state even openly critical thoughts in very strong terms. Sept-Épées speaks with la Bouchère of the religious mission they are beginning, and compares herself and her companion to the *alouette*, a bird frequently associated with spiritual purity (IV iii 7; 879). She then goes on to correct her own image: (IV iii 8; 879)

> Moi, du moins, je suis *une alouette*, et toi, tu n'es qu'*une grosse mouche à viande*. Ça ne fait rien, je t'aime tout de même.

Sept-Épées's reversal indicates that she realizes that la Bouchère is too tied to physical needs to be of much help in carrying out this spiritual mission. Although she then implies that despite their differences she is in fact fond of her companion, her comparison of la Bouchère to a *grosse mouche à viande* remains a strong insult.[14]

When these similarities between the different characters' speech and the popular stereotypes of the three social groups – upper class, lower class, and youth – are recognized by the reader, he is struck by this resemblance of the speakers to real people. Because they thus make the characters seem more 'alive' to him these similarities not only serve to underscore some of the characters' basic attitudes, but also facilitate the reader's emotional identification with the speakers and in this way increase his involvement with the play as a whole.

The psychological qualities that are directly described by the speakers of the *Soulier de satin* generally relate to the characters' emotional responses to specific situations and events, rather than to their basic personality traits. Since most of the narrative-level events that take place within the framework of the play revolve around relationships of love – both mutual and one-sided – the emotions most often described are the joy, encouragement, frustration, and anxiety that such intimate relationships may produce. Four vehicle codes predominate in the expression of these feelings: light and light-producing objects, sickness, life and death, and sense impressions.[15]

Light-code imagery is used to express the joy and hope experienced by a person in love. Rodrigue tells Isidore of the depressing tedium of his daily routine at sea: (I vii 97–8; 696)

... bientôt je ne trouvais plus au firmament que *ce feu de plomb* trop connu,

    L'opaque et sûr falot, triste guide du navigateur sur les eaux inal-térées.

He then adds that Prouhèze appears to him as: (I vii 99; 696)

    ... *ce point de lumière dans le sable vivant de la nuit,*
    ...

The contrast between this light-code vehicle and the absence-of-light imagery both in the preceding versets and in the following reference to *la nuit* implies that, in opposition to the dismal sadness of Rodrigue's days at sea, Prouhèze brings cheer and hope into his life.

TABLE 4
Frequency count: the narrative level

Psychological make-up of characters, codes used		Image elements
Light and light-producing objects, total		21
Star	11	
Other light imagery	10	
Sickness		17
Life		6
Death		25
Sense impressions, total		50
Hearing	41	
Taste	6	
Smell	3	
Actions and events in which the characters take part		
Physical separation of lovers		40
Physical union of lovers		17
Country compared to lover of conqueror		29
Progressive unification of world described through barrier and door codes, total		40
Barrier code	32	
Door code	8	

In addition, the illogical expression *sable vivant* evokes the incessant movement of the sea, and together with the suggestion of darkness in *de la nuit* recalls the frightening precariousness that Rodrigue's adventurous way of life entails. The entire statement then implies through a flashback that in contrast to this state of constant peril the mutual feeling of love between himself and Prouhèze provides Rodrigue with at least one element of reassuring certainty.

Closely related to this use of light-code imagery to express the happiness to which love may give rise is the use of the same code to describe the inspiration and encouragement provided by a beloved person. Rodrigue's expression through references to a star of the idea that Prouhèze stimulates him to look beyond the ordinary, concrete world for ultimate satisfaction was examined in Chapter 2; one passage cited in illustration there was his rhetorical question to Isidore: (I vii 150–1; 698–9)

> ... si je lui demande son immortalité, *cette étoile* sans le savoir *au fond d'elle-même qu'elle est,*
> Ah! comment pourrait-elle me refuser?[16]

The familiar poetic theme of love-sickness is used several times in the *Soulier de satin* to describe the distress of the frustrated lover.

Rodrigue tells Camille that he cannot help loving Prouhèze: (II xi 85; 771)

> Il ne dépend pas d'un homme *sain* que *la peste s'attaque à lui*, ou *la colique*, ou *la lèpre*, ou *toute autre maladie dévorante*.

Although the tenor of this image-sequence is not Prouhèze, but the complex of feelings that Rodrigue experiences as a result of his irresistible attraction to her, the development implies that as the stimulus of his agony she herself is an insidious, destructive being. This series of vehicles thus reveals the tremendous resentment that Rodrigue feels at this moment towards the woman who, by first attracting and then rejecting him, has caused him this great pain.

As is usual in literary texts, when life- and death-code images are used in the *Soulier de satin* to describe the love relationship, the former evoke joyful, inspiring, satisfying emotions, and the latter convey feelings of anxiety and frustration. The characters

who love, however, differ on just which aspects of this relationship cause happiness, and which cause despair.

Early in the play, Camille tells Prouhèze that when a woman
loves a man she forces him to make her the centre of his life: (i
iii 70–1; 676)

> ... Il faut qu'il n'ait plus besoin que d'elle seule.
> C'est *la mort* et le désert qu'elle apporte avec elle.

But Prouhèze responds: (i iii 72; 676)

> Ah! ce n'est pas *la mort* mais *la vie* que je voudrais apporter à celui
> que j'aime,
> ...

Camille's use of the term *mort* here suggests that for himself, at
least, to become deeply involved with a woman means giving up
all other interests in favour of a relationship that has little value
in itself. Prouhèze's reference to life then evokes the opposite
view – love as a fulfilling, enriching experience. The expression
of these different conceptions of love in antithetical terms helps
to stress the sharp contrast in the attitudes of these two speakers
towards such intense emotional involvement.

The vicissitudes of Rodrigue's relationship with Prouhèze are
reflected in his use of death-code images to express his feelings
at different points in the play.

Rodrigue's views are at first very much like those of Prouhèze.
Describing to Isidore the happiness and encouragement his
beloved has brought into his life, he says of their one previous
meeting: (i vii 122–4; 697)

> Déjà elle contenait cette joie qui m'appartient ...
> Déjà elle me regardait avec ce visage qui *détruit la mort*!
> Car qu'est-ce qu'on appelle *mourir*, sinon de cesser d'être néces-
> saire? quand est-ce qu'elle a pu se passer de moi? quand est-ce que
> je cesserai d'être cela sans quoi elle n'aurait pu être elle-même?

The last of these versets functions as a metalinguistic comment
on the phrase *détruit la mort,* and indicates that the mutual
dependence involved in the love relationship – for Camille, *la
mort et le désert* – seems to Rodrigue at this moment not merely
the opposite of death, but the 'death of death,'[17] a satisfying,
reassuring experience that banishes forever feelings of empti-
ness and despair.

Later in the play, after Prouhèze has refused for the second time to leave Mogador with him, Rodrigue again describes his feelings in terms of death; by now, however, his unfulfilled love has caused him great anguish and frustration, and as a result his attitude is much closer to that of Camille. He thus asserts that in the past great men have been led by women they loved to abandon their duties as conquerors and rulers: (III xiii 108; 854)

> Un éclair a brillé pour eux par quoi le monde entier est *frappé à mort* désormais, retranché d'eux,
>
> ...

And he indicates that his own relationship with Prouhèze has left all other areas of his life, too, without meaning or purpose: (III xiii 115; 854)

> Ainsi la vue de cet Ange pour moi qui fut *comme le trait de la mort!* ...

The characters of the *Soulier de satin* often describe the feeling of being linked emotionally to a loved one, and in particular of being able to communicate with this beloved person without physical contact, in terms of sense impressions.

Auditory-code vehicles are used most frequently to express such communication. During Rodrigue's first trip to Mogador, Prouhèze refuses to see him even briefly; Rodrigue, however, declares that he does not actually have to speak with her in order to convey his message: (II xi 76–8; 771)

> Où qu'elle soit je sais qu'elle ne peut pas s'empêcher d'*entendre les mots que je lui dis,*
> Et moi, je sais qu'elle est là *au son que fait mon âme en lui parlant,*
> *Comme un aveugle en chantant sait qu'il est devant un mur ou des buissons ou le vide.*

By describing his contact with Prouhèze in terms of a physical form of communication, Rodrigue makes his connection with her seem more real, and less like simply a wish-fulfilling fantasy on his part.

In addition, the development of the auditory-code image in the second and third versets indicates that he also receives a specific message from Prouhèze in reply. To illustrate the blind man's 'communication' with his surroundings, Rodrigue mentions here three types of obstacles to his progress – *un mur, des buissons, le vide*. The last of these is particularly striking for the reader, because rather than designating a specific physical obstacle, as do the first two nouns, it suggests a dangerous lack of solid objects ahead. This vehicle then reminds the reader of Rodrigue's general situation, and underscores his fear that he might now receive a response that reveals that he, too, is heading towards such a perilous *vide* – towards an empty, futile existence.[18]

The lovers of the *Soulier de satin* also express their feeling of being closely linked with each other through words related to the senses of taste and smell.[19]

In describing the relationship she would like to have with her future husband, Musique exclaims: (i x 45; 709)

Oui, je veux *me mêler* à chacun de ses sentiments *comme un sel étincelant et délectable qui les transforme et les rince!* ...

The verb *mêler* is scarcely effective as an image in itself, but the following metalinguistic simile develops this metaphor through the description of the ways in which salt affects other substances when it 'mixes' with them.

The words *étincelant* and *délectable* evoke the stimulating qualities of this mineral and its ability to bring out the taste of the foods with which it is combined, and thus indicate that Musique hopes to encourage the Viceroy to take more interest and more pleasure in all areas of his life. The verbs *transforme* and *rince* then recall the use of salt as a cleansing agent in various industrial and medical processes, and suggest that she also wishes to have an inspiring, uplifting influence on her husband's thoughts and feelings. (The alliteration of the /s/ sound throughout this sentence helps to underscore the ideas Musique is expressing here.)

ACTIONS AND EVENTS IN WHICH THE CHARACTERS TAKE PART

Almost all of the narrative-level events that take place within the framework of the *Soulier de satin* relate to two types of situations – the love of men and women characters for each other, and the exploration and conquest of various parts of the world.

When relationships of love between men and women are themselves discussed in the text, the characters speak primarily of their feelings – necessarily of greatest importance to those involved in such an alliance –and generally mention only briefly and in literal terms the actions they perform as a result of these emotions.[20]

Because many of the characters remain at a distance from those they love for long periods of time, the related actions and situations that are described in figurative terms involve for the most part the separation of the lovers. Saint Jacques says of the lonely people who turn to him for comfort: (II vi 10; 751)

> ... ceux que *l'abîme* sépare n'ont qu'à me regarder pour se trouver ensemble.

Because the term *abîme* is commonly used as a hyperbolic figurative expression of a division or interval, this image helps to emphasize the distance that lies between the parted lovers. The word *abîme* also functions as a cliché in references to the sea; since Saint Jacques has just been speaking of his position in the sky between the Old World and the New and since the reader knows that Rodrigue is about to leave for America, this association of the term reminds the reader that the Atlantic Ocean will soon act as a barrier between Rodrigue and his beloved.

Most of the images that are used in the play to describe the physical union of lovers are found in scenes in which these characters are in fact separated, but in which they express their longing for each other. Furthermore, these images generally evoke not only a physical proximity, but also emotional and spiritual ties. Sept-Épées tells la Bouchère what would happen if she went to live with Don Juan: (IV iii 64; 883)

> Ah! je serais *un frère* pour lui et *nous dormirions ensemble* côte à côte et je serais toujours à côté de lui pour le défendre ...

The vehicle term *frère* indicates that Sept-Épées hopes to have a close, comradely relationship with her lover. Following this image, the words *nous dormirions ensemble* not only function as a euphemistic reference to her physical union with Don Juan, but also evoke again the intimate emotional relationship she looks forward to enjoying with him.

In passages relating to the conquest and rule of nations and territories, images serve primarily to indicate the significance of the events with respect either to the individual character's own life, or to the relative state of unity or disunity existing among the different parts of the world at the time.

The importance that taking command of a region holds in relation to a character's life is suggested most often by the description of this territory as if it were a woman. In such cases, the conqueror himself is likened to the country's lover, either directly or by implication. The image development then indicates the general nature of both the character's activities in the area and his emotional response to the territory.

The descriptions of Rodrigue's relationship to the Americas contain several examples of this type of personification. Early in the play, the King describes the attitude that the future ruler of the Americas must adopt towards these newly discovered continents: (I vi 61–2; 689)

> ... est-ce pour lui que je m'arracherai cette Amérique ... *s'il ne l'aime de cet amour injuste et jaloux?*
>
> Est-ce dans la raison et la justice qu'il *épousera* cette terre sauvage et cruelle, et qu'il *la prendra toute glissante entre ses bras* ...

The King first uses terms generally associated with a love relationship between a man and a woman; when he continues to develop this love code in the second verset, he employs two expressions that have more definite erotic connotations, referring first to marriage and then to a physical contact suggestive of sexual activity. The passage as a whole both indicates that this conqueror will have to use firm physical force in establishing control over the country, and, since the area is compared specifically to a wife, also implies that the conquest of the New World will serve for him as a substitute for a prolonged relationship with a real woman.

This last suggestion is reinforced by other passages, both literal and figurative, in which Rodrigue's activities as conqueror of the Americas are described. After he has spent ten years in the New World, for example, Ramire speaks of the possibility that someone else may take command of the area: (III vi 54; 810)

> Eh quoi, lui prendre l'Amérique? ce serait lui enlever *plus que sa femme.*[21]

When the significance of a character's activities in relation to the unity of the world as a whole is expressed in the *Soulier de satin*, great emphasis is placed on the necessity of binding together widely scattered territories and peoples.[22] The clearest statement of this idea is found in Rodrigue's explanation to Sept-Épées of the goals he himself has tried to achieve through his activities as an explorer and conqueror. Rodrigue first states that the political and cultural boundaries that presently divide men are far too confining; he then declares: (IV viii 138–41; 920)

> Il n'y a pas d'autre *mur et barrière* pour l'homme que le Ciel! Tout ce qui est de la terre en terre lui appartient pour *marcher dessus* et il est inadmissible qu'il en soit d'aucune parcelle *forclos*.
>
> *Là où son pied le porte il a le droit d'aller.*
>
> Je dis que Tout lui est indispensable. Il ne peut s'en passer. Il n'est pas fait *pour marcher avec une seule jambe et pour respirer avec la moitié d'un poumon.* Il faut l'ensemble, *tout le corps.*
>
> C'est autre chose que d'être limité par Dieu ou par des choses qui sont de la même nature que nous et qui ne sont pas faites pour nous contenir.

In the first verset, the terms *mur* and *barrière* underscore the strength of the man-made obstacles that Rodrigue claims to have no real validity. When he goes on to express his belief that men should have the freedom to travel without restraint, the metonymic expressions *marcher dessus* and *son pied le porte* evoke this movement in specific, familiar, and thus vivid terms. Because walking is a form of locomotion available to all men, these images also imply that every person should be free to explore the world. Although the term *forclos* was formerly used in referring to any type of exclusion, today the word is generally used to express a legal loss of rights and it thus functions here as a metaphor, emphasizing once again the strength of the artificial boundaries set up by men against each other. The body-code development then stresses the importance of unifying the world into a single whole.

The significance of the individual character's explorations and conquests in relation to this progressive unification of the world is most often expressed in terms of two types of objects – doors and barriers.

In the description of his goals just discussed, Rodrigue uses barrier-code images to describe the hindrances to man's freedom of movement that must be eliminated. Door- and barrier-code vehicles are used together in referring to the removal of such obstacles when Prouhèze looks at the Isthmus of Panama on a globe, and says of Rodrigue: (III viii 15–17; 812)

Entre les deux Mers, à l'horizon de l'Ouest,
Là où *la barrière* est plus mince ...
C'est là que tu t'es établi, là est *la Porte* qu'on t'a donné à *ouvrir*.

In these images, Prouhèze implies that Rodrigue's passage through the Isthmus will counteract the divisive effects of this strip of land, and will allow the peoples of the Eastern and Western Hemispheres to mix freely with each other.[23]

Because the Isthmus is compared to a *barrière* in the above passage, this land mass is itself shown to play an important role in hindering the characters' attempts to unify the world. Other land masses are also shown, through the same or different vehicle codes, to function as obstacles to these efforts.

When Rodrigue sends Almagro to establish control over South America, he describes this isolated territory as a closely guarded enemy whose fortifications can be penetrated only with the greatest difficulty: (III iii 71; 803)

... *Ceins la cuirasse,* Almagro! *boucle l'épée sur ta cuisse!* Est-ce qu'il s'agit de cultiver tandis qu'il y a devant toi cet Empire tout en or qui t'attend et dans la nuit antarctique *ces défences monstrueuses à escalader?*

Bodies of water, on the other hand, are generally described as helping to create bonds between different areas and peoples.[24] In speaking of the size of his empire, the King of Spain declares: (I vi 14–15; 686)

... la Mer même, ce vaste Océan à mes pieds,
    Loin de lui *imposer des limites* ne faisait que *réserver* de nouveaux domaines à mon désir trop tardif!

The text of the *Soulier de satin* thus tells a story of lovers and conquerors, of bonds between men and women and of ties among nations. The reader's interest focuses on this narrative level, and as the work progresses he comes to identify emotionally with the individual characters. As will be shown in the following chapters, however, the other levels of meaning conveyed through the work have a much greater impact on both his intellectual and his affective responses to the text.

5   The religious
level

Although many characters of the *Soulier de satin* seem 'true to life' in the ways outlined in Chapter 4, as noted at the beginning of that chapter several of these characters also possess specific nonhuman qualities. To the reader, the presence of these unnatural beings seems inconsistent with the major developments of the story line. Other incongruities are also encountered by the reader on the narrative level – the introduction of characters who have no apparent relationship with the central events of the play, for example, and irregularities in the chronological development of the story.[1]

Faced with these inconsistencies, which give the text a baroque quality, the reader feels compelled to look for an additional stratum of meaning, one which would give greater coherence to the work as a whole.[2] Since many religious concepts are clearly expressed in the play, he looks first for a theological meaning; he then discovers that the text both presents a theologically determined view of the universe as a whole, and indicates the specific religious import of the characters and incidents depicted on the story line.

Because the *Soulier de satin* thus conveys at least two levels of meaning to the reader simultaneously, it may be considered an allegory.[3] As in most allegorical works, the story line serves as the means through which the author expresses a group of abstract ideas in vivid, concrete form; the entire narrative level thus functions, in effect, as a continuous metaphoric vehicle. The allegorical nature of the *Soulier de satin*, however, has a second source as well – Claudel's conception of the nature of the universe.

Claudel's ideas on this subject are based on traditional Catholic dogma, which teaches that every man has both body and soul, and that the soul leads an active life of its own alongside that of the body. This double nature of the individual corresponds to the double nature of the entire universe, in which a spiritual world exists concurrently with the visible or physical world.[4] Some Catholic philosophers – most notably Saint Thomas Aquinas – have developed these concepts further, explaining that each feature of the physical world corresponds to a specific component of the spiritual sphere, and serves in effect as the vehicle through which this spiritual element finds a concrete form of existence. Each person's physical existence is thus a direct reflection of his spiritual being, a kind of metaphoric vehicle for the life of his soul, and terrestrial life in general constitutes a 'living allegory.'[5]

Claudel was greatly influenced by Aquinas, and frequently expressed these and related ideas in his prose writings.[6] When he portrays individual people in a fictional work, the text invariably constitutes a literary allegory in which the terrestrial aspects of the characters' lives make up the narrative level of the work, and the spiritual events to which these earthly pursuits correspond form part of a second stratum of meaning.

The basic allegorical structure of the *Soulier de satin* is thus a direct result of Claudel's belief that all parts of the physical world are concrete representations of spiritual events and functions; the specific development of this allegory – the way in which the multileveled text gradually unfolds – is determined by the exact content of the message he is attempting to express here.

When the reader of the *Soulier de satin* is led by the inconsistencies and incongruities of the story line to look for additional, more abstract levels of meaning in the text, imagery is the principal means through which the religious significance of the work is revealed to him.

DESCRIPTION OF THE SPIRITUAL REALM

The religious level of meaning is presented most explicitly in those passages in which the characters directly describe the spiritual world. Since such a supernatural realm, both because of its totally abstract nature and because of its sacred – and therefore taboo – character, cannot be accurately portrayed in ordinary, literal terms, images play a particularly important role in these portions of the text.

The characters of the *Soulier de satin* use three types of image vehicles in describing the spiritual sphere – expressions whose religious significance has been determined by Catholic tradition; words whose religious meaning is in part determined by tradition and in part established by their use in the *Soulier de satin*; and references to mythological figures.[7]

TABLE 5
Frequency count: the religious level

	Codes
To describe the spiritual world, total	44
Traditional religious expressions	30
Terms whose significance is determined in part by tradition, in part within the play	12
References to mythological figures	2
To give the physical world spiritual meaning, total	70
Traditional religious expressions	41
Terms whose significance is determined in part by tradition, in part within the play	18
References to mythological figures	11

Number of image elements used from codes discussed	Image elements
Spiritual realm described through water code, total	28
Stress is on purity	9
Stress is on Grace	6
Stress is on unity	13
Spiritual realm described through 'three Fates' code	7
Physical world described through Communion code	8
Reciprocal image development, total	40
Spiritual unity expressed through water code	13
Water compared to spiritual unity	27

Terms whose religious significance has been determined by Christian tradition can be divided into two categories: words that designate specific religious events and figures – Mass, baptism, Crucifixion, for example – and terms whose literal meaning is not directly related to theology, but which are frequently used to describe spiritual forces and concepts metaphorically – fire, light, oil, water. Vehicles drawn from the first category bring to mind the religious concepts they traditionally express in virtually any context; those taken from the second function like archetypes in this respect – whether or not the religious associations of these vehicles are evoked in the reader's mind depends on the specific context in which they are found.

The Guardian Angel uses an extended water-code development in telling Prouhèze of the state towards which he has been guiding her: (III viii 196–7; 821)

> L'ANGE GARDIEN: Les connais-tu à présent, *ces eaux* où je voulais te conduire?

DONA PROUHÈZE: Ah! je n'en ai pas assez! encore! Rends-la-moi donc enfin, *cette eau où je fus baptisée*!

This development includes terms from both categories described above. Because the chief functions of the baptismal ceremony are the cleansing of the participant of past sins and his subsequent induction into the Church, the term *baptisée* indicates that these *eaux*, like those used in the ceremony itself, represent metaphorically a spiritual power that purifies and regenerates.[8] The reader thus infers that the situation to which the Angel now introduces Prouhèze will free her from past sins and enable her to enter heaven.[9]

The traditional religious expressions that serve as image vehicles in the *Soulier de satin* are sometimes used in such a way that they not only evoke the theological ideas with which they are customarily associated, but also convey additional, related concepts that are of particular importance for Claudel.

Vehicle terms come to convey these additional concepts through a process described in Chapter 2. As explained there, when a theme is enlarged upon and developed in an extended image, it is apt to assume a certain importance in the reader's mind. If images derived from the same code appear in a subsequent passage of the play, the reader is likely to remember the earlier use of the theme and the meanings it expressed at that time, and he will then understand the new image terms in relation to this remembered group of meanings. Which of these meanings are brought forward most vividly in his mind by any one use of the code depends on the specific context in which the vehicles are used.[10]

In Prouhèze's plea to the Angel for *cette eau où je fus baptisée* the 'water' represents the force that will purify her of past sins and will thus enable her to enter heaven.

A second theological concept often expressed by water-code terms is the existence of a state of Grace or the presence of God.[11] Many biblical passages, for example, describe God's dealings with man through water-code imagery – thus, Psalm 35:8–9 reads: 'Les enfants des hommes à l'ombre de vos ailes seront pleins d'espérances. / ... Vous les abreuverez du torrent de vos délices.'

Terms related to water are also used in this way in the *Soulier de satin*. Before his death, Camille tells Prouhèze that his own fate is inextricably linked with hers, and pleads with her to save him: (III x 203–4; 842)

> Prouhèze, je crois en vous! Prouhèze, je meurs de *soif*! Ah! cessez d'être une femme et laissez-moi voir sur votre visage enfin ce Dieu que vous êtes *impuissante à contenir*,
> Et atteindre *au fond de votre cœur cette eau* dont Dieu vous a faite *le vase*!

The last words of the first verset reveal that Camille's terrible *soif* is a metaphoric expression of his intense longing for redemption. The reader then understands that the *eau* of which God has made Prouhèze the *vase* represents the state of Grace for which Camille yearns, and which he can attain only with Prouhèze's help.

In the *Soulier de satin*, water-code terms frequently suggest to the reader a third religious concept – the unity of all beings and forces within the spiritual realm.

As Musique prays in the Church of Saint Nicholas, she speaks of the quarrels that have divided Eastern Europeans for centuries; her husband, she adds, has halted the warfare among these people by military means, and she herself now offers them spiritual contentment: (III i 48–56; 786–7)

> Au lieu de tout ce mal qu'ils essayaient de se faire à grand labeur, mon Dieu, quelle surprise ce sera pour eux, toute cette joie qu'on n'avait qu'à leur demander pour qu'ils la donnent!
> ...
> Je leur donne rendez-vous *sur un lac d'or*!
> Quand on ne peut faire un pas sans trouver de toutes parts des barrières et des coupures, quand on ne peut plus *se servir de la parole que pour se disputer*, alors pourquoi ne pas s'apercevoir qu'à travers le chaos *il y a une mer invisible* à notre disposition?
> Celui qui *ne sait plus parler*, qu'il *chante*!
> Il suffit qu'une petite âme ait la simplicité de *commencer* et voici que toutes sans qu'elles le veuillent *se mettent à l'écouter et répondent*, elles sont *d'accord*.
> Par-dessus les frontières nous établirons cette république enchantée où les âmes *se rendent visite sur ces nacelles qu'une seule larme suffit à lester*.
> Ce n'est pas nous qui *faisons la musique*, *elle* est là, rien n'y échappe, il n'y a qu'à s'adapter, il n'y a qu'à nous y *enfoncer* jusque *par-dessus les oreilles*.

Since Musique's words are part of a prayer, the reader infers that the *lac d'or* to which she invites these long-suffering people is heaven itself; this impression is reinforced by her use of the archetypal term *or*, generally associated with the idea of supreme value.[12]

After Musique has spoken of the recurrent disputes that divide the Eastern Europeans, she evokes in contrast the *mer invisible* that lies beyond the chaos of earthly life; the reader infers that a key quality of this supernatural 'sea' is the peaceful accord that prevails within its borders. In this context, the reader understands that the references to 'speaking' express tangible forms of communication, and that the 'singing' with which these material interchanges are contrasted represents a purely spiritual relationship. He then realizes that the 'music' produced by these people when they come together to 'sing' on the heavenly *lac d'or* is an expression of the spiritual ties that are established among them, ties so powerful that each individual soul is irresistibly drawn into communion with the others, once he has allowed himself to come within reach of this holy state.[13] This unity is then evoked once more through water-code terms, when Musique speaks of the meeting of individual souls on *nacelles* for which a single tear provides ballast.[14]

Unlike the concepts of purification from sin and the presence of God's power or Grace, the idea of spiritual unity is not commonly expressed through water-code imagery. In the *Soulier de satin*, however, this unity becomes associated in the reader's mind with the water theme through Musique's portrayal of heaven; and as a result, water-code images used to describe the spiritual world in the latter part of the play tend to evoke for the reader not only the theological concepts traditionally expressed through such vehicles but also the interconnection of all beings within the spiritual realm.

Lamenting the failure of European Christians to save their suffering brethren in Africa, Sept-Épées declares: (IV viii 61–4; 916)

Cependant que nos marchands vont jusqu'au bout de la terre pour en rapporter une poignée de perles, quelques tonneaux d'huile, quelques sacs d'épices,
On oublie *une huile plus grasse,*
Un vin plus généreux, cette eau, la vraie, qui nous régénère,
Les larmes sur nos mains des captifs que nous avons délivrés et que nous ramenons à leurs femmes et à leurs mères.

The last three versets of this passage contain a four-part image-sequence. The first two segments of the development designate liquids (*huile, vin*), which are described as being of better quality than the types of merchandise previously named (*plus grasse, plus généreux*); since the word *généreux* is used most often in the sense of 'charitable' or 'beneficent,' the wine also seems to have some general spiritual value. At the end of the verset, the term *régénère* brings to mind the religious rebirth with which this verb is usually associated, and thus indicates that the 'water' being ignored by the Europeans could cleanse them of their sins and introduce them into a totally pure existence. The meaning of *la vraie* then becomes clear by flashback: this water represents the ultimate truth – the power of God himself, which alone can lead the individual to a just and innocent life.

The reader now understands through a second flashback the spiritual significance of the first two images of the sequence – the phrase *huile plus grasse* recalls the use of oil in religious ceremonies to symbolize a state of Grace, and the words *vin plus généreux* bring to mind specifically the wine associated with the Passion of Christ, the ultimate sacrifice through which all men may eventually be saved. The first three segments of this series thus all express the idea of God's redeeming power.

In the final verset cited, the watery substance named – *les larmes des captifs* – first seems to be a metonymic expression of the overwhelming gratitude that the rescued Christians would direct towards their benefactors. Because this statement is placed in apposition to the phrase *cette eau*, however, the reader understands that it also expresses the same tenor concept as the preceding parts of the image-sequence. Since the captives' gratitude and God's power to redeem are thus both expressed by the same phrase, the reader relates these concepts to each other and concludes that by undertaking the mission that will lead to this gratitude the Europeans may attain salvation.

Furthermore, Sept-Épées speaks in this verset not only of the captives and their liberators but also, in the final clause, of the wives and mothers with whom the prisoners will be reunited; her words thus also bring to mind the close-knit relationship that will be re-established in each family following the freeing of these men. Because this earthly form of union is expressed here in connection with a water-code evocation of the saving power of God's Grace, the reader recalls the use of water-code imagery earlier in the play to express the spiritual ties created among all souls who come within reach of this Grace; he then understands that the state of unity that will be created by the Europeans' mission will involve not only the bringing together of families on earth, but also the joining of all those involved on the spiritual plane of life.

The two water-code segments of this image-sequence thus evoke in context not only the religious concepts traditionally associated with the water theme – the cleansing of the sinful individual and the presence of God's Grace – but also the idea so important to Claudel of the unity of all within the spiritual realm.

Terms derived from Greek, Latin, or other European mythologies are generally associated by Westerners with the transcendental forms of life that these mythologies have conventionally been used to describe. In the religiously oriented framework of the *Soulier de satin*, the superhuman forces such words bring to mind are related by the reader to the corresponding Christian spiritual powers.

Having returned to Mogador from the Americas, Rodrigue speaks of the long hours he spent while in the New World trying to reconcile his desires for Prouhèze with his knowledge of the sinful nature of his love. Suddenly he exclaims: (III xii 111–2; 854)

> Laissez-moi m'expliquer! laissez-moi *me dépêtrer de ces fils entremêlés de la pensée!* laissez-moi *déployer aux yeux de tous cette toile* que pendant bien des nuits
> *J'ai tissée, renvoyé* d'un mur à l'autre de cette amère vérandah *comme une navette aux mains des noires tisseuses!*

The weaving-code image through which Rodrigue describes his efforts to sort out and then reorganize his thoughts about his relationship with Prouhèze is particularly attention-getting because the entire development is an extended renewal of the cliché *le fil de la pensée*.[15]

In the second verset, the term *renvoyé* suggests that an unseen force was present during this period, compelling Rodrigue to examine repeatedly all the implications of his guilty love. When the metalinguistic simile *comme une navette aux mains des noires tisseuses* is added, the reader remembers that the forces of fate are symbolized in several mythologies by three women who spin or weave. Earlier in this day (III viii 74–141; 816–9), the Angel explained to Prouhèze that the emotional turmoil Rodrigue was experiencing while in the New World could not be avoided, because this anguish was forcing him to undergo a necessary step in his progress towards religious salvation – an honest self-examination. Rodrigue's statement now stresses both the inevitability and the spiritual significance of this inner torment by implying that the power driving him so relentlessly onward in his quest for self-understanding was an instrument of the Catholic form of fate, divine predestination.[16]

HOW THE PHYSICAL WORLD IS GIVEN SPIRITUAL MEANING

In addition to describing the spiritual realm itself, the characters of the *Soulier de satin* speak of the relationships existing between this transcendental plane and individual parts of the physical world. For the most part these relationships are expressed in the play (as they are in other literary and theological texts) through images that compare specific elements of the physical world to aspects of the spiritual realm. Because the spiritual world is itself usually depicted through concrete vehicles, however, these images must function indirectly, through terms that the reader has come to recognize as figurative expressions of this super-natural realm – in the *Soulier de satin*, the kinds of expressions described in the first part of this chapter.

In pleading with the King to allow all nations to join with Spain in exploring and developing the New World, Rodrigue exclaims: (IV ix 144; 932)

> ... Je veux que tous les peuples *célèbrent la Pâque à cette table énorme* entre les deux Océans *qu'Il nous avait préparée*!

The words *célèbrent la Pâque* are a traditional religious expression, and recall here the taking of Communion – an act through which the individual comes together with the Holy Spirit and all Catholics within the Mystical Body of Christ.[17] The phrase *cette table énorme* both expands upon this religious concept, evoking the altar at which Communion is taken, and also brings to mind the Europeans' enjoyment of the material wealth of the Americas. The first part of this verset thus expresses two tenors – the co-operation of many nations in the physical development of the New World and the spiritual union of these same peoples. Relating these concepts to each other, the reader understands Rodrigue to be saying that by co-operating with each other in material ways the Europeans will also achieve a spiritual union with each other and with God.[18]

The last part of the development – *qu'Il nous avait préparée* – then emphasizes that God is the ultimate source of the natural resources of the Americas. Following the reference to a *table*, this clause also recalls Psalm 22:4 – 'Vous m'avez préparé une table devant moi contre ceux qui me persécutent' – and thus suggests specifically that providing an abundance of material resources is one means through which God protects and encourages those who remain devoted to him.

Once the spiritual significance of a part of the physical world has been suggested to the reader, this link between the two spheres may be emphasized in several ways – by the repetition of the original image, by its elaboration in an extended development, by the expression of the same concept through different vehicle codes, or by the use of reciprocal developments.[19]

In a reciprocal development, the original tenor and vehicle systems are reversed – a concept or group of concepts that has served as a vehicle system is itself compared to the tenor system that it initially expressed. Two ideas exchanged in this way in the *Soulier de satin* are bodies of water and a unifying spiritual situation – on several occasions, transcendental bonds are expressed in water-code terms; in later passages, water is compared to a supernatural power that creates spiritual ties among people, objects, and forces.[20]

Musique's use of water-code terms to describe a spiritual form of communion has been discussed above. Later in the play, Prouhèze speaks of the role of the Atlantic Ocean in bringing her closer to Rodrigue. Separated from her beloved for ten years, she looks at the ocean on a globe and declares that now that Rodrigue has passed through the 'barrier' of Panama, she, too, must go beyond this obstacle and join him on the other side: (III viii 23; 813)

> Comment empêcher qu'on vienne me prendre de l'autre côté de *cette barrière enfoncée*! ce n'est pas la mer dans le brouillard, *ce sont les armées de Dieu d'un mouvement innombrable qui s'avancent à ma rencontre*!

The sea is described here as a vigorous force, the instrument through which God will reunite Prouhèze with Rodrigue; since this is a sacred power, the reader understands that the lovers will be joined by spiritual, as well as physical and emotional, ties.[21] The effect of the reversal of tenor and vehicle concepts is to emphasize strongly the connection between bodies of water and the unification of individuals on the spiritual plane of life.

After the two concepts involved in a reciprocal development have been compared to each other several times, they may be expressed in such a way that the reader cannot be certain whether a particular statement should be understood literally or figuratively.

As Sept-Épées and la Bouchère swim towards the fleet of Don Juan, Sept-Épées expresses her feeling of being closely linked with her friend, and then turns her attention to the sea: (IV x 65–8; 938)

> Je sens directement avec mon cœur chaque battement de ton cœur.
>
> L'eau porte tout. C'est délicieux, l'oreille au ras de l'eau, de per-cevoir *toutes ces musiques confuses,* (Pensé:) les danseurs autour de *la guitare,*
>
> La vie, *les chants, les paroles d'amour, l'innombrable craquement de toutes ces paroles imperceptibles*!
>
> Et tout cela n'est plus dehors, on est dedans, il y a quelque chose qui vous réunit bienheureusement à tout, *une goutte d'eau associée à la mer*! *La communion des Saints!*

Following Sept-Épées's reference to an earthly bond with her companion, her sound-code description of the sea recalls the earlier use of water- and music-code imagery to express spiritual ties, and the reader concludes that the sea through which she is linked with la Bouchère on earth also functions as a concrete actualization of a supernatural unifying force.[22]

In this context, Sept-Épées's final statement becomes ambiguous. The words *on est dedans, il y a quelque chose qui vous réunit à tout* could refer either to the sea itself or to the spiritual power to which this water corresponds. The phrase *une goutte d'eau associée à la mer* at first seems to express the physical link of Sept-Épées with the sea and with other individuals who are simultaneously in contact with its surface; *la communion des Saints,* however, then evokes a purely transcendental form of union.

The ambiguity of this reference to the sea in itself suggests that this water and the spiritual communion of all beings cannot, in fact, be separated, and in this way further emphasizes for the reader this bond between the physical and the spiritual realms.

The entire fourth day of the *Soulier de satin* takes place on the sea. As the day progresses, reciprocal and ambiguous water-code developments such as those discussed above indicate to the reader that the presence of this body of water represents on the religious level of the text the continuous influence of a unifying spiritual force. This idea in itself then underscores important theological implications of the major situations now developing on the narrative level.

The chief events taking place on the story line relate to Rodrigue's acceptance of his humbled way of life and of his approaching death, and Sept-Épées's undertaking of a mission which has as its goal the protection and expansion of the power of the Church in Europe; the importance of uniting the world in more tangible ways is also stressed in this day, and the sea is described as a key means of effectuating such global ties.

After the imagery of the text has repeatedly stressed the religious significance of the sea, the location of this action entirely on the water serves both to emphasize the idea that the physical linking of all parts of the world will involve the formation of spiritual ties as well, and also to suggest that as they carry out their earthly tasks Sept-Épées and Rodrigue are each moving towards a particular form of spiritual unity – Sept-Épées, towards the joining of all Europeans under the rule of the Catholic Church and thus within the Mystical Body of Christ; and Rodrigue, towards participation after his death in the communion of sacred powers in heaven.

The different types of images discussed above convey to the reader the theological significance of most of the events that take place on the narrative level of the *Soulier de satin*.[23] As previously indicated, in so doing, they suggest an explanation for many incidents that seem inconsistent or incongruous when considered only in terms of the story line. Seen from a different point of view, the expression of a religious message in the text can be said to cause many of the inconsistencies of the story line – since the religious level is more important to the author than the narrative,[24] the theological concepts involved are often conveyed at the expense of the story line. In order to explain the spiritual status of the Eastern Europeans after the Battle of the White Mountain, for example, four statues of saints directly address the reader.[25]

All of the narrative-level inconsistencies found in the *Soulier de satin*, however, cannot be accounted for by the religious stratum of meaning. Such incidents as the appearance of the Irrepressible and the substitution of one Actress for another suggest that still other factors are distorting the development of the story line. The reader must therefore look for additional messages in the text, which will reveal the meaning of these narrative incongruities, and will give unity to the work as a whole.

6 The author's
interventions

Claudel frequently intervenes in the *Soulier de satin* in such a way that the reader must consciously recognize his presence in the text. Any fictional work is, of course, entirely a product of its author's imagination and the author is therefore 'present' throughout the work. In most fiction, however, the reader's interest is quickly absorbed by the story line, and he therefore loses his conscious awareness of the author's role in shaping the text. In a play, the author does speak directly, in the stage directions, but these passages are anticipated by the reader and are generally assimilated by him to the narrative level.

In the *Soulier de satin*, Claudel repeatedly violates the reader's expectations in this regard, and thus makes him actively aware of his presence, both in the stage directions and in passages in which he speaks indirectly, through the words of his characters. The ideas conveyed through these interventions do not constitute a single, coherent level of meaning, but are for the most part unrelated expressions of Claudel's personal opinions of other individuals or of himself and his own role as author, or thoughts that help to determine the general perspective from which the reader views the narrative, religious, and emotional levels of the work.

FORMS TAKEN BY CLAUDEL'S INTERVENTIONS

Claudel's first direct appearance is in the Introduction, where he reveals the mocking attitude he has adopted towards at least the story line of his own play.[1] In describing the Announcer's attempts to get the spectators' attention, for example, he states that this speaker is interrupted by several musical sounds, the last of which is a humorous 'rot de saxophone' (p. 664).

After the play itself begins, Claudel continues to make the reader aware of his presence through stage directions that are unusual in content or tone. As III v opens, for example, he explains: (pp. 805–6)

> Mais il est bien clair que nous ne pouvons refuser plus long-
> temps à l'imagination de nos spectateurs, là-haut, tout près des
> cintres, cette rangée de fenêtres dans un platras agréablement rose
> ou bleu d'une maison de Gênes transportée pour les besoins de la
> couleur locale à Panama.

The use of the editorial *nous*, the reference to the audience and
the description of the artificial stage setting all serve to remind
the reader that the narrative level is being shaped by the author
himself, rather than by some independent structure inherent in
the story line.[2]

Claudel also intervenes in the text less directly, through statements he attributes to several of his characters. His presence is
most obvious behind three characters who function outside of
the basic narrative framework of the text – the Announcer, the
Irrepressible, and the Landlady. The role of these characters as
spokesmen for the author is revealed both by the detached perspective from which they view the other characters, and by the
content of their remarks.[3]

The Announcer's function is clearly evidenced by his title and
by his appearance before the first scene begins. His separation
from the story line is emphasized when he addresses the audience directly and when he describes the setting of the opening
scene from the point of view of an outsider.

The Irrepressible, who also addresses the audience directly,
explains himself that he is a personification of the author's
imagination; his name as well as his first words and actions
reveal that the specific aspects of this imagination he embodies
relate to the driving enthusiasm and excitement that stimulate
the author's literary creation but that are usually kept under firm
control.

The Landlady, who beats the body of Léopold Auguste until
it releases Prouhèze's letter, describes the narrative situation
from the perspective of an outsider when she says to Léopold's
corpse: (III v 7–8; 806)

> ... Il me faut absolument cette lettre pour que la pièce continue et
> qu'elle ne reste pas bêtement suspendue entre ciel et terre.
>
> Tu vois bien là-dessous ce monsieur et cette dame tristement qui
> nous attendent.

Although the Landlady's title and the rest of her speech indicate
that she also plays a role within the story line, both her detached

view of the narrative here and her concern with the overall progress of the play suggest that she, too, functions as a spokesman
for the author; the reader therefore infers that her harsh mocking
of Léopold throughout the scene is an expression of Claudel's
own attitude towards this character.

A less overt way in which Claudel reveals his presence behind
a character is by attributing to him statements he himself would
not – or could not – have made.

In praising Fernand for his recognition of the importance of
tradition, Léopold Auguste makes a statement that he clearly
intends to be taken seriously, but that strikes the reader as
humorous: (III ii 34; 793)

> Comme on voit que vous avez fréquenté les livres de notre *solide*
> Pedro, comme nous l'appelons, *le rempart de Salamanque,* le profes-
> seur Pedro de las Vegas, *plus compact que le mortier*!

The description of Pedro as *solide* is itself metaphoric, and
stresses the dependability of this Spaniard's teachings. The vehicles that enlarge upon this image – *le rempart de Salamanque* and
plus compact que le mortier – are humorous, because they are
highly exaggerated when applied to a person. The final vehicle
is also ironic, evoking for the reader two conflicting qualities –
the reliability to which Léopold apparently intends to refer, and
a different kind of mental 'solidity,' a denseness that borders on
stupidity.

Léopold obviously wishes to praise Pedro here; by causing
him to speak humorously and to suggest the opposite of what he
intends to say, Claudel reveals his own scornful opinion both of
Léopold and, by implication, of those whose attitudes conform
with the reactionary views he expresses during this scene. At the
same time, he reminds the reader that Léopold is not an independent person with an integral identity of his own, but a fictional
creation of the author's mind who can be made to say whatever
Claudel wishes.

Related to these indirect appearances of the author through the
speech of his characters are situations and events that are incongruous in context and that are understood by the reader to reflect
the author's opinion of individual characters and the kinds of
people they represent, or of the story line itself.[4]

Mendez Leal is first described in a stage direction as 'une simple silhouette découpée dans de l'étoffe noire' (IV ii; 867). When

this character later takes the shape of a human being and speaks to Rodrigue and Daibutsu, the reader understands by flashback that his original flat shape was the author's way of emphasizing that obsequious hangers-on like Mendez Leal are figuratively 'shallow' people, in that they have no significant identity of their own.[5]

IMAGES USED IN CLAUDEL'S INTERVENTIONS

The passages cited in illustration above reflect the fact that most of the images used by Claudel when he intervenes in the text, either directly or indirectly, are humorous. These mocking remarks are directed at three types of objects – the characters of the play as representatives of real people, the narrative level of the work in itself, and Claudel's own efforts as creator of the text.

As in the cases of Léopold's mocking of the *solide* Pedro and the Landlady's mocking of Léopold, when the object of Claudel's derision is a character or group of characters, the reader usually infers that the author is expressing his own disdain for the type of people whom they represent in the play.

In a more direct statement by Claudel, three of the King's ministers are designated by ironic periphrases – *le Ministre de l'Hygiène, le Ministre de l'Instruction Publique,* and *le Ministre des Exercices Physiques* (IV ix 153, 155, 167; 932–3). The first two titles are anachronistic, because the posts named were not created in Western governments until long after the time at which the play ostensibly takes place; in the third, the position cited both contrasts with the serious functions generally assumed by government officials, and echoes earlier comic descriptions of the courtiers' efforts to maintain their balance while the King's ship was being tossed about by the sea. Through these ironic titles, Claudel expresses his contempt for the self-seeking parasites who surround most powerful authorities.

Humorous remarks directed at the characters and the settings in which they appear in their roles as constitutive elements of the story line (as opposed to, or in addition to, their roles as representatives of real people and situations) suggest to the reader that the narrative level as a whole is relatively unimportant.

Characters are mocked in this way, for example, when Claudel attributes anachronistic statements to them. In telling Rodrigue of his attempt to investigate the band of men who are camped nearby, Isidore declares: (I vii 8; 691)

> ... j'ai vu des armes à la lueur de *ce coup de pinceau phosphorique*,
> ...

The lofty tone of this periphrastic reference to a match in itself makes the expression humorous for the reader, because it contrasts with the lowly social status of the speaker. The reader's awareness that matches did not exist at the time the play ostensibly takes place both heightens the comic effect and – as with other types of unintentionally humorous remarks – reminds the reader that the speaker has no independent identity, but is merely a reflection of the author's own thoughts and desires.

The settings are similarly ridiculed in several of the stage directions. In IV v, after naming the fishermen who are searching for treasure under the sea, Claudel adds: (p. 894)

> On voit les jambes de ces messieurs au-dessous du bordage des bateaux qu'ils manœuvrent puisque aussi bien chacun sait que, sans *jambes*, les bateaux ne sauraient *marcher*.

The final words of this remark recall the children's song, 'Maman, les p'tits bateaux qui vont sur l'eau ont-ils des jambes?' As used in context, the statement is ironic, both because of the contrast between this song and the tone and content expected in a stage direction, and because the usual functions of the two meanings of *marcher* that are evoked here are reversed – the figurative 'to work,' generally understood to apply when mechanical objects are involved, is accepted as literal in this context; while the literal 'to walk,' which comes to mind following *sans jambes*, becomes a figurative means of describing the motion of the boat. Following the statement that the fishermen's legs should show beneath their boats, this comment makes the setting for the scene seem simple-minded to the point of absurdity.

By mocking the scenery and props in this way, Claudel both stresses the relative insignificance of these narrative-level aspects of the work, and underscores the freedom he enjoys in determining the details of each setting of the play.[6]

Mocking remarks that serve to discredit the narrative level of the *Soulier de satin* indirectly disparage the reader of the work as well. Although the reader understands that the story line is fictional, his tendency is to accept this narrative as a valid level

TABLE 6
Frequency count: the author's interventions

	Image elements
Direct intervention, total	54
Introduction	12
Stage directions (no. of occasions – 34)	42
Indirect intervention, total	126
Character spokesmen	61
Humour used unintentionally by speaker	65
Direct and indirect intervention, humorous images, total	131
Directed at characters as representatives of real people	91
Directed at narrative level of meaning	22
Directed at Claudel's efforts as creator of the text	18

of meaning and to expect that, taken in itself, it will have intellectual significance for him; in addition, as previously noted, he generally identifies with the characters and responds emotionally to their words and actions. As a result, when the author ridicules any narrative-level aspect of the play, he is by implication also belittling the reader's intellectual and affective involvement with the work. To the extent that the reader responds to this indirect derision, his impression that the narrative level is relatively insignificant is intensified, and his involvement with this story line is diminished.[7]

On the other hand, because the narrative is shown so emphatically to be unimportant in itself, the reader infers that the other level of meaning clearly conveyed by the text and not mocked by the author – the religious level – is of far greater importance.

Furthermore, as explained in Chapter 5, the narrative level expresses the terrestrial aspects of the characters' lives, and the religious level, the spiritual occurrences that parallel these earthly events. By ridiculing the story line of the play, Claudel also indicates that the terrestrial world is itself inconsequential when compared with the spiritual plane of life. (Depending on his own attitude towards religion, the reader might well assume the religious level of meaning and the spiritual plane it expresses to be more important than the story line and terrestrial life, even without the author's mocking of the narrative; the author's remarks, however, help to keep this basic Christian frame of reference vividly in the reader's mind as the work progresses.)

Humorous remarks are also directed by Claudel at his own efforts as creator of the text. To some extent, Claudel's mocking of the narrative level reflects not only on the reader who becomes involved with the story, but also on himself, since – as he so often reminds the reader – in the last analysis it is he who controls all aspects of this story line. Claudel also makes fun of his own role more directly, however, through the Irrepressible's bantering comments.

Because the Irrepressible clearly functions as a spokesman for the author, the reader interprets his remarks on the composition of the play as an appraisal by Claudel of his own work as a writer. He therefore infers that Claudel is deliberately belittling his own creative ability when the Irrepressible explains his sudden appearance in the text by such mocking statements as: (II ii 2–4; 730)

> ... je n'ai pas eu la patience de *moisir dans cette loge* où l'auteur me tient *calfeutré* ...
>
> ...
>
> ... l'auteur me tient en réserve, *un en-cas* si je puis dire, avec tout un peuple de figurants *qui font un grand bruit de pieds dans les greniers* de son imagination ...

The Irrepressible describes the author's mind here in terms of two concrete locations; both expressions are ironic because the commonplace nature of the locales mentioned contrasts with the dignity and esteem usually accorded the mind of an artist.

Claudel's self-mockery in the *Soulier de satin* has puzzled many critics; in reviewing their reactions to the text, Pierre Brunel offers his own explanation:

> Claudel ... est à la fois le premier critique de ses critiques et son premier critique. Tout se passe comme si le dramaturge avait prévu et voulu prévenir, dans le courant de son drame, les reproches de ses détracteurs futurs ... La 'bienfaisante ironie' de l'auteur, répandue dans le drame, s'est arrogé d'emblée la place de l'ironie que le critique aurait voulu répandre sur elle. Pour éviter les rires et les sarcasmes, Claudel les a suscités, en riant le premier. Qu'on me pardonne cette comparaison: il a vacciné sa pièce contre la rage des critiques.[8]

Whatever Claudel's reasons for deliberately including this self-directed humour in the play, the chief effect for the reader is to disparage more strongly those parts of the text most completely under the author's control, and thus, by implication, to emphasize further the relative importance of the religious level of meaning.

As seen from the above discussion, the author's interventions in the *Soulier de satin* – like the expression of the religious level of meaning – in some cases interfere with the expected logical development of the story line; again, Claudel deliberately distorts the narrative in order to convey a number of specific ideas to the reader.

In the following two chapters, a final level of meaning whose expression in the text affects the development of the story line is considered. This level differs from those previously discussed and from the author's interventions, in that Claudel himself probably remained for the most part unaware of both the exact nature of the concepts involved and the extent of their influence on the reader's response to his work.

7 The emotional level

The strong appeal of the *Soulier de satin* to readers of many different ages, nationalities, and religions suggests that the work not only conveys a narrative-level tale, a theological message, and the author's thoughts about certain people and situations, but also expresses a number of feelings that are experienced at some time by most individuals, whatever the circumstances of their personal lives, and that therefore evoke definite affective responses from almost all readers when they are encountered in the text.

Although as a rule the reader does not consciously recognize the presence of this emotional level of meaning in the text, his unconscious apprehension of the feelings involved is the source of much of the pleasure he experiences as he peruses the work. In addition, this affective message reinforces and heightens the impact on his mind of the other, consciously perceived levels of the text.[1]

Imagery plays a particularly important role in conveying the unrecognized emotional message to the reader. Simon Lesser writes:

> For the most part ... images register upon our minds *as images*. Only occasionally is their meaning – or at any rate, a considerable portion of their meaning – transcribed into words ... Images are often too thick with meaning and they succeed one another too rapidly to be anatomized ... Our desire to learn what happens next, to take in the entire story, reinforces our natural tendency to depend upon our immediate, intuitive understanding.
>
> Curiosity and our tendency to avoid unnecessary effort exert a more or less constant influence in deterring us from formulating the significance of each [image] as it is read. A third factor operates selectively. This is the censorship of the unconscious ego, which, out of its reluctance to offend the superego and its desire to spare us pain, opposes the conceptualization, and in general the conscious apprehension, of those meanings of images which are likely to arouse revulsion and anxiety ... Obviously a language which lends itself to this kind of partial and selective apprehension is an ideal one

for dealing with emotional problems. It encourages honesty without jeopardizing security; it permits things to be said and understood without being conceptualized and brought to awareness.[2]

The universally experienced emotions conveyed through fictional works are as a rule similar to those expressed in myths and rituals. In examining the presence of myths in literature, Northrop Frye explains:

> The poet ... imitates the universal, not the particular ... His subject-matter is ... the typical or recurring element in action. There is thus a close analogy between the poet's subject matter and those significant actions that men engage in simply because they are typical and recurring, the actions that we call rituals. The verbal imitation of ritual is myth, and the typical action of poetry is the plot, or what Aristotle calls *mythos*, so that for the literary critic the Aristotelian term *mythos* and the English word myth are much the same thing.[3]

For this reason, the emotional stratum of a fictional work can be described in two different ways. First, where pertinent, the similarities between the consciously perceived levels of meaning and the events related in a group of actual myths and rituals can be pointed out; this process helps to identify the affective concepts involved and to underscore their universality.[4] Second, the feelings thus identified can be described in terms currently used by psychologists to explain similar affective responses in people; this approach deals more directly with the feelings themselves and with the role they play in the life of each individual. Both of these procedures will be used in the following study of the emotional level of meaning of the *Soulier de satin*; the way in which the imagery helps in conveying this affective stratum to the reader will be underscored in both cases. In addition, the specific effects of the expression of this emotional level on the reader's response to the play will be discussed in detail.[5]

The central events occurring on the narrative and religious levels of the *Soulier de satin* relate to the love of Prouhèze and Rodrigue for each other; the basic emotional message conveyed by the text is also expressed most clearly and most fully in passages that deal with the interaction of these two characters. These parts of the text will therefore be examined first; their narrative and religious meaning will be outlined briefly, and their emotional significance will then be discussed in the two ways mentioned above. To simplify the presentation, only those passages dealing with Rodrigue's role in this relationship are considered in this chapter; the emotional meaning of passages that convey Prouhèze's feelings alone and of those that relate the thoughts and actions of other characters are examined in Chapter 8.[6]

Rodrigue is introduced indirectly in the first scene of the play by his brother, the Jesuit, who speaks briefly of the difficulties Rodrigue has been experiencing in finding personal satisfaction and suggests that the source of his problems is his impatience and aggressive ambition – 'Son affaire à ce qu'il imagine n'étant pas d'attendre, mais de conquérir et de posséder' (1 i 25; 668). The Jesuit then prays to God for appropriate help: (1 i 33–7; 668–9)

> Et déjà Vous lui avez appris le désir, mais il ne se doute pas encore ce que c'est que d'être désiré.
> ... Liez-le *par le poids* de cet autre être ...
> Faites de lui un homme *blessé* parce qu'une fois en cette vie il a vu *la figure d'un ange!*
> Remplissez ces amants d'un tel désir qu'il implique ...
> *L'intégrité primitive* et leur essence même telle que Dieu les a conçus autrefois dans *un rapport inextinguible!*

The Jesuit implies here that the *désir* that led Rodrigue to seek satisfaction first through religion and then through world conquest should now be redirected towards a woman, for after he has dealt with this woman's own *désir* and has suffered as a result he may finally obtain, with her help, the fulfilment and gratification he seeks.

The Jesuit's reference to the distress Rodrigue will experience through a love affair may evoke a corresponding combination of erotic desire and anxiety in the reader, but his emotional response to these words remains limited because their exact significance is unclear at this point in the text. When Rodrigue describes his own feelings in more precise terms later in Day 1, the reader is able to identify with him more closely, and his affective response to Rodrigue's story then becomes both more specific and more intense.

When he first appears in the *Soulier de satin,* Rodrigue tells Isidore that he feels himself to be both spiritually and physically attracted to Prouhèze: (1 vii 141–3; 698)

Ai-je dit que c'était son âme seule que j'aimais? c'est elle toute entière.

Et je sais que son âme est immortelle, mais le corps ne l'est pas moins,

Et de tous deux *la semence est faite qui est appelée à fleurir dans un autre jardin.*[7]

Rodrigue, however, soon finds himself in a dilemma – although he cannot bring himself to give up hope of attaining happiness through Prouhèze, he must recognize that his love for her is forbidden by his society and his religion. On the most basic affective level of the text, his predicament takes the form of an inner conflict between his erotic desires for Prouhèze and the persistent reminders by his own conscience that these desires are strictly prohibited. As a result of this conflict, Rodrigue's narrative-level disappointment over his failure to establish a satisfying relationship with Prouhèze and his knowledge of his social and religious culpability are paralleled and heightened by emotional-level feelings of frustration and guilt.[8]

Since the reader responds both intellectually and emotionally to the basic concepts expressed through the text and to the words through which these ideas are conveyed,[9] he, too, consciously or unconsciously experiences a conflict between erotic drives and their proscription as he follows Rodrigue's adventures through the first part of the play. Furthermore, it has long been recognized by psychologists that no individual can grow to adulthood without passing through an 'oedipal' period, a span of time when he directs erotic feelings towards the parent of the opposite sex, and during which he must learn not only that his desires can never be satisfied, but also that these feelings are strictly forbidden by family and society.[10] This conflict between oedipal drive and prohibition and the specific means by which the individual resolves his personal dilemma remain important unconscious influences in the behaviour of every adult.[11] For this reason, when a similar erotic conflict – such as Rodrigue's – is encountered in a literary work, it may bring forward in the reader's mind specifically the sexual impulses that he himself experienced in childhood and the disappointment and guilt that the proscription of these drives eventually caused him.[12]

Rodrigue first attempts to relieve his frustration by giving in to his most urgent desires. Having been left behind in Spain when

Prouhèze accepts a post at Mogador, he follows her to Africa and tries to persuade her to return to Europe with him. Although he must abandon his hope when Prouhèze refuses even to discuss this possibility, he does meet with her once again before he leaves Mogador and succeeds in experiencing for a brief moment the fulfilment he so impatiently seeks. The Double Shadow describes this final encounter to the reader: (ii xiii 7–14; 776–7)

> Car comme *ce support et racine de moi-même,* le long de ce mur vio-lemment frappé par la lune,
> Comme cet homme passait sur le chemin de garde, se rendant à la demeure qu'on lui avait assignée,
> L'autre partie de moi-même et *son étroit vêtement,*
> Cette femme, tout à coup commença à le précéder sans qu'il s'en aperçût.
> Et la reconnaissance de lui avec elle ne fut pas plus prompte que *le choc et la soudure* aussitôt de leurs âmes et de leurs corps sans une parole et que mon existence sur le mur.
> Maintenant je porte accusation contre cet homme et cette femme par qui *j'ai existé une seconde seule pour ne plus finir* et par qui *j'ai été imprimée sur la page de l'éternité!*
> Car ce qui a existé une fois fait partie pour toujours des *archives indestructibles.*
> Et maintenant pourquoi ont-ils *inscrit* sur le mur, à leurs risques et périls, *ce signe* que Dieu leur avait défendu?

Critics of Claudel's works have drawn different conclusions from the Shadow's speech – some have thought that the meeting between the two lovers actually takes place; others believe that a joining of their souls alone is being described.[13] For most readers, both types of reunion are involved. When the Shadow declares that this meeting has been recorded *sur la page de l'éter-nité,* the reader infers that the encounter does entail the forma-tion of a spiritual bond. The imagery of the earlier versets, how-ever – in particular, the reference to Rodrigue as *ce support et racine de moi-même,* followed by the description of Prouhèze as *son étroit vêtement* – evokes the physical joining of a man and a woman;[14] for this reason, the reader at least unconsciously rec-ognizes that the Shadow also represents, if not an actual erotic experience of the lovers, then their intense desire for such an event.

The fulfilment that Rodrigue experiences during this brief

encounter with Prouhèze is thus both spiritual and erotic in nature, and the Shadow's *accusation* underscores on the narrative, religious, and emotional levels of the text simultaneously the gravity of the transgression he has committed.[15]

The manifold consequences of this violation of social, religious, and moral codes are revealed by the Moon in the following scene.[16] The Moon first declares that Prouhèze and Rodrigue are bathed in its light – a glow it describes as a 'drink' for the soul: (II xiv 13; 778)

> Une lumière non pas pour être vue mais pour être *bue,* pour que l'âme vivante y *boive,* toute âme à l'heure de son repos pour qu'elle y *baigne et boive.*

After explaining that the lovers have separated once again, the Moon quotes their words as each grieves over the loss of the other. Prouhèze's lament is cited first: (II xiv 34–49; 779–80)

> 'Il y a quelqu'un pour toujours de la part de Dieu qui lui interdit la présence de mon corps
> 'Parce qu'il l'aurait trop aimé. Ah! je veux lui donner beaucoup plus!
> ...
> 'Ah! j'ai de quoi lui fournir ce qu'il me demande!
> 'Oui, ce n'est pas assez de lui manquer, je veux le trahir,
> 'C'est cela qu'il a appris de moi dans ce baiser où nos âmes se sont jointes.
> 'Pourquoi lui refuserais-je ce que son cœur désire? pourquoi manquerait-il quelque chose à *cette mort* du moins que je puis lui donner, puisqu'il n'attend point de moi la joie? Est-ce qu'il m'a épargnée? pourquoi épargnerais-je ce qu'il y a en lui de plus profond? pourquoi lui refuserais-je *ce coup* que je vois dans ses yeux qu'il attend et que je lis déjà au fond de ses yeux sans espoir?
> 'Oui, je sais qu'*il ne m'épousera que sur la croix* et nos âmes l'une à l'autre *dans la mort* et *dans la nuit* hors de tout motif humain!
> 'Si je ne puis être *son paradis,* du moins je puis être *sa croix!* Pour que son âme avec son corps *y* soit *écartelée* je vaux bien *ces deux morceaux de bois qui se traversent!*
> 'Puisque je ne puis lui *donner le ciel,* du moins je puis *l'arracher à la terre.* Moi seule puis lui fournir *une insuffisance* à la mesure de son désir!
> 'Moi seule étais capable de le *priver de lui-même.*

'Il n'y a pas *une région* de son âme et pas *une fibre* de son corps dont je ne sente qu'elle est faite pour être *fixée à moi,* il n'y a rien dans son corps et dans cette âme qui a fait son corps que je ne sois capable de *tenir avec moi pour toujours dans le sommeil de la douleur,*

'Comme Adam, quand il dormit, la première femme.

'Quand je le *tiendrai* ainsi *par tous les bouts de son corps* et *par toute la texture de sa chair* et de sa personne par le moyen de *ces clous en moi profondément enfoncés,*

'Quand il n'y aura plus aucun moyen de s'échapper, quand il sera *fixé à moi* pour toujours *dans cet impossible hymen,* quand il n'y aura plus moyen de s'arracher à *ce cric de ma chair puissante* et à ce vide impitoyable, quand je lui aurai prouvé son néant avec le mien, quand il n'y aura plus dans son néant de secret que le mien ne soit capable de vérifier,

'C'est alors que *je le donnerai à Dieu découvert et déchiré* pour qu'il *le remplisse* dans un coup de tonnerre, c'est alors que *j'aurai un époux* et que *je tiendrai un dieu entre mes bras!*

On the narrative level, the imagery of these lines evokes the great distress Rodrigue will experience while he is separated from his beloved; the anguish suggested by the references to death and night is reinforced by the more detailed description of this torturous state in terms of the Crucifixion.

On the religious level, the Cross-code imagery indicates that the sorrow and frustration Rodrigue will experience as a result of his decision to leave Prouhèze at Mogador will serve as his own personal Crucifixion, a painful experience through which he can atone for the sins he has committed by his desires for this woman.[17] As the passage continues, the sacrificial aspects of his ordeal are emphasized by Prouhèze's insistence that she will destroy his earthly ties and that she will 'deprive' him of the very self he now is.

Throughout her lament, Prouhèze stresses the active role that she herself will play in Rodrigue's expiation. In a religious sense, she is the source of Rodrigue's suffering because it was she who first aroused his desires and thus created the need for this act of atonement. Prouhèze, however, explains at the end of this passage that she will also be the cause of her lover's salvation. Her comparison of Rodrigue and herself to Adam and Eve underscores the theological significance of this two-sided role. In context, this image recalls the Catholic belief that, just as the first man was led to his Fall by a woman's temptation, so all mankind will eventually be redeemed through a woman's actions – those of Mary, the second Eve; and that similarly, each individual man must be brought to such a failing by a woman before he can be saved through her intervention and made whole again in heaven.[18]

Prouhèze thus implies that, although she is the cause of Rodrigue's current reprobacy, she alone can lead him back to a state of Grace, and for this reason she herself must act as the 'Cross' through which he expiates his sins.[19]

The marriage-code imagery found in this passage suggests another aspect of Prouhèze's relationship to her lover's spiritual mortification. Early in her lament, Prouhèze says of Rodrigue, *je sais qu'il ne m'épousera que sur la croix*. At this point, the reader understands her words to mean that because Rodrigue's love violates Church laws, it can never lead to the earthly union of the two lovers, but only to an agonizing period of atonement.

The meaning of this 'wedding on the Cross' becomes clearer later, when Prouhèze first describes her contact with Rodrigue while she acts as his 'Cross' as an *impossible hymen*, but then adds that after God has 'filled' him, she will have an *époux*, and will hold a *dieu* in her arms. In the first phrase, the adjective *impossible* emphasizes that so long as Rodrigue has not gained final remission for his sins, he is in a state of *néant*, and cannot attain any kind of satisfaction through his contact with Prouhèze. The later statement, however, then indicates that after he has completed his penance and has submitted totally to God's power, he will finally be able to achieve a true sense of fulfilment, both as an individual and as an *époux* – that is, through spiritual union with another being.

The comparison of Rodrigue to Adam underscores a specific quality of this sense of fulfilment by implying that when Prouhèze holds Rodrigue again in *le sommeil de la douleur*, they will be as completely united as were man and woman originally, in the person of Adam, before the creation of Eve. According to Christian tradition, before Eve's creation woman existed within Adam, who was thus androgynous; Christ, too, is believed to have created within himself this more complete, and thus more perfect, bisexual condition.[20] When the individual believer identifies with Jesus and is introduced into an ideal spiritual state through a ritual such as baptism or penance and absolution, he is also thought to become temporarily androgynous.[21] The comparison of Rodrigue to Adam, together with the indication that he will ultimately be redeemed through his own Crucifixion, thus imply that he, too, will attain this particular form of totality.[22]

Finally, Prouhèze makes several references here to death. At first, these images function as hyperbolic assertions of the severity of Rodrigue's ordeal. Later, when Prouhèze explains that Rodrigue's torment will eventually lead him to a totally new way of life, these terms suggest by flashback that before he is reborn into this pure form of existence his old, sinful nature will be completely destroyed.[23]

The Moon's 'liquid light' now also gains religious significance by flashback. The illogical description of this light in itself originally suggests that the Moon represents an unearthly substance or quality. When Prouhèze now indicates that Rodrigue will be regenerated into a new and holy existence, the reader recalls the use of water in many Church rituals – in particular in the traditional ceremony of rebirth, baptism – as a symbol of purification; the continuing presence of the Moon in this scene then helps to underscore for him the cleansing nature of Rodrigue's painful experience.[24]

The religious concepts expressed in this central passage of the play correspond closely to the ideas conveyed through the initiation myths and rituals of many other societies.

Thus, just as Rodrigue's penitential sacrifice involves the destruction of his sinful way of life and his admission into a new form of existence, so all initiation ceremonies by definition celebrate the induction of the participant into a different phase of life. Like Rodrigue, the initiate generally undergoes a cleansing 'death' – usually in the form of a physical ordeal – prior to his acceptance into a new, as yet unspoiled, situation.[25] The symbolism of the Moon's 'liquid light' is paralleled in these rituals by the use of water to represent both the cleansing of the individual during his symbolic death and the womb from which his subsequent rebirth takes place.[26]

As noted above, the Cross-code imagery of this passage implies that as he atones for his sins Rodrigue identifies with Jesus and takes part in the supernatural mystery of the Crucifixion. The initiation rites of other cultures enable the novice to take part in a similar transcendent experience. Mircea Eliade explains:

We find initiatory death already justified in archaic cultures by an origin myth that can be summarized as follows: a Supernatural Being had attempted to renew men by killing them in order to bring them to life again 'changed'; for one reason or another, men slew this Supernatural Being, but they later celebrated secret rites inspired by this drama; more precisely, the violent death of the Supernatural Being became the central mystery, reactualized on the occasion of each initiation. Initiatory death is thus the repetition of the death of the Supernatural Being, the founder of the mystery. Since the primordial drama is repeated during initiation, the participants in an initiation also imitate the fate of the Supernatural Being: his death by violence ... By dying ritually the initiate shares in the super-natural condition of the founder of the mystery.[27]

In most initiation ceremonies, the ritual death that enables the novice to identify with this 'Supernatural Being' involves his physical mutilation, either symbolic or real. Furthermore, the way in which the novice is maimed during this ordeal generally suggests that he becomes androgynous, thus attaining the more complete form of existence that, as has just been shown, charac-terizes Christian spiritual perfection as well.[28]

Since in most cultures young men are initiated by older men, when Rodrigue's experience is compared with other ceremonies of induction, Prouhèze's role may at first seem incongruous. In fact, however, several features of primitive initiation rites – including the presentation to the women of the tribe of blood, teeth, or foreskins lost during the rites – suggest that they are in part sacrificial offerings to mother figures.[29]

Furthermore, as noted above, Prouhèze's role in the execution of Rodrigue's sacrifice is actually a double one – although she is the cause of his intense suffering and the instrument of his muti-lation, she is also responsible for his eventual salvation. The uni-versality of such an ambivalent view of woman's relationship to man is underscored by the continuing presence in literature, mythology, and religion of two conflicting feminine archetypes – the threatening woman or *femme fatale* (e.g., Medusa, Delilah, the witch) and the saving woman or Great Mother (Demeter, the Virgin, Dante's Beatrice).[30]

The religious concepts expressed by Prouhèze in her lament that are paralleled by the ideas portrayed in initiation myths and ritu-als thus include the termination of an undesirable form of existence, the purification of the individual by means of a painful ordeal involving submission to more powerful figures, and the subsequent achievement of a new and unspoiled way of life involving a sense of completeness or totality of existence.[31]

The similarity in the myths of so many cultures of the means of attaining a more desirable form of existence and of the nature of the coveted state itself suggests that the feelings that lead men to choose these means and objectives are experienced to some degree by virtually all individuals, regardless of the specific circumstances of their lives. The exact nature of these feelings, however, must still be explained.

On the emotional level of the text, the undesirable situation from which Rodrigue seeks to escape is, as previously noted, the conflict between his erotic desires for Prouhèze and the taboos instilled in his conscience by family and society. The penitential ordeal described by Prouhèze here functions on this level as a voluntarily accepted punishment, through which Rodrigue can allay the guilt feelings that his forbidden desires have provoked. Otto Fenichel explains:

> The need for punishment is a special form of the need for absolution: the pain of punishment is accepted or even provoked in the hope that after punishment the greater pain of guilt feelings will cease. Thus the need for punishment can be understood as the choice of a lesser evil ... The sacrifice is actively undertaken and is less unpleasant than the passive waiting for something to happen.[32]

The theological concepts of sacrifice and atonement, Fenichel notes, are directly related to such punishment:

> The ideas that any suffering entitles one to the privilege of a compensating pleasure and that a threatening superego may be placated and forced to renew its withdrawn protective powers by means of voluntary suffering are very archaic ones. The same ideas are expressed in the attitudes of sacrifice and prayer. In both practices, the sympathy of God is bought, and more intense punishments are avoided by means of the active and voluntary acceptance of an unpleasantness as 'prophylactic punishment.'[33]

The Cross- and deprivation-code imagery through which Rodrigue's punishment is described here implies in context that this ordeal is specifically a self-sacrificing act through which he offers a vital part of himself to an all-powerful father figure and submits totally to his will; several details of Prouhèze's speech indicate that what Rodrigue sacrifices to this omnipotent father is his masculinity.

Thus, Prouhèze declares that when she has succeeded in 'depriving' Rodrigue of a key part of himself, he will be left *découvert et déchiré* and she will then turn him over to God to be 'filled.' Since from both the physiological and the psychological points of view 'openness' and the need to be 'filled' are feminine qualities, these expressions imply that after Prouhèze's 'depriving' act Rodrigue's attitude towards his heavenly father will be not simply passive and submissive, but, more precisely, feminine.[34]

This interpretation of Rodrigue's sacrifice is confirmed by the fact that from a psychological standpoint such an emasculating punishment would best resolve his basic conflict – it would both match the original crime[35] and also ensure that it could not be committed again.[36] If Rodrigue's forbidden desires are associated by the reader specifically with his own unconscious oedipal wishes, this penalty is understood to suit his crime in yet another way – by agreeing to undergo this emasculating punishment and to submit passively to an omnipotent father figure, Rodrigue in effect assures the parent whom his incestuous desires have offended that he no longer challenges either his overall authority or his dominant sexual position; if he succeeds in placating the wrath of his father by this self-offering, he may be allowed to regain the comfort and protection that this parent can provide.[37]

As noted above, Prouhèze's task of helping to lead Rodrigue first through this punishing experience and then on to redemption recalls the two opposing roles commonly played by women in literature, mythology, and religion. Psychoanalysts believe that this ambivalent status of woman reflects the conflicting feelings experienced by most boys towards their mothers during the oedipal period – although the mother now seems to be a source of intense sensual gratification, the son also fears on occasion that the desired erotic experience will itself result in his castration.[38] In addition, in this particular passage, since Prouhèze reveals that she is the instrument through which God will force Rodrigue to comply with his demands and that Rodrigue will thus be compelled to submit both to an all-powerful father figure and to his feminine helpmate, Prouhèze's double role brings to mind the ambivalent feelings experienced by all children towards both of their parents – at times, parents seem to the child to be domineering, frustrating taskmasters who should be hated and feared; at other moments, they appear to be all-forgiving providers and protectors who should be dearly loved.[39]

Since Rodrigue will not reach the satisfying state promised by Prouhèze until after he has been punished for his erotic desires in such a way that he cannot repeat his wrongdoings, from an emotional point of view he will be completely innocent by the time he reaches the coveted situation. While in this faultless state, he will be united both with Prouhèze – as her *époux* – and with God himself – who will 'fill' him; furthermore, his bond with God will involve not simply the linking of their two beings, but Rodrigue's identification with this omnipotent figure, for Prouhèze declares that Rodrigue will now become *un dieu*.[40]

Because the ideal state evoked by Prouhèze thus involves both Rodrigue's complete innocence and his identification with an all-powerful being, her words recall a desire that is deeply rooted in the unconscious of all adults, and that was first described by Sigmund Freud in *Civilization and its Discontents*:

An infant at the breast does not as yet distinguish his ego from the external world as the source of the sensations flowing in upon him. He gradually learns to do so, in response to various promptings ... Originally the ego includes everything, later it separates off an external world from itself. Our present ego-feeling is, therefore, only a shrunken residue of a much more inclusive – indeed, an all-embracing – feeling which corresponded to a much more intimate bond between the ego and the world about it. If we may assume that there are many people in whose mental life this primary ego-feeling has persisted to a greater or lesser degree, it would exist in them side by side with the narrower and more sharply demarcated ego-feeling of maturity, like a kind of counterpart to it. In that case, the ideational contents appropriate to it would be precisely those of limitlessness and of a bond with the universe ... the oceanic feeling.[41]

As part of this sensation of union with the entire world – which parallels the androgynous totality sought by the novice through his initiatory ordeal – the infant feels himself to be omnipotent;

when he is forced to recognize that he is not himself all-powerful, he seeks to regain his lost strength by identifying with others. Fenichel explains:

> When the child is forced through experiences to renounce his belief in his omnipotence, he considers the adults who have now become independent objects to be omnipotent, and tries by introjection to share their omnipotence again. Certain narcissistic feelings of well-being are characterized by the fact that they are felt as a reunion with an omnipotent force in the external world ... Religious ecstasy, patriotism, and similar feelings are characterized by the ego's participation in something unattainably high.[42]

Speaking specifically of individuals who undergo intense religious experiences, Fenichel notes that 'salvations frequently are experienced in a passive-receptive way, showing signs of the narcissistic *unio mystica*, of the deepest oral reunion of the subject with the universe, and the re-establishment of the original "oceanic feeling." '[43]

The idyllic state promised Rodrigue by Prouhèze is thus in part an answer to the deeply buried wish of all adults to regain these early feelings of all-inclusive, all-protective merger with the outside world, and of identification with the omnipotent beings by which it is ruled.

In summary, Prouhèze reveals in this passage that in order to regain his lost innocence Rodrigue will have to submit completely to both an emasculating mother figure and an omnipotent father substitute, but that the guilt-free situation he will thereby attain will involve two extremely pleasurable relationships – a union with a beloved woman, and a feeling of merger with the gratifying, protective world that surrounds him, and, in particular, with the powerful forces that rule this realm.[44]

Rodrigue's emotional-level dilemma and the means of resolution suggested by Prouhèze may now be outlined as follows:

STAGE 1 Conflict between erotic desires and their prohibition
STAGE 2 Frustration and guilt
STAGE 3 Punishment involving emasculation
STAGE 4 Achievement of innocent yet satisfying union with universe as a whole, including omnipotent father figure; bond with beloved woman

In the following pages, several key passages of Days 3 and 4 will be examined; they will show that Rodrigue does follow the emotional-level course of action outlined by Prouhèze. He may repeat some stages of this course of action several times, or slip back to an earlier stage and have to regain lost ground, but by the end of the play the reader is assured that he will succeed in reaching the multiple goals that Prouhèze offers him here.

The progress that Rodrigue makes towards the resolution of his difficulties may also be considered from the point of view of the tension and anxiety that the relation of his adventures evokes in most readers of the work.

As explained above, the expression in the text of the conflict between Rodrigue's erotic desires for Prouhèze and their prohibition causes the reader to re-experience unconsciously similar emotional conflicts that he himself has known in the past; most readers therefore feel considerable tension as they peruse the passages discussed above. As a rule, the reader's interest in a fictional work is increased when the situation described in the text creates anxiety in him in this way. He has learned from previous experience that such a work will almost inevitably present at its close a tension-relieving solution to the difficulty it relates, and his unsettlement therefore creates a desire in him to continue reading until he has reached this point.

In general, if some degree of tension is not maintained in the reader's mind almost continuously as a fictional work progresses, his interest in the text is likely to lapse. If, on the other hand, his anxiety becomes too great, he may relieve his unsettlement by abandoning the work altogether. A balance between the creation of anxiety and its relief must therefore be sustained throughout the text.[45]

In the final passage cited above, the tension elicited in the reader by the original exposition of Rodrigue's predicament is at first increased by Prouhèze's description of the penitential agony he must still endure. By the end of her lament, however, Prouhèze has revealed that this suffering is leading Rodrigue towards a very pleasurable situation. Because she seems so certain here that her lover will eventually reach this goal, the reader's anxiety is lessened somewhat as her speech draws to a close.

The following discussion of Rodrigue's adventures as recounted in the rest of the *Soulier de satin* will show how a balance is maintained between tension and relaxation as the play progresses. When the emotional-level implications of the actions of the other characters are discussed in Chapter 8, additional means through which this balance is sustained will be shown.

When Prouhèze has ceased grieving over her lost lover, the Moon speaks again, developing now the comforting thought expressed by Prouhèze in the final words of her lament. Referring to Rodrigue, the Moon explains: (II xiv 59–63; 780)

> Il dort ...
> *Le sommeil sans bords d'Adam et de Noé.*
> Car *comme Adam dormait quand la femme lui fut enlevée du cœur,* n'est-il pas juste que de nouveau il
> Dorme en ce jour *de ses noces où elle lui est rendue* et succombe à *la plénitude?*
> ...
> Non point sommeil, ce qu'il dort est *la prélibation* d'un autre système.

This comparison of Rodrigue to Adam indicates on the religious and myth levels of the text that while he sleeps Rodrigue momentarily attains the androgynous state evoked earlier by Prouhèze.[46] On the emotional level, the Moon's words suggest that, as predicted by Prouhèze, Rodrigue now enjoys a sense both of merger with all parts of the universe (*sommeil sans bords*; *succombe à la plénitude*), and of union with a beloved woman (*ce jour de ses noces*).

In the last verset, the term *prélibation* brings to mind the religious ritual generally designated by this term – the offering to God of the 'first fruits.'[47] As in other sacrificial offerings of food, the worshippers ate part of the offering itself during the ceremony, and were believed to identify with the Supreme Being as they did so. This image therefore suggests that Rodrigue not only experiences at this moment a general 'foretaste' of life in the heavenly realm, but also becomes one with God himself.[48]

On the emotional level, this association of the term *prélibation* indicates that Rodrigue now identifies with this father figure, and thus shares in his omnipotence. In addition, the image underscores the orally satisfying nature of the promised contentment. Since the infant loses his original feeling of total accord with the world through his sensations of hunger,[49] the adult's unconscious wish to recover a sense of communion with the universe is frequently associated with a longing for an oral form of gratification; the 'foretaste' image thus implies that part of what Rodrigue strives for is the feelings of security and comfort that he received in earliest childhood through oral satisfaction.[50]

Rodrigue's moment of happiness passes quickly, however, and the Moon then quotes his response to Prouhèze: (ii xiv 70–7; 781)

'Ce paradis que Dieu ne m'a pas ouvert et que tes bras pour moi ont refait un court moment, ah! femme, tu ne me le donnes que pour me communiquer que j'en suis exclu.

...

'O femme, tu l'as découverte, cette place que tu ne pouvais en moi atteindre que les yeux fermés! La voilà donc au fond de moi, cette blessure que tu ne pouvais me faire que les yeux fermés!

...

'Chaque pulsation de ton cœur avec moi me rend le supplice, cette impuissance à échapper au paradis dont tu fais que je suis exclu.
'Ah! c'est en cette blessure que je te retrouve! C'est par elle que je me nourris de toi comme la lampe fait de l'huile,
'De cette huile dont brûlera éternellement cette lampe qui ne réussit pas à en faire de la lumière.'

On the narrative level of the text, Rodrigue expresses here his frustration and discouragement at having to abandon all hope of regaining the joy he knew so briefly with Prouhèze. On the religious and emotional levels, the repeated references to 'paradise' again recall Adam and Eve, and, in context, emphasize for the reader the double role played by woman in each man's life.

As noted above, from a religious point of view, once Rodrigue has been led to his personal Fall by Prouhèze, he can be redeemed only through her intervention. Here, Rodrigue admits that because Prouhèze has refused to leave Mogador with him, he feels himself to be without her indispensable help and he therefore fears that he has lost contact forever with the heavenly sphere.

In this context, Rodrigue's reference to his blessure recalls the Crucifixion imagery used earlier by Prouhèze and reminds the reader that he has been able to experience a state of Grace even momentarily only by submitting first to the penitential ordeal demanded by this woman. His use of the word nourris to express his relationship with Prouhèze in itself emphasizes that his love serves for him as a means of reaching heaven, because it recalls the belief that the worshipper identifies with Christ during the Communion ceremony through the act of eating.

This idea is stressed further when Rodrigue describes his frustrated desires in terms of two objects commonly used in religious contexts to represent the power of Grace or the presence of God – oil and light.

When these religious concepts are compared to the ideas expressed through the myths of other social groups, the paradise for which Rodrigue yearns is seen to correspond to the long-lost primeval utopias described in many of these narratives. As noted above, in these myths, too, the individual is frequently said to be able to re-establish contact with the ideal state through a ceremony involving the consumption of food.

On the emotional level, Rodrigue's paradise- and food-code imagery again brings to mind the infantile bliss he now despairs of regaining. The light-code imagery used in the last two versets then evokes a second form of sensual frustration – because the idea of burning is so often associated with sexual desire,[51] Rodrigue's use of this imagery here to recount his discouragement underscores his fear that he will also be deprived in the future of adult erotic satisfactions which, again, he can achieve only through Prouhèze. Rodrigue cannot yet accept unreservedly his need to undergo a long period of penitential suffering, because he still doubts that he will ever gain through this punishment the satisfactions he desires; nevertheless, he finds no better solution for his dilemma, and he can therefore see before him only frustration and impotence.

Day 2 now comes to an end, and the reader is left in a state of suspense, which heightens the tension created in his mind by this evocation of Rodrigue's despair; this tension then increases his interest in the coming scenes, which he expects will present a reassuring solution for Rodrigue's dilemma.

After leaving Prouhèze at Mogador, Rodrigue attempts to relieve his frustration in a less direct way, through his activities as an explorer and conqueror. As indicated in the discussion of the narrative level in Chapter 4, several male characters of the *Soulier de satin* approach the territories and nations they govern as if these countries were seductive women, and the men themselves were their lovers. The King's description of the attitude Rodrigue must adopt if he is to succeed in subduing and ruling the newly discovered Americas is one passage cited above to illustrate the way the imagery of the text conveys this idea to the reader: (I vi 61–2; 689)

> ... est-ce pour lui que je m'arracherai cette Amérique ... *s'il ne l'aime de cet amour injuste et jaloux?*
>
> Est-ce dans la raison et la justice qu'il *épousera* cette terre sauvage et cruelle, et *qu'il la prendra toute glissante entre ses bras,* pleine de refus et de poison?

On the emotional level, this love-code imagery reveals that the energy Rodrigue devotes to the conquest of the Americas is in great part a displacement of the erotic feelings he could not satisfy through his relationship with a real woman.

As explained in Chapter 4, however, Rodrigue seeks to conquer more than the Americas; he hopes to gain control of vast areas of the world in order to unify all of its nations and peoples. The religious motivation for this ambition – his belief that the physical joining of these peoples will lead to their spiritual unification as well – was discussed in Chapter 5. On the emotional level, the imagery used by Rodrigue in describing his objectives reveals that his ultimate goal in conquering the world is the same as in his relationship with Prouhèze – the regaining of a sense of merger with a satisfying, protective universe.

Having told Sept-Épées, for example, that the political and cultural boundaries that divide men are far too restrictive and that the world must be made into a single 'body' again, Rodrigue adds: (IV viii 142–6; 920)

> Je veux *la belle pomme parfaite.*
> SEPT-ÉPÉES: Quelle pomme?
> DON RODRIGUE: Le Globe! *Une pomme qu'on peut tenir dans la main.*
> SEPT-ÉPÉES: *Celle-là qui poussait autrefois dans le Paradis?*
> DON RODRIGUE: Elle y est toujours! ...

When Sept-Épées refers specifically to the Apple of Eden, the reader recalls the traditional belief that Adam and Eve were driven from Paradise because they committed the 'Original Sin' of forbidden sexual activity.[52] This recollection, together with the concept of oral satisfaction evoked by the apple itself, emphasizes that when Rodrigue attempts to bring all parts of the world together into a single *belle pomme parfaite,* he seeks to

regain specifically the innocent, primarily oral form of gratification and sense of totality that the individual knows in the
'paradise' of infancy, before he first experiences his own forbidden sexual desires – i.e., before he suffers his personal Fall.

As Day 3 begins, Rodrigue's drive to conquer the Americas
appears to be successful, and the reader therefore infers that
through his activities in the New World he has been able to dis-
charge at least some of the ardent feelings that had been provoked and then frustrated by Prouhèze. The tension created in
the reader by earlier descriptions of Rodrigue's distress is therefore somewhat reduced during the first part of this day.

As the play continues, however, other passages reveal that
because Rodrigue had not yet renounced his wrongful erotic
desires his burden of guilt remains. Since his activities as an
explorer and conqueror have become equivalents for him of the
conquest of a woman, it is through this substitute sphere of
action that he will now begin to experience the punishments that
his transgressions warrant.

Thus, in III viii, the Angel tells Prouhèze that, having achieved
his immediate goals in the Americas, Rodrigue must continue to
explore the world, and that through the difficulties he will
encounter during this second phase of his adventurous career,
he will begin to expiate his sins: (III viii 227–8, 255–62; 823–5)

DONA PROUHÈZE: C'est pénitence qu'il va faire, lui aussi?
L'ANGE GARDIEN: *Les voies directes de Dieu,* le temps est venu pour lui
qu'il commence à les fouler.
...
   Pendant que tu vas au Purgatoire, lui aussi sur terre va recon-
naître *cette image du Purgatoire.*
...
   L'Inde pendue *cuit sur place dans une vapeur brûlante,* la Chine
éternellement *dans ce laboratoire intérieur où l'eau devient de la boue
piétine ce limon mélangé à sa propre ordure.*[53]

The Angel now openly discusses woman's role in leading man
to salvation, and reveals that although Prouhèze's earthly life
will soon be ended she will continue to influence Rodrigue's
progress through Purgatory towards redemption as he travels
around the world: (III viii 130–6, 221–3; 818–23)

DONA PROUHÈZE: L'homme entre les bras de la femme oublie Dieu.
L'ANGE GARDIEN: Est-ce L'oublier que d'être avec Lui? est-ce ailleurs qu'avec Lui d'être associé au mystère de Sa création,
  Franchissant de nouveau pour un instant *l'Éden par la porte de l'humiliation et de la mort?*
DONA PROUHÈZE: L'amour hors du sacrement, n'est-il pas le péché?
L'ANGE GARDIEN: Même le péché! Le péché aussi sert.
DONA PROUHÈZE: Ainsi il était bon qu'il m'aime?
L'ANGE GARDIEN: Il était bon que tu lui apprennes le désir.
  ...
DONA PROUHÈZE: Ces Iles mystérieuses au bout du monde dont je t'ai vu surgir.
  Pour l'y *tirer*, comment faire, maintenant que tu n'as plus mon corps *comme amorce?*
L'ANGE GARDIEN: Non plus ton corps, mais ton reflet sur les Eaux amères de l'exil,
  ...

The importance of the religious-level conclusion to be drawn from this dialogue – the idea that woman may lead man into sin by tempting him sexually, but that this sin can be 'useful' because through it man may be shown the way to atonement and thus to redemption – is underscored by the repetition here of one of the epigraphs of the play, Saint Augustine's 'Etiam peccata' – 'Le péché aussi sert.'

On the emotional level, both the Angel's indication that man regains a state equivalent to salvation during the sex act and his suggestion that the *désir* initially awakened by Prouhèze will play a role in helping Rodrigue to reach this paradise emphasize the erotic nature of the entire experience being described. When he says that man returns to this 'Eden' only by submitting *de nouveau* to a *humiliation* while in a woman's arms, he stresses once more that, having shamed himself and lost his original happiness by indulging in forbidden desires for a woman, man can again experience true gratification only after making up for his initial wrongdoing by undergoing a matching penalty – by allowing a woman to inflict upon him a second, similar degradation.[54]

The Angel thus prepares the reader in this passage for the final meeting of Prouhèze and Rodrigue, when Prouhèze will reject Rodrigue's offers in such a way that he will be motivated to travel to the Far East alone and to suffer there the punishment he deserves, and will thus move within reach of both his religious- and his emotional-level goals.

Having received a plea for help sent by Prouhèze ten years earlier, Rodrigue sails to Africa; but when Prouhèze meets with him on his ship she refuses his offer of aid and announces her decision to remain at Mogador despite the certainty that she will be killed during an impending Arab attack. Rodrigue's bitterness then overwhelms him: (III xiii 115–22; 854–5)

> Ainsi la vue de *cet Ange* pour moi qui fut *comme le trait de la mort*! Ah! cela prend du temps de mourir et la vie la plus longue n'est pas de trop pour apprendre à correspondre à *ce patient appel*!
> *Une blessure* à mon côté *comme la flamme peu à peu qui tire toute l'huile de la lampe*!
> ...
> Pourquoi ... la perfection de notre être et de *notre noyau substantiel* serait-elle toujours associée à *l'opacité* et à la résistance,
> Et non pas l'adoration et le désir et la préférence d'autre chose et ... *de se fendre enfin et de s'ouvrir enfin* dans un état de *dissolution ineffable*?
> *De ce déliement, de cette délivrance* mystique nous savons que nous sommes par nous-mêmes incapables et de là ce pouvoir sur nous de la femme *pareil à celui de la Grâce*.
> Et maintenant est-il vrai que tu vas me quitter ainsi sans aucun serment? *le paradis que la femme a fermé*, est-il vrai que tu étais incapable de *le rouvrir*? ...

As explained in Chapter 4, on the narrative level the death-code imagery used in the first of these versets expresses Rodrigue's feeling that because of his passion for Prouhèze all other areas of his life have been deprived of meaning. As at the end of Day 2 – and using many of the same images – Rodrigue now emphasizes his despair of ever escaping from his unhappy situation.[55] The *blessure* that Prouhèze has inflicted on him seems to [*tirer*] *toute l'huile de la lampe* – one after another, the opportunities for attaining happiness have slipped by, and soon no hope at all will remain.

The religious-level significance of this highly coveted, but apparently unattainable, satisfaction is underscored by the images that compare Prouhèze first to *cette Ange* and then to *la*

Grâce; on the emotional level, these vehicles again evoke for the reader the guilt-free, gratifying state known by all in infancy.[56]

When Rodrigue goes on to speculate on the nature of man in general and on his attempts to gain such satisfaction, his references to a desired *dissolution, déliement,* and *délivrance* emphasize his wish to destroy his present self and begin a completely new existence. Because this destruction would involve specifically his being 'opened' (*se fendre, s'ouvrir*), his words suggest on the emotional level that he himself now begins to recognize, at least unconsciously, the desirability of adopting the submissive, emasculated attitude that would make clear both his acceptance of a just punishment for past misdeeds and his determination not to err in this way again.

Rodrigue, however, also understands that despite his own efforts he will never achieve his objectives without further help from Prouhèze, and he cannot yet bring himself to trust her completely. He still sees her in an ambivalent light – she not only seems to be *cet Ange* and *la Grâce*, but she also appears as *le trait de la mort*, the cause of a *blessure* that never heals. Woman has led man from paradise, Rodrigue recalls, and he doubts that she will ever fulfil her promise to bring him back.

As the scene continues, Prouhèze attempts to assure Rodrigue that he can still achieve happiness, if only he will do what she advises: (III xiii 158–60, 175–6; 857–8)

> LE VICE-ROI: A quoi me sert cette joie si tu ne peux me la donner?
> DONA PROUHÈZE: *Ouvre* et elle *entrera.* Comment faire pour te donner la joie si tu ne lui *ouvres cette porte seule* par où je peux *entrer?*
> On ne possède point la joie, c'est la joie qui te possède ...
>
> ...
>
> Sois généreux à ton tour! ce que j'ai fait, ne peux-tu le faire à ton tour? *Dépouille-toi! Jette tout!* Donne tout afin de tout recevoir!
> Si nous allons vers la joie, qu'importe que cela soit ici-bas à l'envers de *notre approximation corporelle?*

On the religious level of meaning, Prouhèze stresses here the unassuming, submissive attitude that Rodrigue should adopt towards the heavenly powers. From an emotional point of view, her repetition of the contention that he should 'open' himself to the joy he desires and her statement that all individuals must approach this gratifying state *à l'envers de notre approximation corporelle* again emphasize that he should exhibit specifically a more feminine frame of mind.

Prouhèze then repeats her promise that if Rodrigue obeys her injunctions, he will attain a two-fold happiness: (III xiii 180–4; 858)

> Là où il y a le plus de joie, comment croire que je suis absente?
> là où il y a le plus de joie, c'est là où il y a le plus Prouhèze!
> ...
>
> Prends, Rodrigue, prends, mon cœur, prends, mon amour, prends ce Dieu qui me *remplit*!
> La force par laquelle je t'aime n'est pas différente de celle par laquelle tu existes.
> Je suis unie pour toujours à cette chose qui te donne la vie eternelle!

On the emotional level, the reader is again assured that with Prouhèze acting as intermediary Rodrigue can achieve both a satisfying bond with a beloved woman and a close tie with the all-powerful beings who ruled his world during his earliest months of life.

Prouhèze's certainty that Rodrigue can still be saved allays the reader's anxiety somewhat. Nevertheless, since Rodrigue refuses fully to accept the validity of her words ('Si tu t'en vas,' he exclaims, 'il n'y a plus d'étoile pour me guider, je suis seul!' 189; 859), the final outcome of his story remains in doubt as Day 3 comes to an end. The reader is again left in a state of suspense, and his interest in the coming scenes is increased as a result.

The opening pages of Day 4 reveal that, as predicted by the Angel, Rodrigue has encountered his personal *Purgatoire* in the Far East. Having failed to attain his military objectives in the Orient, he has returned to Spain in political and social disfavour; his physical disfigurement adds to his general disgrace.

The emotional-level meaning of Rodrigue's defeat and subsequent humiliation is underscored by the nature of his physical injury – his loss of a leg evokes specifically the castrating punishment demanded earlier by Prouhèze.[57] The passive, detached attitude that Rodrigue now maintains even in the face of harsh insults and mockery emphasizes that he himself fully accepts this punitive emasculation.

Because Rodrigue ungrudgingly endures both his physical impairment and the complete reversal of his worldly fortunes, his burden of guilt is somewhat lightened, and he begins to experience a gratifying sense of fulfilment. As he explain to Daibutsu in speaking of the religious pictures that he now paints and sells: (IV ii 60–7; 871–2)

> Ces images auxquelles vous me provoquiez, *ces grandes possibilités* de moi-même que je dessinais sur des morceaux de papier.
> ...
> Ils me ressemblent bien plus que je ne le fais à moi-même avec ce corps flétri et cette âme avortée!
> C'est quelque chose de moi qui a réussi et qui a obtenu *son avènement*!
> ...
> ... moi, j'ai construit avec mes dessins quelque chose qui passe *à travers toutes les prisons*!
> ... Qui reçoit par les yeux *à l'intérieur de son âme* la figure de *cette espèce d'engin inépuisable qui n'est que mouvement et désir,*
> Adopte une puissance en lui désormais *incompatible avec toutes les murailles*!

From a religious point of view, the holy figures in Rodrigue's pictures represent potentialities of his own spiritual being that he is finally able to realize, now that his sinful, earthly self has been chastened. The description of the impact of these paintings on others stresses the tremendous power of the spiritual forces that he portrays. On the emotional level, these versets imply that since Rodrigue is being appropriately punished for his original erotic crimes he becomes able to fulfil his sensual needs in ways more acceptable to his conscience; the erotic nature of the satisfaction he obtains is underscored by the reference to the *engin inépuisable* that is only *mouvement* and *désir*.

Rodrigue's conversation with Daibutsu also reveals that his present activity is particularly satisfying to him because his behaviour now conforms with the religious- and emotional-level attitudes that are most acceptable within the framework of the *Soulier de satin*; for although Rodrigue speaks of the intense power of his paintings, this artistic work – unlike his earlier adventures – involves both physical passivity and unquestioned submission to the omnipotent forces that rule his world. From a religious point of view, he thus exhibits the humble acquiescence demanded of all by God. Emotionally, he has yielded completely to the all-powerful father who opposed his earliest erotic drives.

As Day 4 continues, the reader's tension is sustained by repeated references to Rodrigue's punishing defeat in the Far East and to the injury he suffered there, as well as by passages in which he is ridiculed by everyone from simple soldiers to the King and his Court. At the same time, however, the reader is reassured by increasingly frequent descriptions of the heavenly realm that Rodrigue is now drawing near to a satisfactory resolution of his painful dilemma.

In the concluding scene of the play, Rodrigue declares himself willing, even eager, to submit to the last and most extreme phase of his penitential ordeal, his own death. Although his generally distressing situation is aggravated at this time by the mocking of the soldiers who accompany him, he calmly and confidently prepares to ascend to heaven.[58]

For a brief time, his thoughts do return to the disappointments and frustrations he endured over so many years; now, however, he is finally able to see that although his feelings for Prouhèze were the source of his torment in the past they are also the reason that he is about to attain satisfaction. Speaking to Frère Léon of Prouhèze, Rodrigue exclaims: (IV xi 96–100; 945)

> Elle est morte, morte, morte! Elle est morte, mon Père, et je ne la verrai plus! Elle est morte et jamais elle ne sera à moi! Elle est morte et c'est moi qui l'ai tuée!
> FRÈRE LÉON: Elle n'est pas *si* morte *que ce ciel autour de nous et cette mer sous nos pieds ne soient encore plus éternels!*
> DON RODRIGUE: Je le sais! C'était cela qu'elle était venue *m'apporter avec son visage!*
> La mer et les étoiles! *Je la sens sous moi!* Je les regarde et je ne puis *m'en rassasier!*
> Oui, je sens que nous ne pouvons leur *échapper* et qu'il est *impossible de mourir!*

Rodrigue thus realizes that through his love he has come to experience a profound sense of unity with his physical surroundings and with the eternal spiritual powers that created them. On the emotional level, the erotic quality of his feeling of union with Prouhèze, and, through her, with the entire universe, is underscored by the expressions, *je la sens sous moi* and *je ne puis m'en rassasier*. Rodrigue's final declaration that it is impossible to die then implies that the effects of his earthly death will be negated by his induction into a totally new way of life, and suggests that in the future, too, omnipotent forces will guard him from possible harm.[59]

Frère Léon now assures Rodrigue that, once he has completely surrendered himself to these divine forces and has given up his last ties to earthly objects and events, he will be united with God: (IV xi 101; 945)

> ... Il n'y a plus moyen de leur *échapper* et d'être ailleurs! On a retiré autre chose que Dieu! On a enchaîné *l'exacteur*! Tout ce qui en vous s'accrochait misérablement aux choses une par une et successivement! ... On *a mis aux fers vos membres, ces tyrans,* et il n'y a qu'à *respirer* pour *vous remplir de Dieu*!

On the emotional level, Léon's declaration that the physical drives that have despotically ruled Rodrigue's earthly life have been deprived of their potency emphasizes the emasculated quality of the humble attitude he now displays, and, in context, suggests once more that because he has accepted appropriate punishment for his misdeeds he can again become one with his omnipotent father.[60]

The solution Rodrigue has found for his dilemma is now unconsciously related by the reader to his own past conflicts between desire and prohibition and to his fears that he could be punished for his wrongful wishes. The reader then infers that these difficulties, too, could be resolved in a pleasurable way; his tension is thus dissolved and as the book comes to an end he is left with a feeling of agreeable satisfaction.[61]

The emotional-level course of action followed by Rodrigue in the *Soulier de satin* was summarized and presented schematically on p. 128 above; the relationship between this emotional-level message and the concepts conveyed on the narrative and religious levels of the text is shown in the expansion of this schema in Chart 1.

As can be seen from this chart, the same basic message is conveyed simultaneously on all levels of the text; only the forms through which this message is actualized, either in the text itself or in the reader's mind, vary.[62] More precisely, the narrative and

CHART 1
Structure of Rodrigue's adventures

Levels	Stage 1 Conflict	Stage 2 Outgrowth of conflict	Stage 3 Means of resolution	Stage 4 Resolution of conflict
Narrative (1)	Forbidden love for Prouhèze	Frustration	Agonizing separation from Prouhèze	Resignation to loss of Prouhèze; satisfaction through religion
Narrative (2)	Desire for vs. difficulty of conquest of distant lands	Failure to achieve goal of unifying world	Defeat, disfigurement, and humiliation	Acceptance of humble role in society; satisfaction through religion
Religious	Forbidden desires (sin)	Guilt	Penitential sacrifice	Salvation; rebirth to pure, heavenly life; union with God and spiritual ties to beloved woman
Myth	Imperfect state	Dissatisfaction	Mutilation and death	Initiation into complete (androgynous) and satisfying state; identification with supernatural founder of social group
Emotional	Forbidden erotic desires	Frustration and guilt	Punishment involving emasculation	Innocent yet erotically satisfying union with universe as a whole, and in particular with beloved woman and omnipotent father-figure

religious levels are variant forms of the emotional-level line of action pursued by Rodrigue, and the impact of both of these levels of meaning on the reader's response to the text is due less to the specific narrative and religious ideas they convey than to the emotional message to which these ideas give form.

As explained in Chapters 5 and 6, the expression of the religious level of meaning and the author's interventions in the play result in some instances in inconsistent developments on the narrative level of the text. The role of the author's interventions in relation to the emotional level is considered further in Chapter 8; as for the religious level, Chart 1 underscores the fact that the theological ideas whose expression causes such inconsistencies are themselves variant actualizations of emotional-level concepts, and that it is thus the expression of the emotional level of meaning that is the ultimate source of these incongruities in the story line. Thus, Rodrigue's attempt to conquer and unify all peoples of the world would have been unthinkable at the time the *Soulier de satin* ostensibly takes place, but on the religious level of the text this development is consistent with the desire expressed by many characters of the play to see all forces and beings inextricably bound together on the spiritual plane of existence. This religious concept, however, is itself a variant actualization of an underlying wish to recover the infant's feeling of merger with all parts of the universe.[63]

The relationship of the emotional level of meaning to other aspects of the *Soulier de satin* is explored further in Chapter 8, where the structure of the play as a whole and the adventures of each of the other major characters are examined.

PART THREE

STRUCTURE

AS EXPRESSED

THROUGH IMAGERY

The structure of *Le Soulier de satin*

The story of each major character of the *Soulier de satin* actualizes in whole or in part the same basic emotional-level message as does Rodrigue's. In some cases, a character does not pursue this sequence of affective responses to its conclusion; in others, he is able to avoid the first, most distressing stages. Almost all of the emotional-level responses manifested by these characters, however, can be found within this sequence. Furthermore, as in Rodrigue's case, when the other characters' activities are related in the text, the affective message is often actualized on several different levels of meaning simultaneously. The basic emotional-level message is thus repeated many times, both diachronically and synchronously, as the work continues.

The importance in poetry of repetition on all linguistic levels was noted in Chapter 3. The patterns of repetition examined there are limited to relatively brief passages of the *Soulier de satin*; repetition, however, can now be seen to be an essential characteristic of the play as a whole. Indeed, it is the reiteration of the same emotional message both sequentially and simultaneously throughout the work which gives the text the internal coherence and unity that make it a single, complete poem.[1] Because the emotional-level message thus functions as the basic system of concepts around which the play as a whole is constructed, it may be considered to constitute the 'invariant structure' of the work.[2]

Paradoxically, the story of the first character to appear in the *Soulier de satin*, the Jesuit, actualizes only the final stage of this invariant structure.[3]

As the play begins, the Jesuit, realizing that he is about to die, expresses his desire to atone for his sins in the manner prescribed by Catholic dogma – by offering himself to God in imitation of Jesus: (I i 5–22; 667–8)

> Et c'est vrai que je suis *attaché à la croix,* mais *la croix* où je suis n'est plus attachée à rien. Elle flotte sur la mer.
>
> ...
>
> Tout a expiré autour de moi, tout a été *consommé* sur *cet étroit autel*

> qu'encombrent les corps de mes sœurs l'une sur l'autre ...
>
> ...
>
> Et maintenant voici *la dernière oraison de cette messe que* mêlé déjà
> à la mort *je célèbre par le moyen de moi-même* ...

The Jesuit's official religious status – that is, his membership in the priesthood – indicates on the emotional level of the text that he has committed no unexpiated sins through lust for a woman, but that on the contrary he has voluntarily decided to suppress his sexual drives, and to give himself over to his Supreme Father. Now he need only reaffirm his wish to surrender himself unreservedly to this omnipotent parent figure: (I i 4; 667)

> Mais aujourd'hui il n'y a pas moyen d'être plus *serré* à Vous que
> je ne le suis et j'ai beau vérifier *chacun de mes membres, il n'y en a plus
> un seul qui de Vous soit capable de s'écarter si peu.*

The Jesuit finds it a simple matter to abandon himself completely to the powers that reunite him with the parental realm – 'ces grandes forces continues qui de toutes parts nous adoptent et nous engagent' (21; 668) – and to identify fully with his Holy Father, existing 'à l'intérieur de Sa sainte volonté, ayant renoncé à la [sienne]' (13; 667).[4]

Because this first character of the play attains the pleasurable goal he seeks without undue suffering, his story suggests to the reader that other characters will also find satisfactory solutions to the problems they face, and that the work will thus have a 'happy ending.' When the Jesuit goes on to outline in the last versets of the scene the difficulties Rodrigue will encounter in the future (in the versets discussed in Chapter 7), his words do introduce an element of suspense, but the reader's concern over Rodrigue's fate is tempered somewhat almost immediately by the Jesuit's promise: 'Et ce qu'il essayera de dire misérablement sur la terre, je suis là pour le traduire dans le Ciel' (38; 669).[5]

In the second scene, the reader's anxiety is again increased, but this time without prompt relief; for the text now introduces two unhappy, frustrated men – Balthazar and Pélage – neither of whom can foresee a satisfactory resolution of his emotional difficulties.

On the narrative level, Balthazar is a lonely, discouraged bachelor, who permits himself to be killed in order to punish himself for having allowed his charge to flee to her wounded lover's side. On the religious and emotional levels, however, Balthazar's crimes begin long before he gives in to Prouhèze's pleas and tears.

Balthazar admits to Pélage that he has been strongly attracted to Musique for some time, but that a lack of money has prevented him from marrying her (i ii). His attraction to Prouhèze, his good friend's wife, is revealed less directly, by his reluctance to escort her alone on a journey (i ii; i v), by his confusion in relating her escape from the inn to l'Alférès (i xiii), and by his answer to her when she asks permission to speak freely with him as they travel: (i v 12–13; 680)

> DONA PROUHÈZE: Mais moi aussi, n'aurai-je pas licence de dire un mot parfois?
> DON BALTHAZAR: *Sirène,* je ne vous ai prêté déjà les oreilles que trop!

Although he has not tried to satisfy his desires directly, Balthazar recognizes that he is guilty of grave wrongdoing, and his indirect suicide is an attempt to placate both the social and religious powers he has offended by his erotic crimes, and his own outraged conscience.

Balthazar fails to achieve this goal, however, because he does not fully accept the demands of the forces he has affronted. On the religious level, the description of his position as he dies reveals that, like all faithful Catholics, he offers himself to God in imitation of Jesus – sitting beside the table that has been spread with sumptuous foods, the stage directions note, Balthazar 'tombe mort, la face au milieu des fruits, tenant la table dans ses bras' (i xiv; 725). Because this position recalls the Crucifixion, it suggests by flashback that the lavish meal Balthazar has just described so ironically is, like the Communion ceremony, a re-creation of the Last Supper. The reader understands, however, that this character's self-offering will be rejected because he in effect takes his own life, in violation of Church laws, rather than submitting blindly to God's will. The mocking attitude he displays as he prepares for his death underscores his own knowledge that he will never attain the salvation for which he longs.

On the emotional level, Balthazar is unsuccessful in his quest for happiness because he refuses to submit either to the father figure whom his desires have angered or to the woman through whom he has sinned, but attempts to retain his independence even while undergoing a penalty he knows he deserves. From a psychological viewpoint, such a self-inflicted punishment is far less threatening than one administered by another person, because its intensity and timing can be determined by the victim; at the same time, however, it cannot effectively placate the parent figure who demands total surrender.[6] During the final moments of Balthazar's life, Musique, the Negress, and the Sergeant appear on a screen behind him; the water on which these three now sail off evokes the innocent state of communion with others that Balthazar has failed to attain.

Because Balthazar's experiences actualize only the first two stages of the invariant structure, his story creates considerable tension in the reader, in whose mind a corresponding dilemma is brought forward and left without a satisfying conclusion. Pélage's story then heightens this tension, because he, too, progresses only to the second stage of this sequence of emotional responses.

Although Pélage's desires for Prouhèze violate no specific social or theological laws, they do bring him into conflict with the unwritten rules of his society and religion – for Westerners generally disapprove of unions between older men and young women, and in the eyes of the Church a physical bond which produces no children and which is marked by the emotional and spiritual disaccord of the participants, as in this case, is unjustified. On the emotional level, Pélage's love for Prouhèze evokes a particular form of forbidden erotic desire, the 'reverse oedipal' love of a father for his daughter. Pélage himself must now admit that his marriage to Prouhèze was an error on his part: (II ii 41–2; 736)

> C'est ma faute. Oui ... c'est moi qui ai mal fait
> De l'épouser, vieux déjà, elle si jeune, et ne sachant pas à quoi
> elle consentait.

Although on all levels of meaning Pélage has thus committed, if not a wrongful, at least a highly questionable act in marrying Prouhèze, he cannot allow himself to be punished or even corrected at her hands. On the contrary, he can envisage their relationship only in terms of his total domination. He tells Honoria, for example, in speaking of Prouhèze: (II iii 50–1; 736)

... Mais ne savais-je pas mieux qu'elle ce qui la rendrait heureuse?
étais-je un tel ignorant de cette vie qu'elle ne connaissait pas?

Qui connaît le mieux *une plante? elle-même qui a poussé au hasard
ou le jardinier qui saura la mettre où il faut?*

On the emotional level, Pélage is apparently reluctant to give up
his role as Prouhèze's master because he believes she will then
reject him completely, and he is afraid to face openly this distressing possibility.

Like Rodrigue, Pélage attempted during one period of his life
to gain through the conquest of a nation the satisfaction he could
not find with a woman. Speaking of his mission to Africa, he
explains: (II iv 27–33; 741)

Oui, je *l'ai aimée. J'ai désiré sa face sans espoir* ...

...

La croisade n'a pas cessé pour moi. Dieu n'a pas fait l'homme
pour vivre seul.

A défaut de cette femme, il ne faut pas lâcher cet ennemi qu'il m'a
donné. Il ne faut pas que *le Maure et l'Espagnol* oublient *qu'ils ont été
faits l'un pour l'autre;*

Pas que *l'étreinte* cesse *de ces deux cœurs qui dans une lutte farouche
ont battu si longtemps l'un contre l'autre.*

As previously explained, the love-code imagery used here
implies on the emotional level of meaning that Pélage sought to
gratify through his militant actions in Africa some of the erotic
drives that had remained frustrated in his relationship with
Prouhèze.[7] Eventually, however, he had to admit that even in
Africa he could not attain a lasting sense of fulfilment. 'L'Afrique
aussi fait partie de ces choses auxquelles je ne crois plus,' he
finally confesses (II iv 25; 741).

Emotionally, the reason for Pélage's disappointment in Africa
is the same as that of his failure with Prouhèze. The sexual drives
Pélage attempted to release through his activities on this continent were wrongful ones; yet here, too, he refused to expiate his
crime by submitting to a suitable punishment at the hands of the
'woman' through whom he had sinned. On the contrary, the
imagery of the above passage indicates that he fought aggres-
sively in Africa to achieve total domination of the Arabs.
Whatever the virtues of his obstinate struggle from a religious

point of view, on the emotional level, because he refused to yield to this 'woman,' also, his combat could provide only a temporary outlet for his pent-up erotic drives, and not the complete, innocent gratification he actually sought.[8]

As noted above, Pélage's inability to satisfy his emotional needs heightens the tension evoked in the reader by the description of Balthazar's unhappy ending; as the play continues, the relation of Camille's story increases the reader's anxiety still further.

On both the narrative and the religious levels of the play, Camille is clearly a renegade, for he rejects the moral and ethical standards of his society as well as the basic principles of Catholicism. The emotional-level significance of his rebellion is revealed by an extended image in which he compares himself to the *Enfant Prodigue*. After describing through this vehicle code his exploits in Africa and the disapproval of his family and society, Camille adds: (I iii 93–5, 677)

> Et croyez-vous que ce soit le Fils Prodigue qui ait demandé pardon?
>
> ...
>
> Moi, je tiens que *c'est le Père, oui, pendant qu'il lavait les pieds blessés de cet explorateur.*

This entire image development, and in particular the lines cited, suggests that Camille's rebellion is the oedipal revolt of a son against his father – rather than submit to his father's domination, Camille wants to reverse the situation, to affirm his own superiority by freely choosing the rules by which he will live, and to see all authority figures yield to his self-proclaimed supremacy.

Speaking again of his Heavenly Father, Camille then declares: (I iii 98; 677)

> Je veux qu'il soit *aveugle comme Jacob* pour qu'il *ne me voie pas.*

This double image conveys two emotional-level ideas in context. First, Camille's wish to see God 'blinded' reveals his own sense of guilt, for the eyes he would like to avoid include those of his own disapproving conscience.[9] Second, because the idea of blindness often functions as an expression of castration, this image reinforces the impression that Camille's religious and social rebellion is on the emotional level an oedipal revolt against a sexual rival.[10]

When Camille is forced to admit that it is the son who is in fact impotent when compared with his father, he seeks to remove himself entirely from his father's sphere of influence: (III x 159–63; 840–1)

> Qu'Il reste Dieu et qu'Il nous laisse à nous notre néant ...
>
> ...
>
> Lui à sa place et nous à la nôtre pour toujours!
>
> ...
>
> La chose par quoi Il est ce qu'Il est puisqu'Il ne peut nous la donner, qu'Il nous laisse donc où nous sommes ...

Like other men of the *Soulier de satin*, when Camille attempts to satisfy the desires of which this father figure disapproves, he turns for a time to a country – in this case, Africa – as a substitute for a woman; unlike the others, however, Camille makes no attempt to justify his militant actions by invoking patriotism and religion, but speaks proudly of his unethical, self-aggrandizing dealings with the Arabs.

The erotic quality of Camille's attraction to Africa is revealed by his description of the continent, which reads in part: (I iii 108–9; 677)

> ... *cet appel du feu capable de les* [les cœurs humains] *consumer.* L'appel de l'Afrique!
>
> La terre ne serait point ce qu'elle est si elle n'avait *ce carreau de feu sur le ventre* ...

Both the fire-code imagery, which evokes feelings of sexual arousal, and the phrase *sur le ventre* suggest on the emotional level that Camille's attraction to the continent is an outgrowth of his persistent, aggressive search for erotic gratification.[11] This impression is confirmed later in the passage when he declares that he wishes to 'penetrate' the continent so that he can devote himself to the exploration of 'ses rives au delà du lac ardent' (I iii 120; 678).

As previously explained, however, on the religious level of the text, one fire-code vehicle applied by Camille to Africa in this scene – 'ce fourneau où vient se dégraisser l'ordure de toutes les respirations animales' – also indicates that Africa serves as a purgatory for men like himself, a place where the sinful can come to be tested, punished, and eventually cleansed of evil by spiritual forces. Camille, too, may thus be led to salvation by the same 'temptress' through whom he now sins. On the emotional level, Camille's use of this vehicle here suggests that his strong attraction to Africa stems not only from his evil desires but at the same time from an unconscious wish to be suitably punished for these crimes and thereby relieved of his heavy burden of guilt.[12]

In Africa, Prouhèze actually fulfils the double role evoked by these fire-code references to the continent – having aroused Camille's desires, she leads him to accept the emasculating punishment through which he finally moves within reach of salvation.

When Camille first tries to persuade Prouhèze to come to Africa with him, in I iii, he self-confidently implies that in any relationship with a woman he would surely have the upper hand. Nevertheless, his eventual surrender to her is foreshadowed by his immediate acceptance of her command at Mogador – for, although he occasionally tortures or beats her, he always obeys her orders.[13] Camille's compliance with Prouhèze's rule stems initially from his feeling that her power over him is stronger than his own will. As he tells Rodrigue soon after her arrival at Mogador: (II xi 126–33; 773)

> Je lui ai cédé ma place ...
>
> ...
>
> ... que vous me croyiez ou non, oui, je l'aurais déjà renvoyée si j'avais pu.
>
> ...
>
> La raison et le hasard, l'ambition et l'aventure, je ne voulais point d'autre *maîtres*.
>
> La voici qui intervient contre moi *comme la destinée*, sur laquelle je n'ai aucune prise.

Although Camille succeeds in marrying Prouhèze after Pélage's death, he soon must admit that their physical union brings him no real gratification, and he eventually abandons his attempt to satisfy his desires through this relationship. During their last hours together, he explains to Prouhèze: 'J'ai juré de ne plus vous toucher. J'ai cédé à votre indifférence insultante' (III x 3; 832). On the emotional level, Camille's abandonment of his sexually aggressive behaviour and his adoption instead of a submissive, emasculated attitude suggests that under Prouhèze's influence he has recognized his need to be suitably punished for his past erotic misdeeds.[14]

As he prepares to die, Camille again denounces the Christian God, and thus rebels one last time against his parent-like authority; he finally admits, however, that he is willing to give Prouhèze his soul – the most vital part of himself – if she will only lead him back to the comforting, protective realm of this Supreme Father: (III x 198–204; 842)

> ... mon âme ne peut être rachetée que par la vôtre ...
> ...
> Prouhèze, je crois en vous! Prouhèze, je meurs *de soif*! Ah! cessez d'être une femme et laissez-moi voir sur votre visage enfin ce Dieu que vous êtes *impuissante à contenir,*
> Et atteindre *au fond de votre cœur cette eau* dont Dieu vous a faite *le vase!*

As explained in the discussion of this passage in Chapter 5, on the religious level of meaning, the 'water' Camille so avidly desires represents a state of Grace.[15] On the emotional level, because water is often associated with the idea of a return to an all-providing mother, Camille seems to be expressing here his desire to regain through this woman the idyllic state he knew in infancy; the water-code imagery also underscores the innocence of the desired state.[16]

Prouhèze's reluctant agreement to grant Camille's request is finally revealed by her facial expression, for after she has repeatedly refused his demand Camille asks: (III x 206; 843)

> Mais d'où viendrait autrement *cette lumière* sur votre visage?[17]

As the anxiety-producing stories of Balthazar, Pélage, and Camille are being told in the first three days of the *Soulier de satin,* Prouhèze's own search for happiness is also related to the reader.

Although Prouhèze is very strongly attracted to Rodrigue, she quickly recognizes the threat posed by her love to herself and her husband. At first, she turns to others for help in suppressing her sinful desires – to Balthazar, who she hopes will prevent her from actually running off to join Rodrigue, and to the Virgin, whose statue stands at the door of her husband's home, and to whom, as she prepares to travel to the inn where she has planned   eet

Rodrigue, she presents one of her slippers and prays: (I v 112–25; 685–6)

> Vierge, patronne et mère de cette maison,
>
> ...
>
> Empêchez que je sois à cette maison dont vous gardez la porte, *auguste tourière*, une cause de corruption!
>
> ...
>
> Je ne puis dire que je comprends cet homme que vous m'avez choisi, mais vous, je comprends, qui êtes *sa mère comme la mienne*.
> Alors, pendant qu'il est encore temps, *tenant mon cœur dans une main* et mon soulier dans l'autre,
> Je me remets à vous! Vierge mère, je vous donne mon soulier!
> Vierge mère, gardez dans votre main *mon malheureux petit pied*!
>
> ...
>
> Mais quand j'essayerai de m'élancer vers le mal, que ce soit avec *un pied boiteux*! la barrière que vous avez mise,
> Quand je voudrai *la franchir*, que ce soit *avec une aile rognée*!
> J'ai fini ce que je pouvais faire, et vous, gardez mon pauvre petit soulier,
> Gardez-le *contre votre cœur*, ô *grande Maman effrayante*!

From a religious point of view, Prouhèze's plea conforms with the traditional Catholic practice of asking the Virgin or the saints for guidance and support in time of need.[18] The offer of her shoe, however – the importance of which is emphasized by the title of the play – has no specific parallel in Christian tradition, and serves for Prouhèze as a symbolic means of asking the Virgin to control her earthly actions in the future.

The meaning of this offer is more limited on the emotional level of the text, where Prouhèze's prayer is a plea to an all-powerful and all-pure mother figure for help in suppressing the erotic urges she knows to be wrong. This interpretation is first suggested by Prouhèze's request to the Virgin to keep her from becoming a cause of 'corruption' to Pélage's 'house'; in context, this reference to a hollow cavity evokes the female vagina or womb.[19]

The satin slipper is a second such cavity that Prouhèze now asks the Virgin to protect. As a rule, the vaginal symbolism of the shoe or slipper is reinforced by the phallic associations of the foot that is placed within it.[20] Such associations are evoked in this passage, as elsewhere in the *Soulier de satin*, by the use of foot-code terms to suggest castration – thus, Prouhèze asks the Virgin here to keep her from trying to satisfy her sexual drives by holding back her *malheureux petit pied*, or by causing this erring foot to become *boîteux;*[21] similarly, as explained in Chapter 7, Rodrigue's later loss of a leg functions on the emotional level as a castrating punishment for his erotic misdeeds of the past.[22] By calling upon the Virgin to guard her 'satin slipper,' Prouhèze is thus asking the Holy Mother to make certain that the physical purity this object represents remains unspoiled in the future.[23]

Prouhèze ends her appeal to the Virgin with the striking exclamation: *ô grande Maman effrayante!*[24] This expression reveals to the reader the ambivalent feelings that Prouhèze now experiences towards the mother figure to whom she has submissively turned for help – for, like other mothers, this *Maman* can seem to her daughter both a comforting, protective presence, and at the same time a frightening power who is swift to punish when her teachings are disregarded – as they clearly have been by Prouhèze.

When Prouhèze later runs off to join the wounded Rodrigue, her Guardian Angel's decision not to stop her as she struggles along the way emphasizes that her agonizing dilemma cannot be permanently resolved by appeals for help from outside forces – not even from the Virgin – but only by her own determination to give up her sinful drives. The reader soon learns, however, that there is one means through which she can at least be encouraged to change her wrongful course.

When Pélage arrives at Rodrigue's home unhappy and bewildered, Honoria explains to him that Prouhèze will again find contentment only after she has been punished for her wrongful thoughts and desires: (II iii 62–3; 737)

> DON PÉLAGE: ... N'était-ce pas *le paradis* où je l'avais mise au milieu de choses excellentes?
> DONA HONORIA: *Le paradis* n'est pas fait pour les pécheurs.

Pélage now recognizes that his wife's situation is like that of the criminals he used to sentence; for such wrongdoers, he agrees, only harsh punishment can bring true 'quittance et libération' (83–90; 738). He decides to offer Prouhèze the command of Mogador, for he understands that the physical, emotional, and spiritual hardships she will endure at this African fortress will serve as the punishment she not only deserves, but at this point actually desires – 'A la place d'une tentation une tentation plus grande' (97; 739).

On the narrative and religious levels of the text, these punitive hardships take several different forms; on the emotional level, however, each one parallels in reverse Prouhèze's earlier erotic crimes.

Thus, Prouhèze's first refusal to leave Mogador with Rodrigue represents on the narrative and religious strata a renouncing of her own desires in favour of the unpleasant, but in the long run inescapable, restrictions of her society and religion. The emotional-level significance of this painful act is revealed by the Moon when it describes her great unhappiness after her lover's departure: (II xiv 25–6; 778)

> Cela a commencé par ces grandes larmes, *pareilles aux nausées de l'agonie*, qui naissent au-dessous de la pensée, au fond de l'être *profondément entaillé*,
> L'âme qui *veut vomir* et que *le fer pénètre*!

Two vehicle codes, a nausea code and an attack code, are developed alternately in this passage. On the emotional level, the attack-code references to Prouhèze's being 'cut open' by a 'sword' evoke specifically a sexual assault – Prouhèze has erred through her aggressive attempts to satisfy her erotic drives, and a similar type of aggression is now being directed back at her.[25] The nausea-code images emphasize the intensity of her suffering at this moment.

Prouhèze's later marriage to Camille represents a similar sexual punishment – having desired a man she could not have, she is now forced to submit to a man she abhors.

Finally, the penitential ordeal through which she is led by her Guardian Angel, described in the text primarily in religious terms, has this same emotional-level significance. In III viii, the Angel allows Prouhèze to experience briefly the effects of the spiritual force that will purify her and then lead her to an innocent form of existence; as this force begins its work, Prouhèze describes her sensations in a long, illogical image-sequence: (III viii 199; 281)

> Elle [l'eau] *me baigne* et je n'y puis *goûter!* c'est *un rayon qui me perce*, c'est *un glaive qui me divise*, c'est *le fer rouge effroyablement*

appliqué sur le nerf même de la vie, c'est *l'effervescence de la source qui*
s'empare de tous mes éléments pour les dissoudre et les recomposer, c'est
le néant à chaque moment où je sombre et Dieu *sur ma bouche qui me*
ressuscite, et supérieure à toutes les délices, ah! c'est *la traction*
impitoyable de la soif, l'abomination de cette soif affreuse qui m'ouvre et
me crucifie![26]

As noted in the previous discussion of this verset, the description of the *source,* the mention of God's activity directly on
Prouhèze's mouth, and the relation of simultaneous sensations of
pleasure and pain all underscore the erotic nature of this purifying experience. At the same time, the punishing quality of the
experience is emphasized by the references to weapons and
actions used in attack – *un glaive, le fer rouge, me perce, me divise,*
sombre, m'ouvre et me crucifie – and by several modifying terms
– *effroyablement, impitoyable, l'abomination, affreuses.* Three of
these vehicles suggest specifically an opening action – *me perce,*
me divise, m'ouvre; in context, these images imply that Prouhèze
surrenders herself to God by submitting in a passive, charac-
teristically feminine way to his harsh assault.[27] The joy she feels
simultaneously with great pain now also seems to reflect her
pleasure at being relieved at last of her burden of guilt and being
allowed to return as a result to the good graces of this omnipotent
parent.

The Angel then tempers Prouhèze's joy somewhat by explaining that before she can offer herself unreservedly to God Rodrigue must agree to her self-sacrifice: (III viii 241–2; 824)

L'ANGE GARDIEN: Cette mort qui fera de toi une étoile, consens-tu à la
recevoir *de sa main?*
DONA PROUHÈZE: Ah! je remercie Dieu! Viens, cher Rodrigue! je suis
prête! sur cette chose qui est à toi *lève ta main meurtrière! sacrifie* cette
chose qui est à toi! Mourir, mourir par toi m'est doux!

From a religious point of view, Prouhèze now needs Rodrigue's
help because she has pledged him her soul and she can therefore
give herself completely to God only after he has released her from
her promise. On the emotional level, because she has sinned
through Rodrigue, her punishment will correspond more closely
to her original wrongdoing, and will thus be more effective, if
it is suffered at least in part at his hands.

When the Angel finally declares, 'Maintenant je n'ai plus rien à te dire sinon au revoir à Dieu' (243; 824), the reader feels certain that Prouhèze will reach her goal, and the anxiety evoked by earlier descriptions of her mental and physical distress is thus relieved.[28] The stage directions at the end of the scene are similarly reassuring, for they conclude: (p. 826)

> Tout l'écran est rempli par le Ciel fourmillant au travers duquel se dessine l'image gigantesque de l'*Immaculée Conception*.

The expression *Immaculée Conception* in itself evokes a situation that is sexually pure.[29] At the same time, this periphrastic reference to Mary recalls Prouhèze's earlier plea to the *vierge mère* for help in suppressing her desires for forbidden satisfaction. Coming as a conclusion to the scene, the statement as a whole implies that by following the course of action just outlined by the Angel – by surrendering herself completely to an all-powerful father and accepting the punishment he will administer – Prouhèze will be satisfying the demands of her mother, also, and will return to her protection, as she earlier sought to do.

Prouhèze's ultimate fate, however, is placed in doubt one more time. As she and Camille await the final Arab attack on Mogador, Prouhèze confesses that she has never completely relinquished her forbidden desires for Rodrigue. Although she thus remains in a state of sin, Camille now reveals through fisherman-code imagery – previously used by the Angel to describe his own relationship with Prouhèze and Rodrigue – that he continues the work of the heavenly Guardian in leading her to redemption: (III x 180–4; 841)

> DON CAMILLE: Ainsi peu à peu, *comme un habile pêcheur,*
> *Je vous ai amenée où je voulais.*
> DONA PROUHÈZE: Pourquoi parlez-vous de *pêcheur?*
> *Un pêcheur ... un pêcheur d'hommes ... il me semble qu'on m'en*
> a montré *un* déjà.[30]

Camille then compels her to admit to her own guilt: (III x 186–96; 842)

> DON CAMILLE: ... Il y a les affections que Dieu a permises et qui sont une part de Sa Volonté.
> Mais Rodrigue dans votre cœur n'est aucunement effet de Sa Volonté mais de la vôtre. *Cette passion* en vous.

DONA PROUHÈZE: *La passion* est unie *à la croix.*
DON CAMILLE: *Quelle croix?*
DONA PROUHÈZE: Rodrigue est pour toujours *cette croix à laquelle je suis attachée.*

...

 Tout ce qui en moi est capable de souffrir la croix, ne le lui ai-je pas abandonné?
DON CAMILLE: Mais *la croix ne sera satisfaite* que quand elle aura tout ce qui en vous n'est pas la volonté de Dieu détruit.
DONA PROUHÈZE: O parole effrayante!

When Camille first explains here how she is still guilty, Prouhèze attempts to justify her feelings for Rodrigue by suggesting that the unhappiness and frustration she experiences as a result of their love are the 'Cross' through which she expiates past sins. Camille, however, then reveals the fallacy in this argument by repeating her Cross-code image but changing the tenor – although Rodrigue is the instrument through which Prouhèze is first chastised, her punishment will be complete only when she has agreed to atone for the sins involved even in this painful relationship.[31]

Confronted, by this explanation, Prouhèze must reluctantly agree to make the final sacrifice; when Camille asks, in the passage cited above, 'Mais d'où viendrait autrement cette lumière sur votre visage?' (206; 843) the reader is assured that she, too, will attain the satisfaction she has sought so long.

Prouhèze makes her final appearance in the *Soulier de satin* in III xiv, when she meets with Rodrigue for the last time, on his ship off the coast of Mogador. During this scene, in passages cited in Chapter 7, she urges Rodrigue to adopt a submissive, 'open' attitude towards the Heavenly Father; she also describes her own surrender to God: (II xiii 135, 145; 855–6)

 ... Comment faire pour vouloir quand *j'ai remis à un autre* ma volonté? Comment faire pour *remuer un seul doigt* quand je suis *prise et tenue?* Avec quoi parler quand *l'amour est maître de mon âme et de ma langue?*

...

 Ce que veut Celui qui me possède c'est cela seulement que je veux, ce que veut Celui-là en qui je suis *anéantie* c'est en cela que tu as à faire de *me retrouver!*

Prouhèze thus submerges her own identity in that of her omnipotent father; as part of this union with God, she becomes linked with Rodrigue, too, in an innocent way: (III xiv 183–5; 858)

> La force par laquelle je t'aime n'est pas différente de celle par laquelle tu existes.
> Je suis unie pour toujours à cette chose qui te donne la vie éternelle!
> *Le sang n'est pas plus uni à la chair* que Dieu ne me fait sentir chaque battement de ce cœur dans ta poitrine ...[32]

Drawn by 'cette force qui nous appelle hors de nous-mêmes' (173; 844) into a pleasurable bond with her omnipotent parents, the man she loves, and the infinite universe surrounding them all ('Tu en aurais bientôt fini avec moi si je n'étais pas unie maintenant avec ce qui n'est pas limité!' 149; 856), Prouhèze thus attains on both the religious and the emotional levels of the text the ideal state she has desired so long.

The stories of two other young women who appear in the *Soulier de satin* – Musique in Days 1, 2, and 3; Sept-Épées in Days 3 and 4 – and that of the Viceroy in Day 2 help to relieve the tension evoked in the reader by the adventures of Prouhèze and most of the male characters; for, like the Jesuit, these three are able to reach paradise without passing through the difficult stages of conflict, frustration, guilt, and punishment.

Musique is characterized on the narrative level by a childlike trust in others and a joyous attitude towards life in general; as explained in Chapter 5, from a religious point of view these qualities emphasize her innocence and her strong faith in God. Similarly, in many mythologies the completely pure individual appears as a child-god or child-hero.[33] On the emotional level, her youthful happiness and ingenuous confidence indicate that she still enjoys the comforting feeling of being staunchly protected by her parents and is as yet untroubled by guilty sexual desires.

Musique's spiritual and emotional purity are also evidenced by her dove-shaped birthmark. Because the dove functions both in the Bible and in Catholic ritual as a symbol of the Holy Ghost or God's Grace, Musique's mark suggests on the religious level that she is in close contact with these divine powers.[34] In literature and mythology, the dove is frequently associated with an undefiled sexual relationship; this connection is reinforced in Musique's case by suggestions that the mark is located in an erotically significant place – on or near her breast.[35] The presence of this birthmark thus implies on the emotional level that any erotic feelings Musique experiences in the future will also be free of shame or guilt.

At times, Musique does pursue lines of thought and action that seem to belie her guileless appearance – she runs away from her mother and the husband chosen by Pélage, and, like other adult women, seeks to marry a man she loves. Her innocence is never really threatened, however, not only because she possesses the special gifts symbolized by her birthmark, but also because her devotion to God never falters – even when she leaves home to go in search of the ruler of Naples, she acts on the belief that their union has been preordained by the Supreme Father.

Before Musique meets her future husband, the Viceroy appears with his band of followers (II v). He, too, displays a strong faith both in his fellowmen and in God. On the emotional level, the Viceroy is now free of painful conflict because he is content with the affective satisfactions he gains through his friendship with his noble companions. As he himself explains: 'Comment voulez-vous que je prenne femme, ayant autour de moi de tels amis?' (II v 71; 750).

The love that draws Musique and the Viceroy together is clearly such that it does not destroy their spiritual and emotional innocence, but rather adds new areas of fulfilment to their lives. When Musique, for example, first describes her feelings for the Viceroy to Prouhèze, she compares the effect she wishes to have on him to several types of physical sensation – taste ('un sel étincelant et délectable,' 'l'eau pour la bouche altérée'), hearing ('ce sens en nous de l'ouïe,' 'mon âme à ces cordes ineffables,' 'le murmure de cette pieuse fontaine,' 'le paisible tumulte du grand port'), scent ('la rose qu'on respire tous les jours tant que dure l'été'), and sight ('le soleil') (I x 45–52; 709). On the religious level, three of these vehicles – un sel, l'eau, and la rose – evoke in context the idea of purity; the last two images also bring to mind the union of all beings on the spiritual plane.[36] Musique's words thus imply that she wishes to introduce the Viceroy to this blissful, sin-free spiritual communion. On the emotional level, her description of their relationship in terms of various sense impressions stresses the innocence of their future physical union, because it indicates that the erotic satisfaction the Viceroy will experience through her will be like the polymorphous sensual gratification enjoyed most intensely by the child during his pre-genital, pre-oedipal – and thus most guilt-free – years.[37]

When Musique and the Viceroy finally meet, these aspects of their relationship are underscored by the location of their encounter in a forest clearing – the kind of isolated, enclosed area that often serves in mythology and literature as a place where the human and divine worlds are joined,[38] and which evokes on the emotional level the comforting protection that mothers provide for their still-innocent children.[39]

At this first meeting, the lovers speak in music-code terms of their feelings for each other, and describe in particular the way Musique puts the Viceroy in touch with an unseen force that unites all elements of the world around them. Musique, for example, declares: (ii x 77; 764)

Mon chant est celui que je fais naître.

And the Viceroy responds: (ii x 78–82; 764)

Ce n'est pas un chant, c'est une tempête qui prend avec elle et le ciel et les eaux et les bois et toute la terre!

...

La divine musique est en moi.

On the religious level, because Musique indicated earlier that she would put her beloved in contact with heavenly unifying forces, and because the Viceroy now speaks of this *musique* as being *divine*, the reader understands that the source of this power is God, and that, having freely and trustingly given himself over to the woman he loves, the Viceroy is being introduced by her to the spiritual realm of the redeemed. From an emotional point of view, the feeling of union with his surroundings that the Viceroy now experiences seems to correspond to the infant's gratifying sense of merger with his environment; the music-code imagery used here reinforces this impression in two ways – first, because of its rhythmic quality, all music is associated to some degree with erotic satisfaction; and second, the kind of music described by the Viceroy involves a harmonizing and blending of sounds which is itself often associated with this sense of fusion.[40] Like Rodrigue and Camille, the Viceroy is thus led by the woman he loves to an innocent yet gratifying union with the

Supreme Father and the world over which he rules; but, unlike these men, his initial attraction to his beloved involves no wrongful desires and he is therefore able to avoid the painful experiences of guilt and expiation.[41]

Musique herself appears once more in the *Soulier de satin*, at the beginning of Day 3. Turning to God in prayer, she describes the joyful unity of the heavenly realm in the long music- and water-code development examined from a religious point of view in Chapter 5.[42] On the emotional level, both the water- and the music-code terms used here indicate that Musique speaks specifically of the longed-for sense of merger with the universe, while the water-code terms stress the purity of this feeling.[43]

The stories of Musique and the Viceroy thus actualize only the final stage of the invariant structure of the play. The references Musique makes to this pleasurable state each time she appears help to relieve the anxiety evoked in the reader by other passages of the text; at the same time, the establishment of a mutually gratifying relationship between herself and the Viceroy assures the reader that human love need not always lead to frustration and chagrin.

In the second half of the *Soulier de satin*, Sept-Épées takes over Musique's role on the religious and emotional levels of the text – her adventures, like Musique's, actualize only the final stage of the invariant structure, and her presence in the work is similarly reassuring to the reader.[44]

Sept-Épées's unusual religious qualities are first suggested by Camille in III x, when he admits that Prouhèze's child resembles the absent Rodrigue, and that Rodrigue is in fact her true father. Since her conception was in this sense a purely spiritual event, Sept-Épées has escaped the taint of Original Sin.[45]

Furthermore, because Prouhèze previously indicated that she and Rodrigue would be united spiritually only after they had voluntarily accepted punishment for past wrongs, Camille's statement implies that Sept-Épées, as the product of a spiritual meeting between these lovers, is also an outgrowth of their earlier suffering. The reader concludes that Sept-Épées represents on both the religious and the emotional levels an actualization of the goals her parents hoped to attain themselves through their self-sacrificing acts.

Sept-Épées's name underscores this aspect of her role in the play because it recalls the Catholic tradition that Mary's heart was pierced by seven 'swords,' the Seven Dolours, and thus emphasizes her connection with the ultimate sacrifice that was the cause of Mary's greatest suffering and that Prouhèze and Rodrigue now imitate in atoning for their sins.[46]

When Sept-Épées herself appears, her special religious role is stressed by her frequent expressions of complete devotion to the Supreme Father, of readiness to give her life in his service, and of her feeling that she is in contact at all times with the heavenly realm; as in Musique's case, her childlike speech and outlook underscore both her continuing innocence and her unquestioning religious faith.[47]

On the emotional level, all of these characteristics suggest that Sept-Épées, like Musique, is free of sexual guilt and still enjoys the childlike feeling of being firmly protected by omnipotent parents. Again, these traits recall the role of the child-god or child-hero in mythologies and folk-tales; Sept-Épées, however, resembles these heroes even more closely than Musique, both because of her unusual birth and because she represents a synthesis of masculine and feminine identities and thus embodies within herself the completeness for which all adults long.[48] This androgyny is indicated by several of Sept-Épées's actions – her eagerness to go to war, for example, and her wearing of men's clothing – and is also attested to by la Bouchère's slip of the tongue when she declares: (IV iii 42; 882)

> Si vous étiez un homme, et si vous n'étiez pas le fils, la fille, veux-je dire, de Don Rodrigue,
> De quel cœur n'iriez-vous pas aussitôt rejoindre les enseignes de Don Juan.

Later, Sept-Épées explains that although she and Don Juan are in love, the position he has offered her on his ship is a masculine one ('je serais son page et son aide de camp,' IV iii 58; 883), and their relationship while they are together will be that of very close friends or siblings: (IV iii 64; 883)

> Ah! je serais *un frère* pour lui et *nous dormirions ensemble côte à côte* et je serais toujours à côté de lui pour le défendre, ah! je reconnaîtrais tout de suite ses ennemis!

Sept-Épées's self-completeness parallels her feeling of merger with all other beings and forces. As she swims towards Don

Juan's fleet, in her final appearance in the play, she describes her sense of fusion with the surrounding universe: (IV x 66–8; 938)

> L'eau porte tout. C'est délicieux, l'oreille au ras de l'eau, de per-cevoir toutes *ces musiques confuses*, (Pensé:) les danseurs *autour de la guitare*,
>> *La vie, les chants, les paroles d'amour, l'innombrable craquement de toutes ces paroles imperceptibles*!
> Et tout cela n'est plus dehors, on est dedans, il y a quelque chose qui vous réunit bienheureusement à tout, *une goutte d'eau associée à la mer! La communion des Saints*!

Sept-Épées's experiencing of this feeling of merger in relation to water stresses both the innocence of her pleasurable sensations and their relation to the infant's sense of union with his sur-roundings; the erotic quality of this pleasure is underscored by the image vehicles she uses to describe what she 'perceives' in the water – *musiques, danseurs autour de la guitare, les chants, les paroles d'amour.*[49]

This passage immediately precedes the final scene of the play, in which Rodrigue prepares to die. Because Sept-Épées repre-sents an outgrowth of Rodrigue's painful sacrifice, the reader understands that, despite the humble circumstances in which he ends his earthly life, he, too, will attain after death the happiness and satisfaction that his spiritual daughter now enjoys.

The narrative- and religious-level stories of all the major charac-ters of the *Soulier de satin* – Rodrigue, Prouhèze, the Jesuit, Pélage, Balthazar, Camille, Musique, the Viceroy, and Sept-Épées – are thus variations of all or of parts of the same emotional-level course of action, and a single affective message is conveyed to the reader repeatedly as the play continues – the pursuit of forbidden desires inevitably leads to agonizing frus-tration and guilt; happiness and satisfaction are to be found only through total surrender to the dictates of omnipotent parents, under whose protection a gratifying sense of fulfilment may eventually be attained.

As explained in Chapter 7, a balance between tension and relaxa-tion must be maintained in the reader's mind as a fictional work progresses. In general, tension is created by the expression in the text of anxiety-producing emotional concepts. Other elements of the work act as 'defences' in relation to these concepts – like psychological defence mechanisms, they help the reader to avoid experiencing too strongly the painful or distressing feelings involved.[50]

The different levels of meaning of which the reader is conscious as he peruses the text serve as defences in themselves; the presence of these levels generally helps to control the reader's anxiety in two ways – first, by diverting some of his attention away from the emotional meaning of the text and towards less deeply disturbing thoughts; and second, by satisfying his demands that the work as a whole have 'significance' and 'value,' thus enabling him to rationalize to his satisfaction his overall affective response to the text.[51]

The specific sequence in which the individual parts of the invariant structure are expressed may also function defensively – as is the case, for example, when reassuring elements of the structure are evoked just before or just after distressing passages. Thus, Musique's music- and water-code description of heaven (III i) immediately follows the Moon's citing of the laments of Prouhèze and Rodrigue after their first separation at Mogador (II xiv), and enables the reader easily to shift his attention from disturbing ideas to more comforting thoughts.

These two elements – the levels of meaning of which the reader is aware and the order in which the individual parts of the structure are expressed – are integral parts of all fictional works. Two additional elements that function defensively in the *Soulier de satin* – humour and variations in the reader's frame of reference – may or may not be found in other texts.

The importance of 'comic relief' in the *Soulier de satin* is underscored by the reaction of several critics to the shortened stage version of the play; Pierre Ganne, for example, writes:

> L'humour imprègne la substance même du verbe poétique. Si par exemple, dans la louable intention de rendre supportable au public l'énorme explosion du *Soulier de satin* on l'allège des scènes comiques ou burlesques, le résultat engendre un malaise profond. Non seulement la tension tragique augmente au dépens d'une légitime détente, le sérieux se condense au prix de l'attention du spectateur, mais le centre de gravité se déplace et la vérité du drame en pâtit, à la limite elle disparaîtrait.[52]

In the complete text of the play, humorous passages are most often closely related to distressing ones, and help both to amuse the reader and to distract his attention from the disturbing scenes.[53] When the fishermen appear at the beginning of IV i, for example, their ludicrous names have a comic effect in themselves and their description of their search for treasure at the bottom of the sea includes many humorous plays on words – Maltropillo's reference, for example, to 'Lévy le bijoutier, qu'on a pendu le mois dernier parce qu'il faisait de la monnaie fausse qu'était vraie' (18; 862); later in the scene, the fishermen reveal to the reader Rodrigue's military failure in the Far East, his permanent physical disability, and his social disgrace.

Because an ironic statement evokes two conflicting thoughts in the reader's mind, irony helps to relieve the reader's tension specifically by enabling him to respond to a disquieting situation and then immediately to disassociate himself from it, at least momentarily.

In I viii, Rodrigue tells Isidore of his love for Prouhèze; after describing his feelings in rather poetic terms, he finally exclaims: (I vii 145; 698)

Isidore, ah! si tu savais comme je l'aime et comme je la désire!

to which Isidore responds: (I vii 146; 698)

Maintenant je vous comprends et *vous ne parlez plus chinois.*

The phrase *vous ne parlez plus chinois* is itself a renewal, by grammatical change, of the cliché *c'est du chinois pour moi.* In addition, because Isidore is repeatedly referred to in the speaker designations of this scene as *le Chinois,* not only the usual figurative meaning, but also the literal, and in context, paradoxical significance of his words comes forward in the reader's mind; the cliché is thus doubly renewed, and has an ironic effect. As noted in Chapter 7, on the emotional level of the text Rodrigue's description of his sinful desires – emphasized by the figurative meaning of this cliché – evokes corresponding erotic feelings in the reader and also elicits an unsettling sense of guilt. Because Isidore makes fun of his master's feelings, however, through the literal meaning of his image here the reader is able to adopt for a moment a similar derisive attitude towards Rodrigue's situation; by thus disassociating himself from Rodrigue's desires, he can temporarily allay his own disturbing feelings of guilt.[54]

In Chapter 6, the author's interventions in the *Soulier de satin* were shown to help guide the reader's response to the different levels of the work. It can now be added that in relation to the emotional level, this 'guiding' is specifically of a defensive nature.

The predominance of humour in the author's interventions was discussed above; when this humour is directed at specific characters or situations, it functions defensively, as do the comic and ironic passages just cited. Thus, in iv ix, the Courtiers mock Rodrigue by playing degrading tricks on him; on the emotional level, these pranks serve as part of his punishment for past erotic wrongs. In the stage directions for this scene, the author describes these Courtiers in comic terms; as the sea beneath them swells and rolls, for example, Claudel declares (p. 923) that they

> font de leur mieux; on voit bien qu'ils font tout leur possible pour être là, et ... à l'aide de force hochements de tête, mains jointes, bras croisés, les yeux levés au ciel ou fichés en terre et gestes attestateurs, expriment (en mesure sur un petit air à la fois guilleret et funèbre) leur profonde consternation.

This humorous depiction of the Courtiers reduces the anxiety that Rodrigue's punishment evokes in the reader by diverting his attention to relatively insignificant details, by evoking pleasurable sensations through the comic effects themselves, and, most important, by suggesting that any penalty to be administered by such ridiculous men could not really be too dangerous.

Claudel's humorous interventions in the text of the *Soulier de satin* were also shown in Chapter 6 to have the cumulative effect of emphasizing for the reader the importance of the religious level of meaning relative to the story line. Because the religious level actualizes the basic emotional message in philosophical and theological terms, it conveys this message to the reader in a more sublimated form than does the story line. By directing the reader's attention to this abstract level of meaning, Claudel's remarks thus tend to diminish his overall emotional involvement with the play.[55]

Unexpected variations in the frame of reference from which the reader views the work – a change from 'realistic' characters to 'unrealistic' ones, such as the Double Shadow and the Moon, for example – are still another type of defence used in the *Soulier de satin*. These shifts in frame help to attenuate the reader's affective response to the text in two ways. First, they tend to disrupt his emotional identification with the major characters of the play. Second, most such changes call the reader's attention to the fictional nature of the story line, and thus reassure him that any emotional responses that are evoked in his mind by the narrative will have no consequences in the real world in which he lives; he is then able to experience the feelings elicited by the text with less accompanying anxiety than might otherwise be the case.[56]

In the cases of the Double Shadow and the Moon, for example, the events described by these characters – the secret, forbidden meeting of Prouhèze and Rodrigue and the penalties both must undergo for their wrongful desires – are particularly threatening. The change to an 'unrealistic' frame in these scenes helps to lessen the reader's anxiety by diverting some of his attention to the unusual speakers involved and by underscoring the imaginary nature of the situations being depicted.[57]

The author's interventions in the *Soulier de satin*, both direct and indirect, cause similar changes in the reader's frame of reference and also disrupt his involvement with the narrative level as a result. Because these passages call the reader's attention specifically to the author's role as creator of the text, they are especially effective in emphasizing its fictional nature.[58]

Less marked changes in the reader's frame of reference are caused by the frequent shifts in the narrative-level content of successive scenes from the story of one group of characters to that of another, and by the introduction of many minor characters, some with no direct connection with the basic story line. These shifts both hinder the reader's emotional identification with the major characters, and in the case of minor characters draw his attention away from important figures towards less significant people and events.

The invariant structure of the *Soulier de satin* was summarized in Chapter 7 as follows:

STAGE 1 Conflict between erotic desires and their prohibition
STAGE 2 Frustration and guilt
STAGE 3 Punishment involving emasculation
STAGE 4 Achievement of innocent yet satisfying union with universe as a whole, including omnipotent father figure; bond with beloved woman

The repetition of this structure diachronically and synchronously as the text progresses, discussed and illustrated in the preceding part of this chapter, can also be shown schematically, as in Chart 2 found on the inside back cover.

The purpose of this chart is to show in concise, visual form how the invariant structure of the *Soulier de satin* is actualized through the narrative and religious levels of the text, and how the two types of defences used in the play – humour and variations in the reader's frame of reference – are related to the expression of this structure.

Each stage of the emotional-level message that constitutes the invariant structure is represented by a different pattern, as shown in the key in the upper right-hand corner of the chart. Pages, scenes, and days are marked off along the horizontal axis.

Section 1, the primary horizontal division of the chart, shows the relative intensity with which the different stages of the invariant structure are expressed through the stories of individual characters. Three horizontal rows are assigned to each of the major characters and to the minor characters and countries as a group.[59] As indicated on the rows assigned to the Viceroy, the top row represents those narrative-level passages that express a love story (corresponding to Narrative Level 1 in Chart 1). The middle row represents other narrative-level passages, in most cases dealing with the exploration and conquest of countries (Narrative Level 2 in Chart 1). The bottom row represents the religious level. Each page of the text was considered individually, and the relative intensity was calculated and is shown on a vertical scale of 0 to 5 units of intensity.[60]

When more than one stage of the invariant structure is expressed on a single page, the stages are uniformly shown from top to bottom, from Stage 1 to Stage 4; the construction in Sections 4 and 5 is the same.

The chart represents the structure of the play as perceived through an overall apprehension of the text, involving rereading and remembering. Thus, some of the stages of the invariant structure noted for a specific page may not be expressed directly on this page, but be evoked rather by flashback or recall.

Two types of defences used extensively in the *Soulier de satin* are represented in Section 2 of the chart, humour on the top two rows and, on the bottom row, variations in the frame of reference from which the reader views the work. Comedy (i.e., humour other than irony) and irony are shown separately here, because irony has a different defensive effect on the reader's response to the text than do other types of humour, as explained above. The relative effectiveness of each defence on each page is indicated here on the same vertical scale of 0 to 5 units used in showing the relative intensity of the invariant structure. This section is placed in a central position on the chart so that the defences can most easily be compared with the expression of the structure through the stories of individual characters (Section 1), and with the totals for all characters (Sections 4 and 5).

The number of images per page is charted in Section 3; the scale used here was adjusted for ease of comparison with the other five sections of the chart.[61]

In Section 4 of the chart, the relative intensities with which the four stages are expressed on each page through the stories of the different characters are totalled. These totals are broken down by stages in Section 5 in order to show more clearly the relative intensity with which each stage is expressed and the movement from one stage to another as the play progresses.

The chart clearly illustrates the role of the invariant structure in creating unity within this highly complex, and at first reading often confusing, work – for although the narrative-level content of successive scenes varies greatly, the chart shows that one or more elements of the invariant structure are expressed in each scene; and as explained at the beginning of this chapter, this repetition of the same concepts both simultaneously and sequentially as the work continues gives the play the internal coherence that makes it a single, complete poem.[62] At the same time, the repetition of the invariant structure many times within the work helps to emphasize this emotional-level message for the reader.

In this connection, several sections of the chart point out that although the individual stages of the structure are expressed in varying order and with different frequency as the work progresses, the general movement of the play is from conflict to resolution. Thus, if the direction of movement were marked on Section 5, it would repeatedly run from Stage 1 through Stage 4, from upper left to lower right on the chart. As seen in Sections 4 and 5, the overall movement of the play as a whole follows this same conflict-to-resolution sequence – the first element of the invariant structure is expressed most intensely in the first Day; the second element, in the second Day, and the third and fourth elements predominate from the end of Day 2 to the end of Day 4. These general movements reflect, of course, the advance of individual characters through the four stages of the structure, as diagrammed in Section 1; as seen there, Rodrigue's progress parallels the overall development of the play most closely, for he is the only character whose story is being told from the first scene of the work to the last.[63]

A comparison of the total of all stages (Section 4) with the number of images per page (Section 3) reveals a close correlation between the intensity with which the underlying structure is expressed in a particular passage and the number of images used in this passage. This correlation reflects two factors discussed above – first, images are especially well suited to the expression of an emotional message and therefore play an important role in conveying this underlying structure to the reader in all literary works; and second, as explained in Chapters 1 and 2, images in themselves tend to heighten the effectiveness of the passages in which they are used, and the presence of many images in a relatively brief passage therefore in itself increases the intensity with which ideas seem to be expressed there. Although other stylistic devices are not charted here, they would also tend to heighten this impression of intensity, as seen in Chapter 3. The correlation of Sections 3 and 4 of the chart thus also reflects the general inter-relationship of style and structure in the text and the effect of this interrelationship on the reader's response – that is, the fact that clusters of stylistic devices and the expression of the invariant structure tend to coincide in the text; the devices draw the reader's attention to the words through which the structure is conveyed, and thus help to emphasize this basic message for him.

The specific ways in which the anxiety-producing stages of the structure are actualized in the text are indicated in the character-breakdown section of the chart (Section 1). The frustrating endings reached by Balthazar and Pélage, for example, are shown at the end of Day 1 and at the beginning of Day 2. Tension is seen to increase again late in Day 2 and in Day 3, when the painful experiences of Prouhèze, Rodrigue, and Camille converge – that is, when the first three stages of the structure are actualized through the stories of at least two of these major characters in each of several scenes. The reader's anxiety becomes particularly great in the final scenes of these two days; the break between days that in each case immediately follows in the text then allows the reader to relax for a moment before the work continues.

Both the summary and the character-breakdown sections of the chart (Sections 1 and 4) show how the resolution stage of the invariant structure is actualized in alternation with the anxiety-producing stages; as explained above, the expression of this tension-relieving stage of the structure from time to time through the work helps to keep the reader's distress within acceptable limits.

The chart also shows in detail how three additional defensive factors operate – the introduction of minor characters and shifts in the narrative-level content of successive scenes, discussed above, and the breaks between scenes and days. These breaks are a direct outgrowth of the dramatic structure of the work, and serve to interrupt the reader's emotional identification with the characters.[64] In addition, a comparison of Section 2 and the 'minor characters' rows of Section 1 shows that in Days 1 and 4 the appearance of minor characters is frequently accompanied by irony and comedy.[65] In most cases, this humour is directed at the frustrating conflicts experienced by the new characters, and the dilemmas of the major figures are then also ridiculed by implication. The stories of these minor characters are thus especially effective as defences.[66]

As shown in Section 1, the number of major characters appearing in each day declines gradually from Day 1 to Day 4; in Day 4, the reader is likely to identify emotionally only with Rodrigue and Sept-Épées.

Throughout Day 4, humour, shifts in the frame of reference, the presence of minor characters, and descriptions of the heavenly realm help to relieve the tension that Rodrigue's situation continues to evoke in the reader's mind; the reader's knowledge that Prouhèze and Camille have already attained salvation further reassures him as he progresses through this day.[67] At the same time, however, the many digressions from the main story line found here – including not only the defensive stories of the minor characters but also such threatening incidents as Rodrigue's involvement with the Actress – keep the reader in a state of suspense by delaying the final resolution of Rodrigue's painful conflict.[68]

Furthermore, as seen in the chart, the third stage of the structure is actualized with relatively great intensity in the last three scenes of Day 4; as in most fictional works, the reader's tension is thus heightened markedly just prior to the final, relaxing passages of the text.

As the play draws to a close, the reader is again assured that all individuals can reach a gratifying situation similar to the one to which Rodrigue now accedes. When a trumpet blast signals Sept-Épées's safe arrival at Don Juan's ship, Frère Léon exultantly exclaims: (IV xi 149; 948)

> *Délivrance* aux âmes *captives*!

Because Frère Léon has just explained that Rodrigue is about to enter heaven, the reference to a trumpet blast recalls the role of this sound in the Bible as a signal of entry into a new, purified form of existence.[69] Léon's words then emphasize for the reader one final time that the agonizing emotional conflict evoked in his mind by the text can indeed be happily resolved, because all who submit to the dictates of parents, society, and religion will eventually be freed of the dilemmas that paralyze and frustrate them, and will move within reach of the total fulfilment for which they search.[70]

The satisfaction now experienced by the reader is heightened by his recollection of the first scene of the play – for in this first scene the Jesuit prayed that Rodrigue be allowed to reach the gratifying state that he himself was then entering, and this appeal has finally been favourably answered.[71] The end of the play thus fulfils the promise of the beginning, and the work in this sense closes upon itself.

Notes

INTRODUCTION

1 See Michael Riffaterre, 'The Stylistic Function,' *Proceedings of the Ninth International Congress of Linguists,* ed. Horace G. Lunt (The Hague, Mouton 1964), esp. 316–7; 'Criteria for Style Analysis,' *Word,* xv (1959), 154–74; and 'Describing Poetic Structures: Two Approaches to Baudelaire's "Les Chats," ' *Structuralism,* ed. Jacques Ehrmann, *YFS,* Nos 36–7 (October 1966), 200–42.
   In defining the stylistic device or sd, Riffaterre writes: 'Style is not a string of sds but of binary oppositions whose poles (context/sd) cannot be separated ... If [a group of features] has a stylistic effect, its stimulus consists of less predictable elements encoded in one or more constituents. The microcontext consists of the other constituents which remain unmarked; contrast is created in opposition to these constituents (the reader perceives the degree of unpredictability in relation to them). The group as a whole (context + contrast) forms the sd' ('Stylistic Context,' *Word,* xvi, 1960, 207–9).
2 See Ehrmann, 'Introduction,' *Structuralism,* 7, and Michael Riffaterre, 'La Poétisation du mot chez Victor Hugo,' *Cahiers de l'Association Internationale des Études Françaises,* No. 19 (March 1967), 182.
3 Early attempts to interpret the reader's response in the light of Freudian psychology include Ernest Kris's *Psychoanalytic Explorations in Art* (New York, International Universities Press 1952) and Simon O. Lesser's *Fiction and the Unconscious* (New York, Random House, Vintage Books 1962). More recently, Norman Holland, in *The Dynamics of Literary Response* (New York, Oxford University Press 1968) combines many of the ideas elucidated in these works with a close analysis of particular literary texts and develops a more clearly delineated model of the reader's response.
4 Structuralist and psychoanalytic methods of analysis have been brought together in several studies published during the past fifteen years; these include Roland Barthes's *Sur Racine* (Paris, Seuil 1963) and Charles Mauron's *Des Métaphores obsédantes au mythe personnel* (Paris, José Corti 1963). These studies, however, focus on the literary text and its relation to the author's personality and experiences.
   The 'reader' whose responses serve as point of departure for the three types of studies described above is in fact a combination of several 'informants'; in addition to the critic himself, these may include other cultivated readers, translations of the work, and variant editions of the text. Stripped of all value judgments, the responses of these 'informants' are used as signals of the presence in the text of data of interest to the critic (see Riffaterre, 'Criteria,' 161–6 and 'Describing Poetic Structures,' 214–6). In this study of the *Soulier de satin,* the 'informants' include the present writer and all available criticism of the play.
   The responses of the spectator at a possible performance of the work are not considered in this study. Note is taken, however, of those aspects of the

dramatic structure of the text that do affect the reader's response to the printed work.

5 Jacques Madaule has written: 'Un lecteur qui ne connaîtrait de Claudel que le *Soulier de satin* n'ignorerait rien d'essentiel' (*Le Drame de Paul Claudel*, Paris, Desclée de Brouwer 1936, 208).

Critical opinion of the *Soulier de satin* is reviewed by Pierre Brunel in '*Le Soulier de satin' devant la critique*, Situation, No. 6 (Paris, M.J. Minard, Lettres Modernes 1964). Brunel cites Gabriel Marceau as an example of a critic whose remarks on the play reflect his uncertainty about both the meaning and the literary merit of this text. Marceau, for example, described the *Soulier de satin* in 1930 as 'L'audacieuse prière du plus grand poète chrétien français,' but wrote in a review of the work in 1958 that he was left 'déconcerté' and 'désorienté' by the mixture of 'grandeur authentique' and 'fausse grandeur' in the play (101–11).

6 These include Alexandre Maurocordato, *L'Ode de Paul Claudel* (Geneva, Droz 1955); H.J.W. Van Hoorn, *Poésie et mystique: Paul Claudel, poète chrétien* (Geneva, Droz 1957); Klara Maurer, *Die biblische Symbolik im Werke Paul Claudels* (Lucerne, E. Brunner-Schmid 1941); Brigitta Coenen-Mennemeier, *Der aggressive Claudel: Eine Studie zu Periphrasen und Metaphern im Werke Paul Claudels*, Forschungen zur romanischen Philologie, II (Münster, Aschendorff 1957); and Eugène Roberto, *Visions de Claudel* (Marseille, Leconte 1958).

These studies reflect Claudel's own belief that imagery serves the poet as a metaphysical tool, an instrument through which he can describe, and thus in effect re-create, the union of all elements within the physical and spiritual worlds. In 'Introduction à un poème sur Dante,' for example, he writes: 'Par *l'image*, le poète est comme un homme qui est monté en un lieu plus élevé et qui voit autour de lui un horizon plus vaste où s'établissent entre les choses des rapports nouveaux, rapports qui ne sont pas déterminés par la logique ou la loi de causalité, mais par une association harmonique ou complémentaire en vue d'un *sens*' (*Accompagnements*, in *Œuvres en prose*, eds Jacques Petit and Charles Galpérine, Bibliothèque de la Pléiade, Paris, Gallimard 1965, 422. Claudel's ideas on the union of the physical and the spiritual realms and the role of imagery in expressing these concepts in the *Soulier de satin* are discussed at greater length in Chapter 5 below.)

CHAPTER 1

1 This use of the terms 'tenor' and 'vehicle' is based on their definition by I.A. Richards in *The Philosophy of Rhetoric* (New York, Oxford University Press 1936), 96.

2 The tenor concept being expressed may itself be abstract or concrete.

3 Citations from the *Soulier de satin* are from *Théâtre*, eds Jacques Madaule and Jacques Petit, Bibliothèque de la Pléiade, 2 vols (Paris, Gallimard 1965–7), II. Day, scene, verset, and page numbers are given in parentheses before each citation. For clarity, passages cited as examples are set off from the text; images in these passages that are commented upon in the discussion are in italics. The verset structure of the *Soulier de satin* is followed as closely as possible in these citations. For this reason, when a quotation begins or ends with the beginning or end of a complete sentence, but not of a verset, original capitalization and final punctuation are maintained, and ellipsis points are included to indicate the missing parts of the verset.

A number of passages of the play are discussed more than one time in this study. This reflects, and serves to illustrate, the convergence of stylistic devices and the expression of several levels of meaning simultaneously, and does not result from a lack of additional examples for the points being discussed. References to previous or subsequent discussions of a passage are included only when these discussions are pertinent to the point being considered.

4 *Philosophy of Rhetoric*, 93–100

5 *Ibid.*, 124–5. In this study, the word 'poetic' is used in the sense of 'stimulating to the imagination and emotions.' This definition is in accord with Richards's statement and with the opinions of many other contemporary critics. See Joseph T. Shipley, ed., *Dictionary of World Literature*, rev. ed. (Paterson, N.J., Littlefield, Adams 1962), s.v. 'Poetry and Prose'; and Karl Beckson and Arthur Ganz, *A Reader's Guide to Literary Terms* (New York, Farrar, Straus & Giroux, Noonday Press 1960), s.v. 'Poetry.'

6 In some cases, the connection between tenor and vehicle cannot be completely understood by the reader, and the meaning of the image then remains unclear or ambiguous. Nevertheless, since it is the mental effort demanded of the reader rather than the significance of the image itself that is the chief determinant of the overall impact of the vehicle terms, such expressions may be highly effective.

7 Many critics divide images into the categories of metaphor, simile (or comparison), and metonymy; see, for example, R.A. Sayce, *Style in French Prose* (Oxford, Oxford University Press, Clarendon Press 1965), 57–68. Michael Riffaterre adds the category of concretization; see *Le Style des 'Pléiades' de Gobineau* (Geneva, Droz 1957), 166–71.

Table 1 shows the specific numbers of images found in the *Soulier de satin* that are characterized by each of the stylistic factors described in this chapter. In computing these figures, image developments of all types (as described in Chapter 2) were counted in terms of component vehicle elements. The calculation of these totals, and of totals given in frequency counts in later chapters, necessarily involved some arbitrariness and subjectivity. Nevertheless, since an attempt was made to keep these calculations as consistent as possible, the numbers are believed to be of a useful degree of accuracy.

8 It would thus be misleading to distinguish systematically between the effects of the metaphors used by an author and those of his similes. There is, however, one difference in the effects that metaphors and similes may have on the reader's response that should be taken into consideration in studying specific images. In most similes tenor and ground are expressed first, followed by the vehicle; the statement of these terms retards the appearance of the vehicle and thus tends to attenuate its effectiveness. The metaphor, on the other hand, is a more concentrated expression; the impact of the vehicle on the reader is more immediate, and is therefore usually stronger. This difference in the relative effectiveness of the two types of images is probably the chief reason why most authors, Claudel included, use far more metaphors than similes.

9 The suggestive power of these metonymies is reinforced by the phrase *cet immense remuement,* which evokes in context the swarming crowds of people also commonly associated with the Far East.

10 See Sayce, *Style in Prose,* 62; and Stephen Ullman, *Language and Style* (New York, Barnes & Noble 1964), 178.

11 The important role played by the face in direct, intimate communication between two people is reflected in the archetype of the face of the all-powerful ruler – god, emperor, king – which ordinary mortals are not permitted to view.

12 The use of the word 'absolute' to describe these images is based on the use of the expression *métaphore absolue* by Riffaterre in *Gobineau*, 185.

13 In *A Grammar of Metaphor* (London, Martin Secker & Warburg 1958, 160–2), Christine Brooke-Rose calls this particular type of absolute image 'Pure Attribution,' and explains that such an image 'expresses a somewhat artificial split of one idea into two terms which are basically identical' – in other words, the 'unshod feet' of Musique's mind in fact represent here her mind itself; thus, the 'abstract notion is being divided into a person and an object.' The effect of Pure Attribution, Brooke-Rose explains, is to change the object to which the metaphoric term is ascribed; in this case, when the phrase *les pieds déchaussés* is attributed to Musique's mind, it changes this mind into a body which can express her feelings and attitudes through its appearance and gestures.

14 That is, the terms of the vehicle are semantically incompatible according to commonly accepted linguistic norms; when taken literally, such expressions designate impossible objects or situations.

15 See George Smith, ed., *The Teaching of the Catholic Church*, 2vols (New York, Macmillan 1952), II, 681.

16 Because this particular illogical vehicle includes terms derived from two very different areas of meaning, it may be considered a 'mixed metaphor'; in the *Soulier de satin*, mixed metaphors are found most often in long image developments, and this type of vehicle will therefore be discussed in detail in Chapter 2.

17 In *A Grammar of Metaphor*, Brooke-Rose explains that in personification the verb of the noun-verb statement is technically a 'replacement' metaphor, because it 'takes the place of' an action or condition generally associated with the stated noun, while the noun itself is literal in context. The relationship of the verb with the noun, however, is much stronger than its relationship with the verb it replaces and its primary effect is to change implicitly the meaning of this noun. In the above example, the verb *m'inviter* replaces a literal statement referring to the appearance of the sun, but from the reader's point of view the principal effect of this verb is to change the sun into an active force, which serves as an instrument of God (206–9).

18 In context, the term *tapis* may also evoke for the reader the wake of the ships that connect Spain with these *régions disjointes*.

19 The associations that any word evokes in the mind of an individual reader depend to a great degree on the reader's own past experiences. Some words, however, have commonly evoked a number of specific feelings and thoughts in the minds of most people; the associations of these words are thus to some extent standardized. Such words, and the objects or situations they designate, are referred to in this study as 'archetypal.'

20 The Americas are referred to metonymically here, through the term *sierra*; since this is a foreign word, it evokes the exotic light in which the New World appeared to Spaniards at this time. (The phrase *toute bleue* suggests the way a distant *sierra* might appear at certain times of the day.)

21 All biblical citations in this study are taken from the Bible used by Claudel, *La Sainte Bible selon la Vulgate, traduction nouvelle* (1866).

22 In the general historical context of this play, the phrase *corde chrétienne* may also evoke for the reader the autos-da-fé of the Spanish Inquisition. The Captain then seems to mock as well this organized killing in the name of the Church.

23 See above, p. 13.

24 Critics and philosophers have long differed on the exact nature of humour. Kant, Schopenhauer, and Spencer are among those who have supported the 'incongruity theory,' the idea that the perception of an incongruity – that is, a contrast with the immediate context – and the resulting disappointment of one's expectations are the source of the feeling that something is humorous; see 'Dialectic of Aesthetic Judgement,' in *Kant's Critique of Aesthetic Judgement*, trans. James C. Meredith, (Oxford, Oxford University Press, Clarendon Press 1911), 196–203; Arthur Schopenhauer, 'On the Theory of the Ludicrous,' *The World as Will and Idea*, trans. R.B. Haldane and J. Kemp, 3 vols (Boston, Ticknor 1886), II, 270–84; and Herbert Spencer, 'The Physiology of Laughter,' *Illustrations of Universal Progress* (New York, Appleton 1964), 194–209.

25 Beckson and Ganz, *Literary Terms*, s.v. 'Irony.' General statements made below about humorous expressions also apply to irony.

26 Critics have also differed on the degree to which aggressive impulses, in particular the desire to see oneself as superior to others, play a part in humour. Those who have developed the view of humour as an expression of aggression include Aristotle, Hobbes, Bergson, and Freud. See, for example, Henri Bergson, *Le Rire* (Paris, Presses Universitaires 1962), esp. 103–6, 147–50; and Sigmund Freud, *Jokes and their Relation to the Unconscious*, trans. James Strachey (New York, W.W. Norton 1963), esp. 102–15.

27 Claudel believed strongly that all natural objects are gifts of God, and should therefore be employed and appreciated in a form as close to their original state as possible; for him, any individual who, like Léopold, is repelled by the natural condition of objects and creatures both deprives himself of great pleasure and commits the sin of rejecting God's work (see 'Le Jardin aride,' *Figures et paraboles*, in *Œuvres en prose*, eds Petit and Galpérine, 930–3).

28 In Table 1, frequency counts are given for each of the three ways in which humour is related to the poetic nature of the text. These counts refer only to brief passages – at most, four printed lines – in which humour and poetry are related in the ways described. This limitation should be kept in mind in considering these subtotals, because in the broadest sense humour and poetry alternate throughout the text and humour thus almost always appears 'within an otherwise poetic passage.'

29 This phrase may also bring to mind in contrast the prestigious knight-errant, who rode about the countryside redressing wrongs and settling disputes.

30 Pélage explained to Balthazar that because a judge represents a potential threat to most individuals he is more feared and resented than admired and cherished: 'On n'aime pas un juge' (I ii 15; 670). He also stated that as a judge he felt compelled to inflict harsh penalties on criminals: 'J'ai appris tout de suite qu'il n'y avait pas de plus grande charité que de tuer les êtres malfaisants' (I ii 17; 670). Because Pélage makes the ironic reference to his horse during a discussion of the military struggle in Africa, his words may also recall the traditional contrast between the *noblesse d'épée* and the *noblesse de robe*; by implication, he then mocks as well the latter group as a whole – the less vigorous nobility, who served their king through safe and often comfortable judicial activities rather than through physical combat.

31 Later in the scene, the Cavaliers show that their underlying attitude towards the religious aspects of their mission is in fact one of reverence and devotion; their earlier ironic comments then seem to reflect both the disrespectful attitude that many young people exhibit towards all their elders hold sacred, and at the same time, a good-natured, joking outlook on life also characteristic of young people.

32 For Claudel, of course, as for other religious militants, these two concepts do not conflict, because for them the benefits to be gained by the conversion of heathens clearly outweigh any suffering either they or the Christians must undergo in the process.

CHAPTER 2

1 Table 2 gives frequency counts for the *Soulier de satin* of single-element images and of each of the patterns of image development discussed below.

2 The use of the term 'code' to designate the vehicle theme is based on the use of this word by Michael Riffaterre in 'La Poétisation du mot chez Victor Hugo,' *Cahiers de l'Association Internationale des Études Françaises*, No. 19 (March 1967), 186–7.

In the following discussion, the term 'element' is used in designating individual parts of either the vehicle system or the tenor system; which system is referred to will be clear in each case from the context.

3 As a rule, only children describe geographic locations in this pictoral way, and the image thus adds an element of light humour to the statement.

4 See John F. Sullivan, *The Externals of the Catholic Church*, rev. by John C. O'Leary (New York, P.J. Kenedy 1951), 298. The reader may also remember that earlier in the *Soulier de satin* two individuals were compared to a *colombe* and that in both cases the image suggested in context that this person helped to bring those with whom he came in contact within reach of a state of Grace: the King referred to Columbus as 'fils de la Colombe' (I vi 34; 688 – the dove image is, of course, commonly used in relation to Columbus), and Prouhèze told Musique: 'C'est toi qui es la colombe' (I x 17; 707).

5 The use of metonymies within metaphoric developments is discussed further on pp. 36 and 37 below.

6 The meanings of these two vehicles are stressed because the disjunctive *sans fin* separates verb and subject in this clause, and thus creates a moment of suspense, which leads the reader to pay more attention to the compound subject when it finally appears.

7 Since the reader is familiar now with all parts of the image, even though he may reread each successive part of the vehicle system separately, as he does so he relates each element to the ideas already suggested to him by other parts of the image development and by the passage as a whole.

8 The ideas conveyed by this dove-code development also reflect Claudel's belief that the physical unification of all parts of the world and the intellectual collaboration of its peoples will lead eventually to their spiritual union under God's rule; the repeated expression of this idea in the *Soulier de satin* will be discussed in Chapters 5 and 8.

9 The alchemists, of course, performed their operations in the opposite direction, attempting to change worthless metal into gold; cf. Racine, *Athalie*: 'Comment en un plomb vil l'or pur s'est-il changé?' (III vii; *Théâtre complet*

de Racine, ed. Maurice Rat, Paris, Garnier 1953, 692).

10 The choice of this expression is based on the use of the term *métaphore autonome* by Michael Riffaterre in *Le Style des 'Pléiades' de Gobineau,* 183.

11 The expression *l'appel de l'Afrique* is a cliché associated with colonialist writings of the first quarter of this century; the image is renewed here by the previous metaphoric designation of Africa as a *feu capable de les consumer* – certainly not what the colonialists had in mind.

12 The illogical quality of the clause – animal breath cannot in fact be purified in a furnace – makes it even more attention-getting for the reader.

13 When autonomous elements are found within extended images that are entirely absolute in nature, the tenor concept to which the autonomous element corresponds may not in fact be more abstract than the other tenor elements. Nevertheless, because the tenor system at first seems to the reader to 'disappear' at this point in the development, from the reader's point of view the distance between tenor and vehicle systems does increase in this segment of the image.

14 Karl Beckson and Arthur Ganz, *A Reader's Guide to Literary Terms* (New York, Farrar, Straus & Giroux, Noonday Press 1960), s.v. 'Metaphor,' 121

15 Claudel's mixing of metaphors often reflects synaesthesia, an appeal to the reader or spectator through more than one kind of physical sensation simultaneously. The image discussed below, for example, involves the senses of hearing and sight. For a more detailed discussion of Claudel's relationship to synaesthesia, see Eugène Roberto, *Visions de Claudel,* esp. 6–8.

16 See below, pp. 98–9.

17 A metonymy is used in a similar manner within a metaphoric development in the Actress's dove-code description of England. As noted above, the phrase *une palpitation d'ailes* is a metonymic expression of the constant movement of the birds as they fly around the dovecote, and this movement is itself a metaphor for the activity of the ships around England.

18 Even if the reader does not consciously recall the previous use of the code, it may influence his understanding of the later image.

Two examples of code developments are given here. Other important code developments found in the *Soulier de satin* are discussed in Chapters 4 to 8, and the way in which these codes function within the text is shown in more detail there.

19 This type of image development is similar to the 'image-sequence' described by Stephen Ullman in *Language and Style,* 183.

20 This association of the vehicle terms is reinforced by the connection of the word *gueules* with the desire to eat encouraged in Eve by the snake.

21 This type of development is similar to that which Ullman calls a 'double analogy' (*Language and Style,* 182).

CHAPTER 3

1 See Michael Riffaterre, 'Criteria for Style Analysis,' *Word,* xv (1959), 172.

2 See Table 3 for calculations of the frequency with which each of these devices converges with images in the *Soulier de satin.* Detailed studies of stylistic devices related to syntax and to repetition can be found in Michael Riffaterre, *Le Style des 'Pléiades' de Gobineau,* 92–163.

3 For a discussion of the ways in which Claudel's writing in general most often departs from commonly accepted forms of French syntax, see Paul Angenendt, *Eine Syntaktische-stilistische Untersuchung der Werke P. Claudels* (Bonn, L. Neuendorff 1932), 40–61.

4 For a discussion of the importance of this spiritual joy for Claudel, see Pierre Ganne, *Claudel, humour, joie et liberté* (Paris, Éditions de l'Épi 1966).

5 As can be seen in Table 3, these devices converge with images less frequently in the *Soulier de satin* than do other syntactic devices; their relative infrequency causes them to be all the more striking for the reader when they do appear.

6 For a more detailed study of the use of ellipsis in the *Soulier de satin*, see Paul Imbs, 'Étude sur la syntaxe du *Soulier de satin* de Paul Claudel (l'ellipse),' *Le Français moderne*, XVI, No. 4 (October 1944), 243–79.

   The asyndeton, or the omission of conjunctions customarily used to connect parts of a sentence, is a specific type of ellipsis found in the *Soulier de satin*; since its most important effects relate to the creation of repetitive rhythmic patterns in the text, however, this device is discussed in a later section of this chapter.

7 The expression 'prose rhythm' is taken from the discussion of rhythm by René Wellek and Austin Warren in *Theory of Literature*, rev. ed. (New York, Harcourt, Brace & World, Harvest Books 1956), 169.

8 Jeanne Varney Pleasants, *Pronunciation of French*, trans. Esther Egerton (Ann Arbor, Michigan, Edwards 1962), 87

9 Since the sequence of accented syllables is determined primarily by the grammatical development of the statement, stylistic devices that involve unexpected syntactic arrangements (such as those discussed in the preceding section of this chapter) usually disturb the normal stress patterns of the statement as well. These rhythmic disruptions are themselves startling to the reader and therefore increase the effectiveness of the words involved, but since they cannot be separated from the corresponding syntactic devices they do not constitute in themselves additional stylistic devices.

10 This statement is printed in the text as part of a sentence beginning with *Ah!*, but because the preceding independent clause, *quel maître as-tu tiré au sort*, could itself constitute a complete sentence (and in fact ends as would a sentence, with an exclamation point), the reader would tend to pronounce this second statement as a separate sentence.

11 Although the two words *un mur* do not constitute a grammatically complete sentence, because they are printed here as a separate sentence, they are perceived, and would be pronounced, as such by the reader, and they therefore constitute an independent rhythmic unit.

12 One reason for the great variation in verset length in most of Claudel's poetic works is suggested by the remarks he makes on the role of verse structure in poetry in the essay 'Réflexions et propositions sur le vers français': 'On ne pense pas d'une manière continue, pas davantage qu'on ne sent d'une manière continue ou qu'on ne vit d'une manière continue. Il y a des coupures, il y a intervention du néant. La pensée bat comme la cervelle et le cœur ... Sur cette matière première l'écrivain éclairé par sa raison et son goût et guidé par un but plus ou moins distinctement perçu travaille, mais il est impossible de donner une image exacte des allures de la pensée si l'on ne tient pas compte

du blanc et de l'intermittence. Tel est le vers essentiel et primordial, l'élément premier du language, antérieur aux mots eux-mêmes: une idée isolée par du blanc' (*Positions et propositions*, in *Œuvres en prose*, eds Jacques Petit and Charles Galpérine, 3). Because the poet's thoughts would tend to vary in nature and complexity, a verse pattern based on the configuration of these thoughts would include units of different length and internal structure.

13 A passage in which bizarre-sounding words have a very different effect is discussed on p. 68 below.

14 It is widely recognized that Pedro de las Vegas is a caricature of Pierre Lasserre, a French critic who wrote disparagingly both of Claudel's ideas and of the style in which he expressed his thoughts; Lasserre himself grew up in the Basque area of France (see *Mémoires improvisés*, ed. Louis Fournier, Paris, Gallimard 1954, 293; this passage is deleted in the 1969 edition of the *Mémoires improvisés*.)

15 See above, p. 52.

16 Some critics believe that a poem can be defined in terms of its repetitive nature. Roman Jakobson comments: 'What is the empirical linguistic criterion of the poetic function? In particular, what is the indispensible feature inherent in any piece of poetry? To answer this question we must recall the two basic modes of arrangement used in verbal behavior, *selection* and *combination* ... The poetic function projects the principle of equivalence from the axis of selection onto the axis of combination.* Equivalence is promoted to the constitutive device of the sequence' ('Linguistics and Poetics,' *Style in Language*, ed. Thomas A. Sebeok, New York, Wiley 1960, 357–8). See also Michael Riffaterre, 'Describing Poetic Structures: Two Approaches to Baudelaire's "Les Chats,"' *YFS*, Nos 36–7, October 1966, 201; and Samuel Levin, *Linguistic Structures in Poetry* (The Hague, Mouton 1962).

   Claudel realized that repetition, especially the repetition of sounds, has an important effect on the reader's response to the poetic text: 'Le poète ... se sert ... des mots ... non pas pour l'utilité, mais pour constituer de tous ces fantômes sonores que le mot met à sa disposition, un tableau à la fois intelligible et délectable. L'habitude qui substitue à la nature réelle des choses une seconde nature, c'est-à-dire une valeur purement pratique, maniable et efficace, est devenue son ennemie, une ennemie qu'il faut dérouter et endormir, comme la flûte d'Hermès jadis fit pour le cruel Argus. C'est à quoi sert la répétition des sons, l'harmonie des syllabes, la régularité des rhythmes et tout le chant prosodique. Une fois que la partie de l'âme ouvrière, quotidienne et servile, est ainsi assujetie et occupée, *Anima* s'avance librement au milieu des choses pures d'un pas infiniment léger et rapide' ('Réflexions et propositions,' *Œuvres en prose*, 48). Claudel thus sees repetition as a key means of heightening the impact of a text on the reader's imagination and emotions – in other words, of intensifying its poetic effectiveness.

17 See Gérald Antoine's study, *Les 'Cinq Grandes Odes' de Claudel, ou la poésie de la répétition* (Paris, M.J.Minard, Lettres Modernes 1959).

18 John Sullivan, *The Externals of the Catholic Church*, rev. by John O'Leary (New York, P.J. Kenedy 1951), 274

19 The frequency count for image-sequences is repeated in Table 3, in order to show more clearly the extent to which semantic repetition occurs in the *Soulier de satin*.

20 These Arab leaders are Tarik Ibn Myad, a Moslem general who crossed the Straits of Gibraltar in 710; Yousouf Ibn Tachfin, who took up the invasion in the eleventh century; and the dynasty of the Almohades, who occupied half of Spain in the twelfth century.

21 Grammatical repetition usually coincides specifically with the reiteration of a concept in different words. As noted above, when vehicle terms are repeated without change in the *Soulier de satin,* the microcontext is generally altered; the grammatical structure of this microcontext is in most such cases also changed.

22 See, for example, Ps. 138: 16.

23 Another type of polysyndeton involves the use of a conjunction such as *et* at the beginning of a sentence, where it cannot perform its usual connecting function. This particular device is used a number of times in the *Soulier de satin,* but it does not serve directly to heighten the effectiveness of image vehicles.

24 Because it expresses an essential quality of the sea, the adjective *mouvante* functions as an *épithète de nature*; almost all such epithets are, like *mouvante* here, redundant.

25 The term *portions* itself suggests the dividing of the area into small, clearly defined units that belong to specific groups of people, and thus underscores the severe restrictions imposed on the Orientals. The final clause of the sentence indicates that these people want to relieve their confining situation not by achieving total freedom, but rather by discovering a balanced, stable way of life. In context, the term *centre* may recall for the reader Claudel's belief that the absolute 'centre' of the universe is God; this image then suggests that the relief these people seek can in fact be found only through the Church (see, for example, *La Rose et le rosaire*, Paris, Egloff 1947, 240).

CHAPTER 4

1 As opposed to spiritual situations and events, discussed in Chapter 5

2 These characters include the Double Shadow, the Moon, the Saints, the Guardian Angel, the Irrepressible, Leal, Isabel, and Ramire. To cite one example – Saint Jacques's appearance as a constellation emphasizes that he is a heavenly being, and thus stresses his role as a representative of a pure, blissful form of existence.

3 Children are treated separately here because in the *Soulier de satin* the childlike traits of the young characters are displayed more obviously in their speech and are more significant in relation to the meaning of the play than is their class background; for the reader, the children thus form a distinct social group. (A character may at times speak in a manner typical of a social group other than his own – through most of the play, for example, Rodrigue's speech reflects his aristocratic upbringing, but near the end of his life he occasionally speaks like a child.)

   No frequency counts are given for the types of images considered in the first part of this chapter, because the relative intensity with which such images convey the narrative-level significance of the text to the reader can best be shown schematically, as in the chart found on the inside back cover; this chart will be discussed in detail in Chapter 8. Frequency counts are given, however, for the specific vehicle codes examined in the second part of this chapter, in Table 4.

4 Although Camille has renounced his position in Spanish society, he was born and raised in aristocratic surroundings, and his speech is very much like that of the other noble characters (see I ii 26; 670 and I iii 20–1; 673).

5 In this context, the term *yeux* also functions as an archetype, evoking both the profound source of this power and the intangible ways in which it was exercised. This archetype, however, serves primarily to reinforce an idea that Rodrigue expresses more directly in the rest of the development – the almost absolute control that women are able to maintain over the men who are attracted to them.

6 *Gentille* is used in this sense today only in poetic texts.

7 The effectiveness of this particular passage is increased by an indication in a stage direction that, as he speaks, Camille moves so that his shadow plays with that of Rodrigue on the wall.

8 The soldiers' remarks in this scene hold special interest for the reader because they present him with a new and different view of Prouhèze; as in other literary works, the description of a character from many points of view gives the reader a more complete picture of him and makes him seem more true to life. In this particular case, the soldier's expression of contempt for Prouhèze also recalls the incomprehension exhibited by most lower-class individuals towards their social superiors, and thus indirectly underscores for the reader Prouhèze's isolation at Mogador.

Other stylistic devices found in the speech of these characters further accentuate their low social rank and lack of education. As seen above, some grammatical forms they use both are incorrect and are generally used only by lower-class individuals. An additional example is the fishermen's repeated use of the term *ça* instead of a noun or personal pronoun as the subject of a sentence. Mangiacavallo, for example, says of the sea, 'Ça goûte tout pareil aussi la même chose que de l'eau salée qu'est salée' (IV i 27; 862).

The orthography of the printed text in itself underscores the speaker's lack of good breeding when it indicates that the way he enunciates certain words deviates from the standard pronunciation of the period. This is the effect of the repeated omission of the letter *l* from the word *il* in the description by the soldiers at Mogador of a Spaniard who has just been executed as a traitor: 'Maintenant c'est fini pour Don Sébastien. I s'en fout / … du moment où notre vieille épousait notre vieux, i n'avait plus qu'à se sauver. Et où est-ce qu'i se serait sauvé autre part que chez les Turcs?' (III iv 7, 15; 805).

The pattern that such grammatical and orthographic devices follow in IV i illustrates how these stylistic factors are used in the play to indicate the social class of the speaker. At the beginning of this scene, there are many such constructions and misspellings. At this point, the fishermen are describing their attempt to bring to the surface the unknown object lying under the sea. Their discussion reveals that for them this is a search for a supernatural solution to all life's difficulties, the magical 'pot of gold at the end of the rainbow' – an activity in itself characteristic of simple-minded people. Form and content thus merge here to underscore the primitive mentality of the speakers. Later in the scene, the fishermen describe first the activities of the King and his followers on the sea and then the appearance of Rodrigue and his paintings; in these passages, there are few such characteristic misspellings. There are two reasons for this change. First, by this point in the scene, the general mentality of the fishermen has been clearly established for the reader; such devices are therefore no longer necessary as indicators of their frame of mind. Second, the subject of conversation now shifts away from the fishermen, centreing first on the King and his court and then on Rodrigue; the use of these devices here would tend to distract the reader's attention from the content of these passages. (Nevertheless, the images used by the characters in describing first the court and then Rodrigue continue to exhibit the lower-class characteristics described and illustrated above.)

9 Musique speaks like a child in at least one passage of every scene in which she appears; Rodrigue's speech is childlike only in Day 4, as he nears the end of his life.

10 In the following section of this chapter, references to the 'children' of the play generally pertain to the childlike moments of Musique and Rodrigue as well as to Sept-Épées and la Bouchère.

11 The relationship between a child's simple-minded view of the world and a strong religious faith accounts for the childlike speech of Musique and Rodrigue at some moments – because their speech then reveals that these characters have adopted the child's simple, uncritical attitude, it suggests that they are, at least temporarily, more easily able to accept without question the existence of God and the spiritual world. (The important role played by a childlike attitude in strengthening religious belief has long been recognized by theological authorities, and is the basis for the original teaching of Jesus: 'Laissez venir à moi les petits enfants ... car le royaume de Dieu est pour ceux qui les ressemblent. Je vous le dis en vérité, quiconque ne recevra pas le royaume de Dieu comme un enfant, n'y entrera point' [Mark 10: 14–15].)

12 The added reference to the *nacelles* and their ballast, on the other hand, is clearly not childlike; these images are conceits and remind the reader that Musique is in fact not a child. The religious significance of these water-code terms will be discussed in Chapter 5.

13 Dragut and Barbarossa were Moslem heroes, fierce pirates who were hired by Suleiman the Magnificent during the sixteenth century to help the Turks in their struggle against the Europeans.

14 One factor that does lessen somewhat the harshness of this insult is the aptness of the expression as a description of la Bouchère, who is by name and by proposed marriage closely linked to *la viande*.

There is only one passage in the text in which an additional stylistic device serves to emphasize specifically the childish nature of the speaker. At the beginning of the first scene in which Sept-Épées and la Bouchère appear (IV iii), there are three orthographic errors that suggest that Sept-Épées pronounces at least some words in a typically childish manner – *vas* for *vais* (1; 878) and *la mé* for *la mer* (1; 878 and 5; 879). These misspellings underscore for the reader Sept-Épées's youth; once this characteristic has been firmly established in the reader's mind, no further indications of incorrect pronunciation are found.

15 As noted above, frequency counts for vehicle codes discussed in this part of the chapter are found in Table 4.

16 Since light-code imagery serves so often to express the lover's feelings of joy and encouragement, it might be expected that vehicles related to darkness

would be used to convey the anxiety and frustration that the love relationship also produces at some moments. Such imagery, however, is used only once in the *Soulier de satin* to describe this particular type of emotional distress, when the Moon quotes Prouhèze as saying of Rodrigue: 'Oui, je sais qu'il ne m'épousera que sur la croix et nos âmes l'une à l'autre dans la mort et dans la nuit hors de tout motif humain!' (II xiii 41; 779). Even here, the phrase *hors de tout motif humain* and the presence in the microcontext of Cross-code imagery indicates that the most important implications of the image relate to the religious, rather than the narrative level of the play. (When Rodrigue refers to Prouhèze as a *point de lumière*, in the passage cited above, he does use absence-of-light imagery to express a feeling directly opposed to the joy that results from his love for her; Rodrigue, however, is referring here not to the pain produced by love itself, but to his dreary existence without Prouhèze.)

17 The phrase *détruit la mort* is thus an adynaton, a form of hyperbole in which an event is magnified by being described in terms of an impossibility.

18 Auditory-code developments that include terms related specifically to music are used a number of times in the *Soulier de satin* to express both emotional and spiritual ties between individuals; see above, p. 36, and below, pp. 164–5.

19 In the *Soulier de satin*, terms related to the remaining physical senses – touch and sight – are not found in images that express only the emotional ties between lovers, although such words are used in both literal and metonymic descriptions of their physical contact.

20 The difference in the way these two aspects of the love relationship are treated in the text can best be seen by examining a scene in which a character discusses both his feelings for another person and the actions to which these emotions lead him.

In I x, pp. 706–10, Musique tells Prouhèze of her love for the Viceroy of Naples. In v. 12 of this scene, she explains why she has left home, using only one image. She then states very briefly, and in literal terms, that she intends to marry the 'King of Naples' (vv. 13–15). In vv. 18–27 and 35–55, Musique continues to talk of her lover, but speaks now of her intense feelings for him and of his eager response to her; in these passages, she uses many images, including a complex sensation-code development, part of which was discussed above. (In the remaining versets of this scene, Prouhèze's, rather than Musique's, situation is discussed.)

21 The conquest of a country is shown to play a similar role in the lives of other male characters of the *Soulier de satin*. A development that suggests that Pélage's activities in Africa were in this respect like those of Rodrigue in America was discussed in Chapter 1; additional implications of images that compare a country to its conqueror's lover will be examined in Chapters 7 and 8.

22 This emphasis reflects Claudel's belief that over the last several hundred years the world's peoples have been rapidly moving towards greater unity on all levels – political, economic, cultural, and spiritual. The vital importance of this unity for Claudel was reflected in many of his actions as a diplomat as well as in a great number of his writings; see, for example, *Mémoires improvisés*, ed. Louis Fournier (Paris, Gallimard 1969), 365–70; and *Cinq Grandes Odes*, in *Œuvre poétique*, Bibliothèque de la Pléiade (Paris, Gallimard 1957), 280–1. In Claudel's mind, a key vehicle of this unification was the

Renaissance, during which the *Soulier de satin* takes place; for a discussion of the relationship of the Renaissance to the play see Frédéric Lefèvre, *Une Heure avec ...*, 5. sér. (Paris, Gallimard 1929), 115.

23 The capitalization of the term *Porte* recalls in context the religious significance of the unity Rodrigue is helping to create; this significance will be discussed in Chapter 5.

24 An exception is Saint Jacques's reference to the Atlantic Ocean, cited above – ' ... ceux que l'abîme sépare n'ont qu'à me regarder pour se trouver ensemble' (II vi 10; 751). In each case, the terms of the text make it clear which role the sea plays – in Saint Jacques's statement, the key word is *sépare*; in the example cited here, the important words are *loin de lui imposer des limites*.

CHAPTER 5

1 These characters include Don Gusman, Ruis Peraldo, Diego Rodriguez, and Professors Bidince and Hinnulus.

An obvious chronological irregularity occurs in II vi – Saint Jacques describes the boats of Prouhèze and Rodrigue as they sail away from Spain, Prouhèze to Africa and Rodrigue to the New World, yet the King does not even decide to send Prouhèze to Mogador until II viii.

Anachronistic references to objects, events, and people abound in the play. For a review of those found in the final day alone, see Michel Autrand, 'Les Énigmes de la quatrième journée du *Soulier de satin*,' *Revue d'histoire du théâtre*, xx (1968), 309-24. Autrand reviews possible reasons for the inclusion of these anachronisms in the play, and concludes that for many, no reasonable explanation can be found: 'Claudel a connu et voulu nombre des irrémédiables bizarreries de son texte' (p. 324).

2 On the baroque aspects of the *Soulier de satin*, see Marie-Louise Tricaud, *Le Baroque dans le théâtre de Paul Claudel* (Geneva, Droz 1967), esp. 269-70; and Alain Baudot, '*Le Soulier de satin* est-il une anti-tragédie?' *Études françaises*, v (May 1969), 120-1.

3 Angus Fletcher notes in *Allegory* (Ithaca, Cornell University Press 1962, 2-3) that most contemporary critics consider any work of art that conveys more than one level of meaning to be allegorical.

4 George Smith, ed., *The Teaching of the Catholic Church*, 2 vols (New York, Macmillan 1952), I, 42-3

5 See Hampus Lyttkens, *The Analogy between God and the World* (Uppsala; Almquist & Wiksells 1952); and Hans Meyer, *The Philosophy of St. Thomas Aquinas*, trans. Frederic Eckhoff (St. Louis, B. Herder 1944), 275-8.

6 See, for example, Claudel's *Journal*, eds. François Varillon and Jacques Petit, Bibliothèque de la Pléiade, 2 vols (Paris, Gallimard 1968-9), I, 284-5, 586-7, 616, 938; also, *Mémoires improvisés*, ed. Louis Fournier, 81-2, 156. In developing the ideas of Aquinas on the origin of the relationship between the physical and the spiritual worlds, Claudel explained that all reality, both tangible and intangible, derives from a single source – a 'state of movement,' which itself results from the reaction of all matter to the Divine Being: 'Que sont, au rapport de l'une à l'autre, les réalités désignées sous le nom de matière et d'esprit? ... On doit ... leur refuser non pas la différence qui est féconde, mais un isolement de nature qui est inconcevable. Toutes deux sont des créatures et relèvent, dès lors, de l'état de mouvement ... L'origine du mouvement est

dans ce frémissement qui saisit la matière au contact d'une réalité différente: l'Esprit' (*Art poétique*, in *Œuvre poétique*, 151–2, 138). Because they derive from a single, divine source, all non-divine aspects of the world – all that are not God himself – are closely connected with each other, as well as with their unique point of origin: 'Nous faisons partie d'un ensemble homogène, et comme nous co-naissons à toute la *nature*, c'est ainsi que nous la connaissons ... Connaître donc, c'est être: cela qui manque à tout le reste ... Chaque note de la gamme appelle et suppose les autres ... Il y a connaissance, il y a obligation de l'une à l'autre, lien donc entre les différentes parties du monde, comme entre celles du discours pour former une phrase lisible' (*ibid.*, pp. 153–4).

Claudel's belief in the common origin of all parts of the physical and spiritual worlds thus led him to accept, in effect, the principle of 'universal analogy,' a concept which attracted much attention during the eighteenth and nineteenth centuries, following its exposition and development by the Swedish philosopher, Swedenborg. Claudel's views, however, differed from those of most earlier proponents of this principle in that for him the spiritual sphere with which physical existence is so closely connected is that which is specifically defined by Catholic doctrine.

7 Frequency counts for the types of codes discussed below and for the specific codes cited as examples are found in Table 5.

8 Smith, *Teaching*, II, 767

9 The Guardian Angel and the saints who appear as speaking characters also function as 'images' whose religious significance has been determined by Catholic tradition. The names and titles of these characters indicate to the reader that they are spiritual essences, and that the concrete forms in which they appear serve primarily to enable them to interact more effectively with earthbound human beings (including the reader himself). In addition, the specific religious roles associated by the reader with each of these traditional names and titles correspond to, and thus emphasize for him, the particular theological function fulfilled by the character within the play.

10 Some of these codes are used in other of Claudel's works to express religious concepts metaphorically; the reader familiar with his writings may therefore recall the usual religious significance of a particular code for Claudel the first time he encounters it in the *Soulier de satin*. The reader's understanding of these codes within this play is not dependent on his familiarity with Claudel's other works, however, because in each case the specific religious significance of the theme in this particular text is conveyed to him by the text itself. (It is for this reason that when codes used by Claudel in other works are discussed in this study, the other texts are as a rule not cited.)

11 References to 'baptismal waters' also imply the existence of a state of Grace, because they evoke the individual's entrance into a spiritually pure form of life; in context, however, such expressions generally bring to mind most vividly the cleansing of the individual of his earthly sins.

12 The interrelationship of gold- and water-code imagery in other of Claudel's works is discussed by Conor Cruise O'Brien in *Maria Cross: Imaginative Patterns in a Group of Catholic Writers* (Fresno, Calif., Academy Guild Press 1963), 175–83.

13 The use of the word *accord* in the fourth verset above in such a way that it evokes two meanings (the entire clause *elles sont d'accord* is used literally here,

but in context the musical associations of the term *accord* are also brought to mind) helps to stress the unity of all beings in heaven.

14 The frequency with which Claudel links music and water in his writings has been noted by Jean-Noël Segrestaa in his article, 'Regards sur la composition du *Soulier de satin,' Revue des lettres modernes,* Nos 180–2 (1968), 79–81. In the above passage, the alternate use of music and water codes to describe the spiritual realm, and in particular their combined use in the final verset (where they form a mixed metaphor), further underscores the unity of all forces within the spiritual world by implying that even areas of reality as different in nature as water and music may function together in perfect accord on this transcendental level of life.

15 The use of the plural *ces fils* in the first verset in itself renews the cliché. Other stylistic devices that contribute to the effectiveness of this development include the disjunctives *aux yeux de tous* and *pendant bien des nuits* in the first verset, and the unexpected occurrence of the verset break between the conjunction *que* and the subject and predicate of the clause it introduces, *j'ai tissée.*

16 As in this passage, the use of a mythological figure to designate a supernatural force generally results in the personification of this power. Such a personification is particularly effective because it both adds dramatic vividness to the text and enables the speaker to describe with greater precision the way in which the spiritual world interacts with human beings. Here, Rodrigue's personification of the power of predestination enables him to relate in concrete terms the specific manner in which this force affected his mental and physical behaviour.

17 Smith, *Teaching,* II, 679–81

18 Claudel's belief that the peoples of the world must continue to move towards greater unity in all areas of earthly life was noted in Chapter 4. The passages cited in the preceding part of this chapter to illustrate the use of water-code imagery indicate that for Claudel the spiritual sphere of existence is also characterized by the close interconnection of all participating forces. Rodrigue's Communion-code plea to the King now reveals the relationship between these two types of unity – since the earthly and the heavenly spheres are closely linked, the physical interaction of peoples and natural elements will ultimately lead to their spiritual unification as well.

19 The 'reciprocal image developments' described below are similar to the 'reciprocal images' discussed by Stephen Ullman in *Language and Style,* 191.

20 The only other concepts repeatedly exchanged in this way in the *Soulier de satin* are earthly love and religious devotion. These particular concepts have been interchanged similarly by many poets in the past; their reciprocal use generally reflects a belief that human love is a reflection of, and in some cases a means to the attainment of, godly love. See, for example, Mary Paton Ramsay, *Les Doctrines médiévales chez Donne, le poète métaphysicien de l'Angleterre, 1573–1631* (London, Oxford University Press 1925), 224–7; and F.A.C. Wilson, *Yeats's Iconography* (London, Gollancz 1960). Claudel expresses this view of love directly in several of his essays, including 'Introduction à un poème sur Dante' (*Accompagnements,* in *Œuvres en prose,* eds Jacques Petit and Charles Galpérine, 422–34).

21 The phrase *armées de Dieu* is especially striking because it is a renewal of the

biblical expression, *le Dieu des armées*. The tremendous power of these *armées* is stressed for the reader by the unexpected modification of the singular noun *mouvement* by the plural adjective *innombrable*, and by the attention-getting, anteposed disjunctive position of this entire prepositional phrase.

22 Here, too, Claudel interrelates music and water.

The references to the *danseurs* who are linked by the rhythm of their movements and to the amorous nature of the *paroles* reinforce the reader's impression that these sound-code images express specifically the presence of a unifying force.

23 The specific theological significance of each of the main characters' thoughts and actions is discussed at length in Chapters 7 and 8.

24 The ways in which the relative importance of the two levels of meaning is suggested to the reader are discussed in Chapter 6.

25 For a discussion of the ways in which the expression of religious concepts causes many of the historical inconsistencies found in the text see Anne-Marie Mazzega, 'Le Soulier de satin, une parabole historique,' *Revue des lettres modernes*, Nos 150–2 (1967), 43–59.

CHAPTER 6

1 Although the effectiveness of these particular scoffing remarks is attenuated somewhat by the reader's knowledge that prefaces to fictional works are traditionally light and humorous in tone, their comic effect is soon reinforced by other mocking passages, as will be seen below.

2 It is shown in Chapter 8 that the narrative level does, in fact, develop according to a specific structure; as is indicated below, however, the source of this structure is in the author's mind, not in the narrative itself.

Frequency counts for types of images used in Claudel's interventions in the *Soulier de satin* are found in Table 6.

3 Several of the religious characters (including the saints in the Church of Saint Nicholas and Saint Jacques) as well as the two object characters (the Double Shadow and the Moon) also remain outside the narrative in that they do not interact with the ostensibly human characters; these speakers, however, function as spokesmen of a supernatural power, as indicated by the content of their speeches and their titles.

4 These incongruous situations are among those that lead the reader to look for more than the narrative level of meaning in the play, as explained in Chapter 5.

5 Other characters involved in incongruous situations that suggest Claudel's opinion of the types of people they represent or of their roles in the play include Léopold Auguste (III v), Ramire and Isabel (III vi), the Actress (IV vi), and the Chamberlain (IV iv).

6 This particular remark also emphasizes for the reader the simple-mindedness of the characters who appear in the following scene.

7 The effects of this mocking on the reader's affective response to the text will be discussed in greater detail in Chapter 8.

8 'Le Soulier de satin' devant la critique, Situation, No. 6, 13–15. Words in quotation marks are taken from Denis Saurat, 'Paul Claudel,' *Perspectives* (Paris, Stock 1938), 166.

CHAPTER 7

1 Numerous critics have acknowledged that the reader's response to a literary work is determined in part by his unconscious reaction to the emotions it conveys; the most thorough and systematic study to date of the relationship between the affective concepts actualized by the text and the reader's subjective experience of the work is Norman Holland's *The Dynamics of Literary Response* (see esp. 3–30, 79–82); see also Simon Lesser, *Fiction and the Unconscious*, 188–211, 238–68.

In the following pages, the emotional stratum is described as being expressed 'in' the text, and is discussed in terms of the characters' lives; it should be understood that as a rule corresponding affective responses are evoked in the reader's mind and are, as explained in more detail below, related by him to his own experiences.

The word 'emotional' is used here with due caution. The narrative and religious levels of meaning do, of course, involve the expression of feelings and evoke related sentiments in the mind of the reader, as has been indicated in the preceding chapters. As will be explained in this chapter and in Chapter 8, however, the narrative- and religious-level emotions can be seen as being primarily reflections of more fundamental affective responses, the nature of which will be made clear below. Although the word 'emotional' can thus be used in different ways, in order to avoid the use of a less accurate designation, this basic affective message is referred to hereafter as the emotional level.

2 Lesser, *Fiction*, 153–4

3 *Fables of Identity: Studies in Poetic Mythology* (New York, Harcourt, Brace & World 1963), 53

4 The fact that these ideas and feelings are experienced at some time by most individuals does not mean that the literary text is merely the direct expression of thoughts common to all men; on the contrary, the author shapes the universal concepts he conveys through his work according to his own intellectual and emotional make-up, and the result is a highly individualized text. As Leslie Fiedler states in explaining the terminology used in his own studies: 'The word Archetype ... I use ... instead of the word 'myth,' which ... becomes increasingly ambiguous, to mean any of the immemorial patterns of response to the human situation in its most permanent aspects: death, love, the biological family, the relationship with the Unknown, etc. ... I use Signature to mean the sum total of individuating factors in a work, the sign of the Persona or Personality, through which an Archetype is rendered ... Literature, properly speaking, can be said to come into existence at the moment a Signature is imposed on an Archetype' ('Archetype and Signature,' *Art and Psychoanalysis*, ed. William Phillips, Cleveland, World Publishing, Meridian Books 1963, 462). Similarly, each reader's personal affective history is different, and each thus responds somewhat differently to any particular aspect of the text. The responses of the 'reader' discussed below are those which might be expected from a majority of the readers of the *Soulier de satin*. The reactions of any individual reader may, of course, be very dissimilar.

5 Although any fictional work undoubtedly expresses many unconscious needs of its author, to attempt to identify the psychological characteristics of a writer through the study of his work necessarily requires considerable speculation, both because the author's mind is far more complex than any one or any group of his works, and because as a rule he cannot be directly questioned by the

critic. This approach is therefore not used at all in this study of the *Soulier de satin* and the conclusions reached below should not be construed as pertaining in any specific way to the psychological make-up of Claudel himself.

6 The relative importance of the story of Prouhèze and Rodrigue on all levels of meaning was determined after study of the entire work and was not a preconceived supposition. The order of presentation followed in this chapter and in Chapter 8 was selected for reasons of simplicity and clarity, and does not reflect the procedures used in studying the text.

In order to demonstrate the relative importance in the play of the types of images discussed in this chapter and in Chapter 8 more effectively than could be done through frequency counts, the role of these images in conveying different levels of meaning is shown schematically in the chart found on the inside back cover; this chart is discussed in detail in Chapter 8.

7 Rodrigue's seed-code image emphasizes the two-sided nature of his love – in context, the word *semence* evokes man's ability to perpetuate his physical existence through his children and thus underscores Rodrigue's sensual attraction to Prouhèze; at the same time, this term recalls the frequent use of seed-code imagery in biblical parables to express the spiritual development of the individual and therefore stresses Rodrigue's hope that his love will also have lasting religious consequences.

The relationship shown in this chapter between religious concepts and erotic feelings may seem improbable or even offensive to some; Claudel himself, however, recognized that strong religious feelings are in many ways related to sexual drives. In 1915, for example, he wrote to Victor Segalen: 'Au point de vue moral comme au point de vue intellectuel, le catholicisme agit violemment en introduisant dans notre vie intime le principe béni de la contradiction, en imposant une exigence si haute et si complète qu'elle ne nous laisse aucun repos, en rinçant notre âme comme par le feu et en lui proposant hors d'elle-même – hors d'elle-même enfin! – à son cœur comme à son intelligence, à toutes ses études, un intérêt si fort que je ne puis le comparer qu'à ce désir sexuel, auquel sa violence est seule supérieure ... Le catholicisme n'est pas autre chose que l'Amour entre l'homme et Dieu, un amour au-dessus de tout sentiment et de toute parole, entre un homme personnel et un Dieu *personnel* à ce degré sublime et transcendant que nous appelons la Trinité ... La vie étrange qu'il vous semble voir dans mes livres, c'est celle de ce Dieu qui est pour moi non pas une abstraction, mais une personne réelle, vivante, extérieure, connue, expérimentée. C'est l'étreinte sur mon cœur de cette deuxième partie de la réalité qui complète et ferme l'univers une fois pour toutes et m'enclôt avec elle dans un paradis de certitude et de béatitude. Pas plus que la vie physique, notre vie morale et intellectuelle pour qu'elle éclose en un jaillissement suprême ne peut se passer de ce quelqu'un hors de nous avec qui nous formions un couple' ('Correspondance avec Paul Claudel,' *Cahiers du sud*, No. 288, 1948, 282–3).

8 Cf. Rodrigue's discussion with Camille, II xi 61–116; 770–3.

9 That is, to the extent that these terms evoke additional thoughts and feelings in the reader's mind; cf. above, pp.13–14.

10 See Calvin S. Hall, *A Primer of Freudian Psychology* (New York, New American Library, Mentor Books 1954), 109–12.

11 Otto Fenichel, *The Psychoanalytic Theory of Neurosis* (New York, W.W. Norton 1945), 108. This is the most comprehensive and systematic study of psychoanalytic principles to date.

12 The connection between the feelings evoked by the text and the reader's oedipal conflict remains, of course, unconscious in virtually all cases.
   Holland stresses the likelihood that the reader will relate a love story like
Rodrigue's to his own oedipal feelings: 'Almost any interpersonal relationship has oedipal elements, and, by the same token, any work of art dealing
in depth with relations of love and hate between people is likely to contain
some oedipal fantasies ... It is safe to say, as a general rule, that a work of literature builds on an oedipal fantasy whenever it deals with relationships
involving more than two persons or whenever it makes us feel fairly realistic
versions of adult love or hate' (*Literary Response*, 46–7).

13 After the play was written, Claudel himself stressed the spiritual aspects of
this encounter; see *Mémoires improvisés*, ed. Louis Fournier, 307–8.

14 On the religious level of meaning, these two phrases suggest that when
Prouhèze and Rodrigue are spiritually joined Rodrigue is the soul, and
Prouhèze the body, of their united being. For Claudel, however, the soul is
specifically feminine in nature (cf., for example, 'Parabole d'Animus et
d'Anima' in 'Réflexions et propositions sur le vers français,' *Positions et propositions*, in *Œuvres en prose*, eds Jacques Petit and Charles Galpérine, 27–8).
In this passage, the expression of the emotional level of meaning thus results
in inconsistencies not only in the story line, but also on the religious level of
the text.

15 The presentation of this meeting through the words of a third party, rather
than through a direct portrayal, helps to lessen the anxiety that the commit-
ting of this sin evokes in the reader's mind; this role of the Shadow is discussed at greater length in Chapter 8.

16 The central position of this scene in the play – this is the last scene of the second of four days – underscores the importance of the ideas being expressed
here.

17 For an explanation of the Catholic teaching that each individual must sacrifice
himself in imitation of Jesus, thus identifying with the Saviour and participating in the mystery of the original Crucifixion, see George Smith, ed.,
The Teaching of the Catholic Church, 2 vols (New York, Macmillan 1958), II,
906, 953. This identification with Christ is believed to be achieved, for example, by all who participate in the Communion ceremony (*ibid.*, I, 508).
   In order to simplify the following discussion, Rodrigue's 'sacrifice' is
described as if he had already consented to the experience related by
Prouhèze here. In fact, Prouhèze is only predicting what Rodrigue will do;
he himself does not fully accept the necessity of this course of action until he
is about to die.

18 Smith, *Teaching*, I, 241, 524

19 For a general discussion of the importance for Claudel of woman's role in leading man through suffering to redemption, see Odile Vëto, 'La Rédemption
et l'amour: étude sur *Paul Claudel interroge le Cantique des Cantiques*,' *La Table
ronde*, No. 191 (December 1963), 49–64. Woman is depicted as fulfilling this
role in several of Claudel's plays. In *Partage de midi*, for example, the spiritual
influence exercised by Ysé over Mesa closely parallels that of Prouhèze over
Rodrigue; Ysé's role, too, is described in Cross-code terms (cf., for example,
Théâtre, I, ed. Jacques Madaule, 1051, 1136, 1226). As is shown in Chapter 8,
the success or failure of other men of the *Soulier de satin* in reaching redemption is similarly dependent on their relationship with a beloved woman.

20 Mircea Eliade, *The Two and the One*, trans. J.M. Cohen (London, Harville Press 1965), 105–7

21 The liturgy for the blessing of the baptismal font, for example, reads in part: 'May [the Holy Ghost] fertilize this water prepared for the regeneration of man by the secret admixture of His light, that by a holy conception a heavenly offspring may come forth from the spotless womb of the divine font as a new creature, and may all who differ in sex or age be begotten by parent grace into one and the same infancy' (E.O. James, *Christian Myth and Ritual*, New York, World Publishing, Meridian Books 1965, 116).

22 As will be explained below, on the emotional level of the text, Prouhèze suggests in this passage that in submitting to God's will Rodrigue adopts specifically a feminine attitude towards this father figure; this implication supports the above-mentioned indications that through his cleansing experience Rodrigue enters an androgynous state.

Although Mary can be seen as the feminine counterpart of God the Father, Christian heaven is generally regarded as being asexual rather than bisexual. Nevertheless, the way in which the individual commonly experiences this ideal state is through bisexuality. Eliade explains: 'The formula of the *coincidentia oppositorum* is always applied when it is necessary to describe an unimaginable situation either in the Cosmos or in History. The eschatological symbol *par excellence* – which denotes that Time and History have come to an end – is the lion lying down with the lamb, and the child playing with the snake. Conflicts, that is to say opposites, are abolished; Paradise is regained ... The fact that the lion lies down with the lamb and the child sleeps beside the snake implies ... that this is no longer *our* world, but that of Paradise ...

'All expressions of the *coincidentia oppositorum* are not equivalent. We have observed on many occasions that by transcending opposites one does not attain the same mode of being ... The element common to all the rites, myths and symbols [just discussed as examples] lies in this: that all seek to come out of a particular situation in order to abolish a given system of conditions and reach a mode of "total" being. But, according to the cultural context, this "totality" may be either a primordial indistinction (as in "orgy" or "chaos"), or ... the liberty and blessedness of one who has reached the Kingdom in his own soul' (*The Two and the One*, 121–3).

23 In *Maria Cross*, Conor Cruise O'Brien points out (p. 233) that several Catholic writers, Claudel among them, see virtually all love in terms of the Crucifixion. For these writers, O'Brien states, 'Man remains nailed to his mother. When he seeks to break loose, to find "paradise" in loving another woman, he becomes aware of his crucifixion. Crucifixion, in which the cross suffers equally with the sacrifice, is punished for being the cross, is the only form of love.' Writing specifically of the *Soulier de satin*, O'Brien notes that 'the mutual crucifixion of the lovers, in an equilibrium of pain and punishment, is a conscious substitute for sexual enjoyment ... This balance of pain and punishment subsists until death. It can ... reach the point of ecstasy where man the crucified identifies himself with his female Cross. Death is then the triumphant and paradisiac hour when the dying hero gives birth to himself' (*ibid.*, 232–3).

24 In baptism, the individual participant is also believed to participate in the Passion and death of Jesus before he is reborn into a new, purified form of existence; see Smith, *Teaching*, II, 675–6, 767–76.

25 Mircea Eliade, *Birth and Rebirth,* trans. Willard R. Trask (New York, Harper 1958), xii-xiv
26 Mircea Eliade, *Patterns in Comparative Religion,* trans. Rosemary Sneed (New York, Sheed & Ward 1958), 188–9
27 Eliade, *Birth and Rebirth,* 131–2. The parallels with Christian tradition are obvious.
28 Eliade explains: 'In a great number of primitive peoples, initiation at puberty implies the ... androgynisation of the initiate. The best-known example is furnished by the initiatory subincision practised by certain Australian tribes, which symbolically gives the initiate a female sexual organ. If we remember that, according to the Australians, and many other primitive peoples elsewhere, non-initiates are considered asexual, and admission to sexuality is one of the consequences of initiation, the deeper significance of this rite seems to be the following: one cannot become a sexually adult male before knowing the coexistence of the sexes, androgyny; in other words, one cannot attain a particular and well-defined mode without first knowing the total mode of being' (*The Two and the One,* 111–12). In many cultures, the belief that androgyny is superior to the unisexual human condition is reflected in the portrayal of the gods as bisexual beings.
29 Bruno Bettleheim, *Symbolic Wounds* (Glencoe, The Free Press 1954), 159–60
30 Gilbert Durand, *Les Structures anthropologiques de l'imaginaire* (Paris: Presses Universitaires 1963), 102–7, 239–50. In the Moon's speech, Prouhèze compares herself directly to one of the most familiar of the threatening women, Eve.
31 In his study of the psychological implications of initiation ceremonies, Bettleheim underscores the resemblance of these rites to the Christian sacraments: 'Initiation into sexual maturity was probably the central ritual of primitive society ... It seems possible that other rituals which later gave meaning to human life were originally part of it. Of the seven sacraments of the Roman Catholic Church, at least five and possibly six can be recognized as components of initiation. Baptism, a ritual rebirth, is one of them. Confirmation in the faith, and possibly also Holy Orders, find their counterparts in initiation proper and, among many tribes, in the admission to secret religious societies that follows initiation. Communion, eating together of food that symbolizes the ritual (if not the god), is also part of initiation. The ordeals imposed on the initiates, often painful and humbling, may be linked to the sacrament of penance. Thus only two of the seven sacraments, marriage and extreme unction, are unaccounted for, and, since initiation among many tribes confers the right to marry, even this may be connected. The process of civilization seems almost to have run parallel to the separation of a single ritual into constituent parts, and their separation from each other in time' (*Symbolic Wounds,* 134). Four of these sacraments are evoked by Prouhèze's words – penance, baptism, the Eucharist, and marriage; Bettleheim's statement thus corroborates the above comparison of the religious ideas expressed here by Prouhèze and the concepts generally conveyed through initiation myths and rituals.
32 *Psychoanalytic Theory,* 105
33 *Ibid.,* 292. Jacques Petit has noted that in many of Claudel's plays, when the more violent and demanding of two rivals 'usurps' the beloved of the other, the 'victim' submits with surprising willingness to this seizure of what had been his (*Claudel et l'usurpateur,* Paris, Desclée de Brouwer 1971, 99–103).

Speaking of the *Soulier de satin*, Petit cites as an example Rodrigue's readiness to abandon Prouhèze to Camille – as seen, for example, in his discussion with Camille in II xi. Petit believes that this compliance on the part of the victim generally arises from a feeling of pride, a desire to be heroically superior to the 'usurper.' In Rodrigue's case, however, the person thus relinquished is the object of a guilty love, and this willingness to lose to a rival represents on the emotional level an expression of his wish for a 'prophylactic punishment' such as is described by Fenichel here.

34 See Erik H. Erikson, *Childhood and Society*, 2nd ed. rev. (New York, W.W. Norton 1963), esp. 104–8.

35 In the sense that, having committed an erotic wrong through his desires for a woman, Rodrigue would be sexually wounded through the influence of this same woman. This particular punishment thus conforms to the archaic talion principle – any deed may be undone, or at least sufficiently punished, by the inflicting of a similar deed upon the doer. From a psychological point of view, the talion principle reflects an animistic way of thinking that is especially characteristic of the undeveloped mind, but that survives in many more advanced individuals in covert form, and is reflected in such myths as that of the weapon which alone can cure the wound that it inflicts (see Fenichel, *Psychoanalytic Theory*, 44).

36 For these same reasons, castration is the punishment most children fear will be provoked by their actual incestuous wishes (see Hall, *Primer*, 109–10). As will be shown below, subsequent passages of the *Soulier de satin* help to confirm this interpretation of Prouhèze's remarks.

37 Similarly, both in Christianity and in many primitive cults the sacrificial death of the supernatural leader which the initiate must imitate has been interpreted as the voluntary submission of a son to his father in order to appease the anger that has been aroused by the wrongdoings of his children (Eliade, *Birth and Rebirth*, 132–3). The emasculation, either symbolic or real, of the participant during these ceremonies may reflect corresponding psychological factors.

38 Fenichel, *Psychoanalytic Theory*, 330–1

39 *Ibid.*, 83–9. In this and other scenes between Prouhèze and Rodrigue, Prouhèze, in contrast to Rodrigue's femininity, acts as the more masculine of the couple. This masculinity is in part a reflection of her own progress towards the attainment of androgyny, which will be discussed in Chapter 5.

40 For an explanation of the psychological mechanism of identification, see Hall, *Primer*, 41–7, 76–7.

Although in the monotheistic tradition *un dieu* is clearly not the equivalent of *Dieu*, this metaphor does suggest in context that through his bond with God Rodrigue will become in some respects similar to this omnipotent being. (A religious person like Claudel would not be likely to compare a character directly to God.)

41 Trans. James Strachey (New York, W.W. Norton 1962), 13–15. The fact that Rodrigue will experience this feeling of union with the divine through a relationship with a beloved woman also supports this interpretation, because, as Freud explains, 'There is ... one state ... in which [the ego does not maintain clear and sharp lines of demarcation]. At the height of being in love the boundary between ego and object threatens to melt away' (p. 13; see also Fenichel, *Psychoanalytic Theory*, 75).

The water-code imagery used in this scene by the Moon to describe its own light not only underscores on the emotional level, too, the innocence of this ideal state, but also helps to verify this interpretation, because water is associated in many cultures with the idea of a return to an all-providing mother, primal source not only of life, but of all happiness as well (Durand, *Structures anthropologiques*, 239–45; Freud himself, it will be noted, calls this sense of merger an 'oceanic' feeling). See also the discussion of Claudel's water-code imagery in O'Brien, *Maria Cross*, 166–75; O'Brien traces here the association of water in Claudel's works with the themes of bitterness, death, motherhood, and love.

42 *Psychoanalytic Theory*, 40

43 *Ibid.*, 425. The emphasis Claudel places throughout the *Soulier de satin* on the union of all spiritual forces within the heavenly realm helps to confirm this interpretation of religious salvation. (See Chapter 5; it should be noted that Fenichel speaks here specifically of an 'oral reunion ... with the universe'; the significance of the oral quality of this communion will be explained below.) The reader now also understands by flashback that on the emotional level it is this sense of totality of which the Jesuit speaks when he prays that Rodrigue and Prouhèze be allowed to achieve together *l'intégrité primitive*, through a *rapport inextinguible*.

44 The providing by a single situation of two different kinds of satisfaction is not unusual from a psychological standpoint. Like individual images and symbols, events and situations in literary works are frequently 'overdetermined'; that is, they convey several different emotional-level meanings simultaneously (see Lesser, *Fiction*, 153–60). Similarly, in life itself, the psychological implications of a single incident for the individual involved may be many and varied, and may not only overlap, as in Rodrigue's case, but even contradict each other (see Fenichel, *Psychoanalytic Theory*, 141–67).

In this particular passage, Rodrigue's future union with Prouhèze is stressed, and his achievement of a sense of merger with the universe is only indirectly suggested; as will be seen below, in other passages of the *Soulier de satin* in which a character's contact with the heavenly sphere is described the feeling of merger with his surroundings is emphasized much more strongly.

45 See Holland, *Literary Response*, 98.

46 In the second verset cited, Rodrigue's extraordinary sleep (*sans bords*) is compared not only to that of Adam, but also to that of Noah. Noah's sleep, like Adam's, led on one occasion to a sexually related humiliation which was to have serious consequences. The incident in question is related in Gen. 9:20–27 – having drunk too much wine, Noah falls asleep; his son Ham enters the tent, discovers his father lying naked, and rushes to tell his two brothers, who refuse to join him in making fun of their father's predicament. When Noah awakens he curses Ham's one Canaan and declares that he will be 'à l'égard de ses frères l'esclave des esclaves.'

47 Following the phrase *non point sommeil*, the entire expression *ce qu'il dort est la prélibation* functions as a renewal of the cliché, *dormir son sommeil*; this stylistic device helps to draw the reader's attention to the image and to stress the ideas it conveys.

48 Arnold Van Gennep, *The Rites of Passage*, trans. Monika Vizedon and Gabrielle Caffee (Chicago, University of Chicago Press 1960), 29. See also Sig-

mund Freud, *Totem and Taboo,* trans. James Strachey (New York, W.W. Norton 1952). Similarly, in Catholic tradition the worshipper is believed to identify with Christ by eating his body and blood during Communion.

49 From a psychological point of view, such beliefs derive from the infant's first attempts to identify with objects by means of oral incorporation; this mode of behaviour remains the basis for many later attempts at identification (Fenichel, *Psychoanalytic Theory,* 37–41).

50 Similarly, in many mythologies those who reach paradise are described as enjoying there an inexhaustible supply of oral gratification. In *The Hero with a Thousand Faces,* Joseph Campbell writes of the hero of his 'monomyth': 'The supreme boon desired ... is uninterrupted residence in the Paradise of the Milk that Never Fails: "Rejoice ye with Jerusalem, and be glad with her, all ye that love her: rejoice for joy with her, all ye that mourn for her: that ye may suck, and be satisfied with the breasts of her consolations; that ye may milk out, and be delighted with the abundance of her glory. For thus saith the Lord, Behold I will extend peace to her like a river ... then shall ye suck, ye shall be borne upon her sides, and be dandled upon her knee" (Isaiah, 66:10–13). Soul and body food, heart's ease, is the gift of "All heal," "the nipple inexhaustible" ' (New York, World Publishing, Meridian Books 1965, 176). Campbell cites many other myths that conform with this pattern, including the feasting of gods and heroes on ambrosia on Mt. Olympus; the consuming of the meat of Sachrimnir, the Cosmic Boar, in Wotan's mountain hall; and the serving of the flesh of Behemoth, Leviathan, and Ziz to the redeemed of Yahweh.

51 Durand, *Structures anthropologiques,* 356–60

52 Smith, *Teaching,* I, 343–9; Durand points out that this interpretation of Original Sin is supported by the erotic associations of the forbidden fruit itself (*Structures anthropologiques,* 116).

53 Several passages of III iii and III ix indicate that during his conquest of the Americas Rodrigue was unusually harsh towards both the native population and rival European adventurers. These passages help to justify on the narrative level of the text his eventual punishment through defeat on the battlefield.

54 The reference to death in this statement stresses once again the severity of the penitential ordeal. In addition, because the Angel declares that when man re-enters Eden he becomes associated with *le mystère de la création,* he emphasizes that man's attainment of this paradise involves his initiation into a totally new way of life.

The fisherman-code imagery used in the last versets of this passage to describe Prouhèze's role in leading Rodrigue to salvation is a development of a vehicle code used extensively in the first part of this scene to express the Angel's relationship to human beings, and elaborated on from time to time as the scene continues. The purifying nature of Rodrigue's experience in the Far East is underscored throughout the scene both by the development of this code and by the frequent direct references to water. When the Angel, for example, speaks of his relationship to Prouhèze, he tells of his desire to lead her to the heavenly 'waters,' 'ces eaux que j'habite' (61; 815); later, Prouhèze expresses her desire to bring Rodrigue, also, to heaven by pleading with the Angel: 'Il ne demandait qu'une goutte d'eau et toi, frère, aide-moi à lui donner l'Océan' (212; 822).

202 / NOTES TO PAGES 136-47

55 In the first scene of the play, the Jesuit also used two of these images – *Ange* and *blessé* – to predict Rodrigue's future suffering and redemption.

56 The innocent quality of this ideal state is underscored indirectly here by the location of the entire scene on the water.

57 Fenichel, *Psychoanalytic Theory*, 341–2

58 Rodrigue's eagerness to surrender himself to parent figures and thus gain their protection and support is underscored at the end of the scene by his plea to the *mère glaneuse* to take him with her to one of the convents of the *Mère Thérèse* (see IV xi 134–5; 947).

59 The statement *je sens que nous ne pouvons leur échapper* underscores Rodrigue's recognition of the need to submit fully and unquestioningly to these powers.

60 Who, it should be noted, is again described as 'filling' him.

61 As noted above, each reader's personal affective history is different, and each thus responds somewhat differently to any particular literary text. For this reason, Rodrigue's solution may not seem satisfactory to some readers – to those, for example, for whom the demand for submissiveness to which he complies represents a greater threat than the more masculine aggressiveness he discards. Some of these readers may abandon the play at the end of the second or third days, when this solution is outlined by Prouhèze; others may be left dissatisfied by the work as a whole. (The reader may, of course, abandon the text before the end for other reasons – general boredom, for example, or lack of responsiveness to religious ideas.)

62 The two parts of the story line outlined in the diagram are not, of course, expressed simultaneously in the text; the other levels of meaning, however, are conveyed at the same time, generally through one or the other of these parts of the narrative. (The religious level is sometimes expressed directly; the emotional stratum, however, is always conveyed through one of the other levels.) The corresponding positions of the two parts of the narrative level in the above diagram underscore the fact that each stage of Rodrigue's emotional-level experience is expressed several times in the text before the final resolution is presented.

63 A passage in which the expression of the emotional level of meaning results in an inconsistent development on the religious level is discussed in n. 14 above; this theological inconsistency confirms the above interpretation of the role of the emotional level in shaping all other levels of the work.

CHAPTER 8

1 Cf. Roman Jakobson's comment in 'Linguistics and Poetics': 'The repetitiveness effected by imparting the equivalence principle to the sequence makes reiterable not only the constituent sequences of the poetic message but the whole message as well. This capacity for reiteration, whether immediate or delayed, this reification of a poetic message and its constituents, this conversion of a message into an enduring thing, indeed all this represents an inherent and effective property of poetry' (*Style in Language*, ed. Thomas A. Sebeok, 371).

2 The expression 'invariant structure' is used here as defined by Riffaterre in 'La Poétisation du mot chez Victor Hugo': 'Toute structure est un système invariable de relations. Peu important les variations des éléments ainsi

organisés: les divers modèles obtenus demeurent interchangeables, formant autant de *variantes* de la même structure. Il va de soi que *l'invariant*, comme toute géométrie, n'est jamais observable dans la réalité: une structure n'est perçue qu'à travers ses variantes. On l'obtient par abstraction à partir de formes dont les constituents sont homologues, dont les rapports internes sont identiques. Dans tout message linguistique, le matériau qui donne forme visible à une structure est le matériau lexical' (*Cahiers de l'Association Internationale des Études Françaises*, No. 19, March 1967, 182).

3 As noted in Chapter 7, in order to demonstrate in the most effective manner the relative importance in the play of the types of images discussed in this chapter, frequency counts are not given, but the role of these images in conveying different levels of meaning is shown instead schematically, in Chart 2, found on the inside back cover; this chart is discussed at the end of this chapter.

4 The location of this scene on the water and in particular the Jesuit's description of the sea as a joyful spiritual force with which he will soon be joined (11; 667) underscore the purity and blissfulness of the new phase of life he is about to enter, and stress the relationship of this state to the 'paradise' of infancy.

5 The reference to the gratifying state towards which Rodrigue will be struggling and the implication that God could not fail to answer the Jesuit's humble yet confident prayer for his brother also help to mitigate the reader's anxiety here.

6 See Otto Fenichel, *The Psychoanalytic Theory of Neurosis*, 105, 360–5.

7 See discussion of this passage, pp. 23–4 above.

8 Although the text does not suggest in Pélage's case that he is denied ultimate spiritual salvation, the rigid, austere manner in which he expresses his religious ideas to Honoria in II iii indicates that he never knows the intense spiritual joy which is described by the more successful characters of the *Soulier de satin*, and which, as many critics have noted, is for Claudel an important aspect of true religious fulfilment (see above, Chapter 3, n. 4).

9 In *Les Structures anthropologiques de l'imaginaire* Gilbert Durand points out that eyes and vision are frequently used in mythology, religion, and literature to express the workings of the conscience or superego (157–9). From a psychological point of view, Camille's attributing of these eyes to God reflects his use of the defence mechanism known as projection (Fenichel, *Psychoanalytic Theory*, 165–6); in this case, the mechanism allows him to deny, at least consciously, his own underlying feelings of guilt.

10 See Fenichel, *Psychoanalytic Theory*, 78.

Later in the play (III x), Camille again expresses his heretical religious views at some length, underscoring the oedipal nature of his revolt by comparing God's interference in men's lives to the presence of a government minister at his clerk's wedding (158; 840), and emphasizing his desire to see this father figure made impotent by describing God as a *Vieillard dangereux*, who is not only *aveugle*, but also *un peu gâteux* (138–40; 839; see also discussion of this passage above, p. 21).

Camille's comparison of God to Jacob by implication also equates his own role with that of Joseph, another biblical son who returned to his father after many years of absence (Gen. 48). Unlike the Prodigal Son, Joseph returned home an influential person, a situation Camille would no doubt like to emulate.

11 The fire-code imagery used in this scene is discussed at length in Chapter 2, pp. 34–5. For a discussion of the sexual connotations of the term *ventre*, see Durand, *Structures anthropologiques*, 118–21 and 213–15. Durand notes that this word is used most often in connection with evil or dangerous qualities, an association which underscores the sinful intentions with which Camille approaches the continent.

12 The fire-code imagery of this passage also recalls a particular kind of initiation myth – that in which the hero descends into the underworld, struggles with a threatening woman, and is finally reborn into the better way of life that is his ultimate goal (see Joseph Campbell, *The Hero with a Thousand Faces*, 109–12). As in Camille's description, fire may function ambivalently in such myths, evoking both the sexual desire aroused by the woman and the eventual purification of the participant (Durand, *Structures anthropologiques*, 180–3; see also Northrop Frye, *Anatomy of Criticism*, Princeton, Princeton University Press 1957, 150). Other statements made by Camille in telling Prouhèze of his attraction to Africa underscore the parallel between his experiences and the destruction of the novice's old way of life during the initiation ceremony; Camille, for example, describes Africa as 'ce rien qui nous délivre de tout' (58; 675).

13 See III iii 42–3; 851.

14 The emasculated quality of Camille's attitude is underscored not only by his agreement to cease all physical contact with his wife, but also by his admission that the daughter she has borne since their marriage is more Rodrigue's child than his own (39–42; 834). The punishing quality of this surrender is emphasized by the sarcasm with which Camille speaks in this scene, for his cynical attitude reveals as well as hides his emotional wounds.

15 See above, p. 98.

16 The innocence of this state is further underscored by Camille's plea, *Ah! cessez d'être une femme*, which in itself stresses his wish to end his former guilty relationship.

17 In his article, '*Le Soulier de satin*, "somme" claudélienne,' Jacques Petit states that Camille, unlike Rodrigue, does not abandon his revolt, does not 'renonce, accepte et se soumet,' but is saved by God nonetheless (*Revue des lettres modernes*, Nos 180–2, III, 1968, 101–11). Petit elaborates this idea in *Claudel et l'usurpateur*, where he asserts that Camille is finally reconciled with his Omnipotent Father not because he gives in to the demands that God conveys to him through Prouhèze, but only because Prouhèze accepts the necessity of her own self-sacrifice and thereby justifies Camille's act of usurpation (see esp. pp. 55–6, 75–6). As just explained, however, Camille does adopt a submissive attitude towards Prouhèze, agreeing even to abstain from the physical contact he so long desired, and finally begs for her help; it therefore seems clear that Camille, too, surrenders his proud independence in order to gain the happiness he desires.

18 This tradition is based on the Catholic belief in the Communion of Saints, a principle that is also reflected in the *Soulier de satin* in the emphasis placed on the unification of all within the heavenly realm (see George Smith, ed., *The Teaching of the Catholic Church*, 2 vols, New York, Macmillan 1952, II, 671).

Since Prouhèze is asking the Holy Mother here specifically for help in fulfilling her obligations as a wife, when her prayer is related to the events portrayed in initiation myths and rituals it recalls that the chief purpose of the initiation of girls in most social groups is the instruction of the novice in the duties and responsibilities of an adult woman towards her husband, children, and society. As in such rites, Prouhèze has recently been secluded from others in a dark, enclosing location – Pélage's home, 'cette maison déserte et sombre' (I v 105; 684) – which is itself reminiscent of the 'womb' through which the initiate seeks rebirth (Mircea Eliade, *Birth and Rebirth*, trans. Willard R. Trask, New York, Harper 1958, 41–3).

19 See preceding note; also Durand, *Structures anthropologiques*, 257.

20 See Fenichel, *Psychoanalytic Theory*, 327, 341–2.

21 Prouhèze's repetition of her plea to be held back by the Virgin in terms of an *aile rognée* emphasizes this idea, because, when cited in connection with erotic desires, the act of flying generally functions as an expression of sexual excitement (Durand, *Structures anthropologiques*, 134–5).

22 The erotic associations of the foot are also evoked in the discussion between Prouhèze and Camille in III x. At first, Camille tells Prouhèze that he can still overcome her physically: 'Il ne tiendrait qu'à moi de prendre ce petit pied nu'; to which she acquiesces: 'Il est à vous, comme le reste. N'ai-je pas l'honneur d'être votre épouse?' (1–2; 832). Later in the scene, Prouhèze warns that she will soon escape Camille's domination: 'Adieu, Señor! je retire mon pied, quelqu'un est venu me chercher et je suis libre' (80; 836; Prouhèze refers here to her Guardian Angel).

23 The great value of this purity is underscored by the references to this shoe in the stage directions of the scene and in the title of the play as *le soulier de 'satin.'*

24 The unexpected use of the intimate term *Maman* to refer to the Virgin makes this expression especially forceful for the reader and emphasizes the Virgin's role as a mother-substitute for Prouhèze. The phrase as a whole is also highly effective because the affectionate term *Maman* contrasts semantically with both modifying adjectives – *grande* and *effrayante* – and because the entire phrase is placed in an attention-getting position at the end of the scene.

25 For a discussion of the erotic symbolism of the sword, see Durand, *Structures anthropologiques*, 166.

26 The religious and erotic implications of this development are also discussed on pp. 44–6 above. Two specific aspects of Prouhèze's purification as described here correspond to the experiences of the novice in initiation ceremonies – first, several images indicate that her sinful existence will be destroyed before she will be allowed to enter a new, innocent phase of life; and second, her cleansing and subsequent rebirth are closely associated here with water.

27 The text thus suggests that, on this level, Prouhèze's punishment is equivalent to the castration undergone by male characters, in that she, too, is compelled by a penalty that parallels her erotic crimes to give up her aggressive search for sexual satisfaction and to abandon herself completely to an all-powerful parent figure.

28 In this general context and following the phrase *au revoir*, both the literal and the figurative meanings of the expression *à Dieu* come to mind, and the phrase is especially striking for the reader as a result.

29 This phrase refers to both the purity of the mother who conceives without sexual activity and that of the child who is thus born without Original Sin (Smith,

Teaching, I, 526–8). When Prouhèze's daughter, Sept-Épées, is later described by Camille as more Rodrigue's child than his own, this stage direction reinforces by flashback the implication that she is a totally pure being (see below, p. 165).

The metaphor *Immaculée Conception* is particularly striking here because the stage directions specify that this is an *image* to be spread across the sky; since the idea of virgin birth is not generally expressed in concrete form, the reader is unexpectedly compelled to use his imagination in order to visualize the setting in question.

30 This fisherman-code imagery is discussed on pp. 134–5, above. Camille's role in relation to Prouhèze, although like that of the heavenly *pêcheur*, differs from the Angel's in an important way. As explained in Chapter 7, all children experience ambivalent feelings towards both of their parents; as a result, there are not only two archetypal feminine figures in literature and mythology, as described above, but also corresponding male figures, who represent on the one hand the power of the father to severely punish, and on the other his role as provider for, and protector of, his family (see also Campbell, *Hero,* 126–49). Although the Angel and Camille both fulfil double roles in relation to Prouhèze in that both speak of her need for punishment yet at the same time lead her towards redemption, the Angel's role, as underscored by his title, is primarily that of the benign father, while Camille's is that of the threatening one. (Theologically, an angel is an innocent, asexual being; see Durand, *Structures anthropologiques,* 145–9. Camille, on the other hand, is clearly irreligious and immoral, and behaves in a dangerously seductive way towards Prouhèze. The splitting of the ambivalently regarded parent figure into two characters is a common phenomenon in literature and has been likened to the psychological defence mechanism of 'splitting' or 'decomposing'; for a discussion of the function of such splitting in literary works and the implications of the procedure for the reader, see Norman Holland, *The Dynamics of Literary Response,* 56; also Marie Bonaparte, 'Poe and the Function of Literature,' *Art and Psychoanalysis,* ed. William Phillips, 67–71.)

31 The unexpected shift in tenor from Rodrigue to the higher power that works through Rodrigue attracts the reader's attention and thus heightens the effectiveness of this development. Similarly, the meaning of *passion* changes when it is repeated in these versets – first the word evokes Prouhèze's intense desire for Rodrigue, and then the Crucifixion; this shift stresses the connection between Prouhèze's desire and the penance demanded of her.

32 On the emotional level, both of these passages evoke erotic relationships – the first, through the lover's cliché *l'amour est maître de mon âme* and the second, through the reference to Rodrigue's heartbeat. (As Durand notes in *Structures anthropologiques,* 359–65, rhythmic activities of all types are universally associated with sexual rhythms; in this case, the association is strengthened by the previous erotic attraction of these individuals for each other.)

33 For a description of the child-god and child-hero figures, see C.G. Jung, 'The Psychology of the Child Archetype' and 'The Special Phenomenology of the Child Archetype,' in *Psyche and Symbol: A Selection from the Writings of C.G. Jung,* ed. Violet S. de Laszlo, trans. R.F.C. Hull (Garden City, New York, Doubleday, Anchor Books 1968; Jung's interpretation of this archetypal figure, however, is not considered valid by the present writer).

34 John F. Sullivan, rev. by John O'Leary, *The Externals of the Catholic Church* (New York, P.J. Kenedy 1951), 298

35 See Durand, *Structures anthropologiques*, 134–5. The most important such indication is Musique's refusal to show the mark either to the Sergeant or, at first, to the Viceroy; the Sergeant's statement that it is located 'au-dessous de l'épaule' (i viii 44; 704) helps to confirm this interpretation.

36 See Sullivan, *Externals*, 43; M.C. Nieuwbarn, *Church Symbolism*, trans. John Waterrens (London, Sands 1910), 51 and above, pp. 98–101.

37 Fenichel, *Psychoanalytic Theory*, 61

38 Frye, *Anatomy of Criticism*, 7; Frye later notes that such 'points of epiphany' are often presented in erotic terms, and thus seem to involve some degree of sexual fulfilment (203–5).

39 Durand, *Structures anthropologiques*, 262–3

40 *Ibid.*, 360, 374–6. When the meaning of the music-code imagery she uses so frequently becomes clear to the reader, Musique's own name helps to emphasize the concepts these images express. The effectiveness of this name as an image is, however, greatly reduced by the repetition of the term within the text; in fact, the name functions effectively as a metaphor only at those few points at which the use of other images makes the reader actively aware of its religious- or emotional-level significance.

41 The reader is also reassured that the union of Musique and the Viceroy will remain free of sin in the future, for as the couple begin to seek shelter for the night, Musique warns, 'Si vous essayez de m'embrasser, alors vous n'entendrez plus la musique!' and the Viceroy responds, 'Je ne veux que dormir près de toi en te donnant la main ... Plus tard quand Dieu nous aura unis, d'autres mystères nous sont réservés' (ii x 120–4; 766).

The continuing religious and emotional submission of this couple to the Holy Father is underscored again later in the play, when Musique offers her son – the product of their union – to God (iii i 84–7; 789).

42 Pp. 98–9

43 Musique speaks in this passage specifically of the *nacelles* on which souls will 'visit each other' in this ideal realm; Durand points out the frequent association of such vessels with the protective, comforting cradle (*Structures anthropologiques*, 267–8).

44 The similarities in the religious- and emotional-level experiences of Musique and Sept-Épées are underscored by parallels in their narrative-level adventures. Jean-Noël Segrestaa has pointed these out in 'Regards sur la composition du *Soulier de satin*': 'Avec Sept-Épées, fille de Prouhèze, c'est aussi la simplicité et la fraîcheur de Musique qui reparaissent; elle nage au-devant du fils de Musique et du Vice-roi de Naples comme Musique et son Sergent doré voguaient miraculeusement vers la Sicile ... Et, de même que le Sergent ... au moment d'arriver, coulait à pic après avoir "flotté un petit peu" au côté de Musique, la brave petite Bouchère se noie' (*Revue des lettres modernes*, 75).

45 iii x 43 –4; 834; Prouhèze confirms this later, when she tells Rodrigue of 'cet enfant que mon cœur tout rempli de vous a fait' (iii xiv 56; 851). See also above, n. 29.

46 See Nieuwbarn, *Church Symbolism*, 111.

47 These aspects of Sept-Épées's religious role also recall the story of Joan of Arc.

In the discussions of the adventures of Rodrigue and Pélage, it was explained that their respective attempts to conquer nations must end in failure because these efforts represent for them the aggressive release of wrongful erotic feelings. This is also true in Camille's case. Both Sept-Épées and the Viceroy, however, apparently meet with success in their militant endeavours. The difference lies in the fact that the successful characters do not use this aggressive activity as an outlet for forbidden sexual drives. In other words, within the emotional-level framework of the *Soulier de satin*, militant aggression is acceptable only when separated from guilty erotic drives.

48 See Jung, 'Child Archetype,' *Psyche and Symbol*, 124–5, 139–41. As is the case with many of these heroes, Sept-Épées's unusual birth involves two fathers – the first, physical father is of lowly status and the second, spiritual one is socially and religiously more worthy (see also Durand, *Structures anthropologiques*, 327–8).

49 As explained in Chapter 5, these lines express on the religious level of meaning Sept-Épées's feeling of being spiritually linked both with other human beings and with heavenly forces (see p. 104 above).

50 See Holland, *Literary Response*, 27–30.

51 *Ibid.*, 183–4

52 *Claudel, humour, joie et liberté*, 82–3

53 Psychoanalytic explanations of the specific means by which comedy facilitates the release of pent-up tension are found in Sigmund Freud, *Jokes and their Relation to the Unconscious*, trans. James Strachey (New York, W.W. Norton 1960); Ernst Kris, *Psychoanalytic Explorations in Art*; and Martin Grotjahn, *Beyond Laughter* (New York, McGraw-Hill 1957). See also Henri Bergson, *Le Rire*, esp. 147–53.

54 A a rule, humorous remarks that are deliberately directed by a character towards himself or his own distressing situation (as, for example, when Pélage mocks himself in the passage discussed on pp. 23–4 above) are less effective as defences than are those in which one character mocks another's difficulties, because in the former case the speaker reveals his underlying anxiety at the same time as he openly displays a relatively detached attitude towards his problems.

55 See Norman Holland, 'Prose and Minds: A Psychoanalytic Approach to Non-Fiction; *The Art of Victorian Prose*, eds George Levine and William Madden (New York, Oxford University Press 1968), 333.

56 See Holland, *Literary Response*, 67–74, 163–90; and Simon Lesser, *Fiction and the Unconscious*, 194.

57 The reader's identification with Prouhèze and Rodrigue is interrupted to some degree in these two scenes by the indirectness of the presentation of their stories in itself; the unexpectedly 'unrealistic' nature of the narrators involved, however, markedly intensifies this disruptive effect.

The appearance in the play of such spiritual figures as the Guardian Angel is probably considered similarly 'unrealistic' by most readers of the work. In such cases, however, the character's role as a representative of a blissful, protective situation is undoubtedly more important in reassuring the reader than is the emphasis drawn by his appearance to the fictional qualities of the work.

58 Author interventions that are humorous are particularly effective as defences because of the convergence of defensive elements. For a more detailed discussion of the way in which these interventions stress the fictional nature of the text, see Michael Wood, 'Providence's Play: *Le Soulier de satin*,' in *Claudel: A Reappraisal*, ed. Richard Griffiths (London, Rapp & Whiting 1968), 48–62.

59 Because Sept-Épées takes over Musique's role on the religious and emotional
levels of the text, these two characters are assigned the same three rows; a
diagonal line marks the end of Musique's role and the beginning of Sept-
Épées's.

The characters and countries included under the heading 'Minor Characters
and Countries' are as follows:

Jesuit	I i; II viii; IV i	Léopold Auguste,	
Arabs, Africa	I iii; II iv; III xiii	Fernand	III ii
Isabel	I iv, ix; III ii, vi, ix, xi	Almagro	III iii
First King,		Soldiers	III iv
Spain	I vi	Ramire	III vi, xi
America	I vi	The Far East	III viii; IV ii
Isidore	I vii, xi, xiv	Rodilard	III xi
Negress	I viii, xiv	Fishermen	IV i, v
Sergeant	I viii, xiv	Daibutsu	IV ii
Guardian Angel	I xii; III viii	Leal	IV ii, iv
Cavaliers	II i	La Bouchère	IV iii, x, xi
St. Jacques	II vi	Second King,	
Ruis Peraldo		Spain	IV iv, ix
and companions	II xii	Courtiers	IV iv, ix
Shadow	II xiii	Actress	IV iv, viii
Moon	II xiv	England	IV vi
Saints	III i	Rodriguez	IV vii
Eastern Europe	III i	Soldiers	IV xi
		Léon	IV xi

60 The calculations of relative intensity and, in the cases of the defences discussed below, of relative effectiveness, were based on the present writer's
response to the play, and they therefore – like the image counts given in Chapters 1 to 6 – necessarily involve a considerable degree of arbitrariness and subjectivity. Nevertheless, since an attempt was made to keep these calculations,
also, as consistent as possible as the chart was being constructed, the relative
intensity or effectiveness of the factors noted for each page is believed to be
shown with a useful degree of accuracy.

61 In calculating the number of images per page, image developments of all types
(as described in Chapter 2) were counted in terms of component elements,
rather than as single images.

62 Claudel himself suggested on several occasions that the various narrative-
level incidents of the *Soulier de satin* all express the same basic concepts and
that the repetition of these concepts as the work progresses helps to unify the
different parts of the play. Thus, writing of Diego Rodriguez's appearance in
the play – an incident often cited as being unrelated to the main events portrayed – Claudel explains: 'L'épisode de Diego Rodriguez se rattache au plan
général du *Soulier* non pas comme une pièce de mécanique à une autre pièce,
mais comme un ton à un autre ton ... Les mêmes sentiments entraînent des
mouvements non pas engrenés mais parallèles qui s'éclairent l'un par l'autre.
C'est comme la Vérité illustrée par des paraboles différents' (cited in Walter
Willems, *Paul Claudel, rassembleur de la terre*, Brussels, Desclée de Brouwer
1962, 209). See also *Mémoires improvisés*, 346.

It should be noted, however, that those versets of the text that convey the narrative level of meaning to the reader do not all directly express part of the invariant structure; some elements of the narrative serve only to give a minimum degree of coherence to the story line. Such passages may be expressive or evocative in themselves, but as a rule they are far less effective for the reader than those passages that do actualize the invariant structure, because, as explained in Chapter 7, it is the presence of this structure that is primarily responsible for the impact of the text on the reader.

63 Since the reader's involvement with the text derives primarily from his emotional identification with individual characters, Rodrigue's presence throughout the play is an important factor in giving the work unity for him.

64 This effect is, of course, strongest at the end of days and when a shift in narrative-level content converges with a break between scenes.

65 This is true to a lesser extent in Day 3.

66 The stories of several minor characters actualize only the first two stages of the invariant structure (e.g., the stories of Isidore, the Negress, and the Sergeant in I vii and viii). Nevertheless, because the feelings evoked by these stories are in each case very strongly defended against by the humorous treatment of the characters, the reader tends to respond with little intensity to the passages involved, and the failure of these characters to reach the final stage of the invariant structure therefore does not in itself arouse marked anxiety in him, as do the similar failures of Balthazar and Pélage.

(The interpretation of the narrative-level stories of several of the minor characters – the Courtiers of Day 4, for example – as expressions of conflicts similar to those experienced by the major characters may be questioned by some; these characters, however, do express various socially unacceptable desires – greedy wishes for wealth and prestige in the case of the Courtiers – that are frustrated and that in some cases result in considerable suffering for the individuals involved.)

67 In three scenes of Day 4 – iv, vi, and ix – the ironic effect of the text is heightened by the ambiguity of the situation. In these scenes, the reader and at least one character know facts of which the other characters are not aware, and many versets convey two levels of meaning as a result; the ambiguity is greatest in IV vi, because in this case the reader, too, is not certain at all times of the exact situation – are the feelings expressed by the Actress about the sea at all sincere, for example, or is she just acting?

68 Roland Barthes has explained the creation of suspense through such digressions in structuralist terms: 'La forme du récit est essentiellement marquée par deux pouvoirs: celui de distendre ses signes le long de l'histoire, et celui d'insérer dans ces distortions des expansions imprévisibles. [By *distortion* Barthes means the separation of the essential elements of the narrative sequence within the story; other, more or less extraneous information is then inserted between these narrative elements.] Le "suspense" n'est évidemment qu'une forme privilégiée, ou, si l'on préfère, exaspérée, de la distortion: d'une part, en maintenant une séquence ouverte (par des procédés emphatiques de retard et de relance), il renforce le contact avec le lecteur (l'auditeur), détient une fonction manifestement phatique; et d'autre part, il lui offre la menace d'une séquence inaccomplie, d'un paradigme ouvert ... c'est-à-dire d'un trouble logique, et c'est ce trouble qui est consommé avec angoisse et plaisir (d'autant qu'il est toujours, finalement, réparé); le "sus-

pense" est donc un jeu avec la structure, destiné, si l'on peut dire, à la risquer et à la glorifier' ('Introduction à l'analyse structurale des récits,' *Communications*, No. 8, 1966, 23–4). See also Lesser, *Fiction*, 139–40. In this connection, it should be noted that Day 4 is the longest of the four days, and that the average scene length is greatest here.

69 See, for example, Matt. 24:31, Apoc. 11:15.

70 André Blanc has written of these last words of the play: 'Le *Soulier de satin* … s'ouvre par la prière d'un père jésuite et la dernière réplique, explication de tout le drame, est mise non pas dans la bouche de Don Rodrigue, mais dans celle de l'humble frère Léon … Car c'est le prêtre seul qui délie et qui peut ainsi constater, comme témoin officiel, cette délivrance' (*Claudel, le point de vue de Dieu*, Paris, Éditions du Ceinturon 1965, 75). In emotional terms the priest clearly represents a father figure – and, in the last analysis, only a father can offer his children unqualified reassurance of forgiveness and admission to the comforting, protective realm over which he rules.

71 The narrative-level parallels between the last scene of the play and the first – the location of the action on the water, the approach of death, the presence of the priest, and the trumpet blast – underscore the relationship between these two parts of the work, and thus reinforce this impression in the reader's mind.

Glossary

This glossary provides definitions for the stylistic and structuralist terms of importance in this book; the definitions given cover only the sense in which these terms are used in this study.

ABSOLUTE IMAGE An image that expresses feelings or concepts that can be described directly only in very general terms, rather than a specific element of reality.

ADYNATON A hyperbole in which an event is magnified by being described in terms of an impossibility.

ALLITERATION The close repetition of a consonant sound at the beginning of words.

ANAPHORA The repetition of the same word or group of words at the beginning of each of a series of phrases.

ANTEPOSITION The placing of a word or phrase before that part of the sentence on which it depends grammatically.

APOSTROPHE Words addressed directly to a person or thing, usually as a digression.

APPOSITION The placing of a word or expression beside another in such a way that the second has the same grammatical construction as the first, and serves to clarify or expand upon its meaning.

ARCHETYPE An object or situation that is associated by most people with a group of specific feelings and thoughts.

ASSONANCE The close repetition of the same or similar vowel sounds.

ASYNDETON The omission of a conjunction that is ordinarily used to link two or more terms.

AUTONOMOUS VEHICLE A part of an extended image development that seems at first not to correspond to any element of the tenor system and that therefore appears to exist independently in the text. Autonomous elements are in fact absolute images conveying abstract concepts which, although not precisely identifiable by the reader, are part of the total system of ideas being expressed.

CODE The thematic material from which vehicle elements are drawn; Crucifixion-code images, for example, are images whose vehicles are terms related to the Crucifixion.

CONCRETIZATION The expression of an abstract concept in concrete form. An abstract concept is concretized when it is expressed in substantive form in a context that ordinarily requires a concrete term.

CLICHÉ A familiar, stereotyped expression.

DISJUNCTIVE A word or group of words that come between, and thus separate, two terms that would ordinarily follow each other directly.

DOUBLE IMAGE A figurative development consisting of two analogies whose vehicles are taken from different thematic areas; the meaning of the first image serves as the tenor of the second.

ELEMENT An individual part of either a vehicle or a tenor system; generally consists of a single word or phrase.

ELLIPSIS The omission of a word or words necessary for the syntactic completion of a statement.

EXTENDED IMAGE A figurative development in which an initial analogy is expanded by the comparison of ideas closely related to the original tenor to vehicles derived from the same theme as the first vehicle.

HUMOUR A general term for the laughable or the amusing; thought by many to derive from the perception of an incongruity and the resulting disappointment of one's expectations.

HYPERBOLE Deliberate exaggeration for purposes of emphasis.

IAMBIC RHYTHM A rhythmic pattern in which one or more unstressed syllables are followed by a stressed syllable.

IMAGE A figure of speech in which one idea is likened to another, different, and generally more concrete idea.

IMAGE-SEQUENCE A series of vehicle elements, drawn from different thematic areas, that express a single thought.

IRONY A form of humour that evokes two distinct, conflicting thoughts; that in effect says one thing and means another.

METALINGUISTIC STATEMENT A statement that functions as a comment on another statement of the text.

METAPHOR An image in which two concepts are compared by the substitution of one for the other in the text.

METONYMY An image in which a concept is likened to another with which it partially overlaps in meaning and which is substituted for it in the text, such as a part for the whole.

METRICAL RHYTHM The rhythm that results from the poetic organization of the text.

MICROCONTEXT The unmarked linguistic elements within which an unpredictable element appears, forming a stylistic device.

MIXED METAPHOR The use of terms derived from more than one thematic area within a single figurative expression.

PERIPHRASE The designation of a person or object through a description of one of its qualities, functions, or actions.

PERSONIFICATION The endowing of inanimate objects, parts of nature, or abstract ideas with human qualities or actions.

PHONEME The smallest discernible speech sound or group of sound features that are relevant to determine meaning in a language.

POLYSYNDETON The use of a conjunction where it is not required.

PROSE RHYTHM The rhythm that derives from the grammatical organization of the words.

RENEWED CLICHÉ A fixed expression whose stylistic effectiveness has been restored through its use in an unusual form or manner.

SIMILE An image in which the connection between the principal concept and the idea to which it is compared is directly stated.

STRESS-GROUP In French, a unit of one or more unstressed syllables followed by a stressed syllable; corresponds to a single grammatical unit.

STYLISTIC DEVICE An unpredictable linguistic element within an otherwise unmarked linguistic context; the context and the contrasting element together form the stylistic device.

SYLLEPSIS The grammatical linking of two or more semantically unrelated expressions by a single term.

SYSTEM A group of closely interrelated concepts that serve either as the tenor or as the vehicle of an extended image development.

TENOR The principal concept being expressed through an image.

VEHICLE The terms through which the principal concept being expressed through an image is conveyed to the reader, and with which this principal concept is compared.

Selected
bibliography

This bibliography lists the works of greatest interest in the preparation of this study. It is not intended as a complete bibliography in any of the designated subject areas.

I / WORKS BY CLAUDEL

Journal edited by François Varillon and Jacques Petit. Bibliothèque de la Pléiade, 2 vols. Paris, Gallimard 1968–9
Mémoires improvisés: quarante et un entretiens avec Jean Amrouche edited by Louis Fournier. Collection Idées. Paris, Gallimard 1969
Œuvres complètes de Paul Claudel 26 vols. Paris, Gallimard 1950–
Œuvres en prose edited by Jacques Petit and Charles Galpérine. Bibliothèque de la Pléiade. Paris, Gallimard 1965
Œuvre poétique Bibliothèque de la Pléiade. Paris, Gallimard 1957
Théâtre edited by Jacques Madaule and Jacques Petit. Bibliothèque de la Pléiade, 2 vols. Paris, Gallimard 1965–7

II / WORKS ON CLAUDEL

Angenendt, Paul *Eine Syntaktische-stilistische Untersuchung der Werke P. Claudels* Bonn, L. Neuendorff 1932
Antoine, Gérald *Les 'Cinq Grandes Odes' de Claudel, ou la poésie de la répétition* Paris, M.J. Minard, Lettres Modernes 1959
Autrand, Michel 'Les Énigmes de la quatrième journée du *Soulier de satin*' *Revue d'histoire du théâtre* xx (1968) 309–24
Baudot, Alain '*Le Soulier de satin* est-il une anti-tragédie?' *Études françaises* v (May 1969) 115–37
Beaumont, Ernest *The Theme of Beatrice in the Plays of Paul Claudel* London, Rockliff 1954
Bernard, Raymond 'La Description de la mer dans *Partage de Midi* et *le Soulier de satin*' *Revue des lettres modernes* Nos 134–6 (1966) 39–48
Brunel, Pierre '*Le Soulier de satin*' *devant la critique: dilemme et controverses* Situation No. 6. Paris, M.J. Minard, Lettres Modernes 1964

Chiari, Joseph *The Poetic Drama of Paul Claudel* New York, P.J. Kenedy 1954

Coenen-Mennemeier, Brigitta *Der aggressive Claudel: Eine Studie zu Periphrasen und Metaphern im Werke Paul Claudels* Forschungen zur romanischen Philologie II. Münster, Aschendorff 1957

Ganne, Pierre *Claudel, humour, joie et liberté* Paris, Éditions de l'Épi 1966

Griffiths, Richard, ed. *Claudel: A Reappraisal* London, Rapp & Whiting 1968

Guillemin, Henri *Claudel et son art d'écrire* Paris, Gallimard 1955

Imbs, Paul 'Étude sur la syntaxe du *Soulier de satin* de Paul Claudel (l'ellipse)' *Le Français moderne* XVI (1944) 243–79

Ince, W.N. 'The Unity of Claudel's *Le Soulier de satin*' *Symposium* XXII (1968) 35–53

Lerch, Emil *Versuchung und Gnade: Betrachtungen über Paul Claudel und sein Schauspiel 'Der seidene Schuh'* Wien, Heiler 1956

Lindemann, Reinhold *Kreuz und Eros: Paul Claudels Weltbild im 'Seidenen Schuh'* Frankfurt am Main, Josef Knecht 1955

Madaule, Jacques *Le Drame de Paul Claudel* Paris, Desclée de Brouwer 1936

– *Claudel et le langage* Paris, Desclée de Brouwer 1968

Maurer, Klara *Die biblische Symbolik im Werke Paul Claudels* Lucerne, E. Brunner-Schmid 1941

Maurocordato, Alexandre *L'Ode de Paul Claudel: essai de phénoménologie littéraire* Geneva, Droz 1955

Mazzega, Anne-Marie 'Le Soulier de satin, une parabole historique' *Revue des lettres modernes* Nos 150–2 (1967) 43–59

O'Brien, Conor Cruise *Maria Cross: Imaginative Patterns in a Group of Catholic Writers* Fresno, Calif., Academy Guild Press 1963

Petit, Jacques 'Pour une Explication du *Soulier de satin*' *Archives des lettres modernes* No. 58 (1965)

– 'Le Soulier de satin, "somme" claudélienne' *Revue des lettres modernes* Nos 180–2 (1968) 101–11

– *Claudel et l'usurpateur* Paris, Desclée de Brouwer 1971

Roberto, Eugène *Visions de Claudel* Marseille, Leconte 1958

Segrestaa, Jean-Noël 'Regards sur la composition du *Soulier de satin*' *Revue des lettres modernes* Nos 180–2 (1968) 59–81

Vachon, André *Le Temps et l'espace dans l'œuvre de Paul Claudel* Paris, Seuil 1965

Van Hoorn, H.J.W. *Poésie et mystique: Paul Claudel, poète chrétien* Geneva, Droz 1957

Vëto, Odile 'La Rédemption et l'amour: étude sur *Paul Claudel interroge le Cantique des Cantiques*' La Table ronde No. 191 (December 1963) 49–64

Wood, Michael 'The Theme of the Prison in *Le Soulier de satin*' *French Studies* XXII (1968) 225–38

III / STYLISTICS AND STRUCTURALISM

Barthes, Roland *Sur Racine* Paris, Seuil 1963

– 'Introduction à l'analyse structurale des récits' *Communications* No. 8 (1966) 15–32

Black, Max *Models and Metaphors* Ithaca, Cornell University Press 1962

Brooke-Rose, Christine *A Grammar of Metaphor* London, Martin Secker & Warburg 1958

Cohen, Jean *Structure du langage poétique* Paris, Flammarion 1966

Cressot, Marcel *Le Style et ses techniques* Paris, Presses Universitaires 1963

Ehrmann, Jacques 'Introduction' *Structuralism, Yale French Studies* Nos 36–7 (1966)

Fletcher, Angus *Allegory: The Theory of a Symbolic Mode* Ithaca, Cornell University Press 1964

Frye, Northrop *Anatomy of Criticism* Princeton, Princeton University Press 1957

Levin, Samuel *Linguistic Structures in Poetry* The Hague, Mouton 1962

Lévi-Strauss, Claude *Anthropologie structurale* Paris, Plon 1958

Richards, I.A. *The Philosophy of Rhetoric* New York, Oxford University Press 1936

Riffaterre, Michael *Le Style des 'Pléiades' de Gobineau: essai d'application d'une méthode stylistique* Geneva, Droz 1957

– *Essais de stylistique structurale* translated by Daniel Delas. Nouvelle Bibliothèque Scientifique. Paris, Flammarion 1971

– 'Sémantique du poème' *Cahiers de l'Association Internationale des Études Françaises* No. 23 (1971) 125–43, 349–62

Sayce, R.A. *Style in French Prose: A Method of Analysis* Oxford, Oxford University Press, Clarendon Press 1965

Sebeok, Thomas, ed. *Style in Language* New York, Wiley 1960

Ullman, Stephen *Language and Style* New York, Barnes & Noble 1964

IV / PSYCHOANALYTIC INTERPRETATION

Bergson, Henri *Le Rire: essai sur la signification du comique* Paris, Presses Universitaires 1962

Bettleheim, Bruno *Symbolic Wounds* Glencoe, The Free Press 1954

Bodkin, Maud *Archetypal Patterns in Poetry* Oxford, Oxford University Press 1934

Campbell, Joseph *The Hero with a Thousand Faces* Cleveland, World Publishing, Meridian Books 1956

Crews, Frederick 'Literature and Psychology' in *Relations of Literary Study*, edited by James Thorpe, 73–87. New York, Modern Language Association 1967

Durand, Gilbert *Les Structures anthropologiques de l'imaginaire* Paris, Presses Universitaires 1963

Erikson, Erik H. *Childhood and Society* 2nd ed. rev. New York, W.W. Norton 1963

Fenichel, Otto *The Psychoanalytic Theory of Neurosis* New York, W.W. Norton, 1945.

Freud, Sigmund *Totem and Taboo* translated by James Strachey. New York, W.W. Norton 1952

– *Civilization and its Discontents* translated by James Strachey. New York, W.W. Norton 1962

– *Jokes and their Relation to the Unconscious* translated by James Strachey. New York, W.W. Norton 1963

Grotjahn, Martin *Beyond Laughter: Humor and the Subconscious* New York, McGraw-Hill 1957

Hall, Calvin S. *A Primer of Freudian Psychology* New York, New American Library, Mentor Books 1954

Holland, Norman *The Dynamics of Literary Response* New York, Oxford University Press 1968

Kris, Ernst *Psychoanalytic Explorations in Art* New York, International Universities Press 1952

Lesser, Simon O. *Fiction and the Unconscious* New York, Random House, Vintage Books 1962

Mauron, Charles *Des Métaphores obsédantes au mythe personnel: introduction à la psychocritique* Paris, José Corti 1963

Phillips, William, ed. *Art and Psychoanalysis* Cleveland, World Publishing, Meridian Books 1963

Index

absolute image 5, 10, 11–12, 19;
  in image development 31–2,
  33–5, 44–6
Actress (character): and
  Rodrigue 6, 28–30, 36, 106;
  and structure of play 110n5,
  172n50, 175
Adam 121–3, 130, 131, 133–4
adynaton 87n7
affective message: see emotional level of meaning
Africa 68–9; and Pélage 23–4,
  151–2; and Prouhèze 30–1,
  157–8; and Camille 34–5, 38,
  153–4
allegory 94–5
alliteration 16, 53, 73–4, 89
Almagro (character) 172n59
Americas 3–4, 12, 14n20, 17–18,
  41–4, 55, 70–1; and Rodrigue
  7, 46–7, 61–2, 91, 93, 102–3,
  132–3, 134n53
anachronisms: see narrative
  level of meaning, inconsistencies in
anaphora 42, 44, 50, 70, 71–3
androgyny 122–3, 124, 127,
  130, 142, 166
angel, as image code 10–11, 88,
  117, 136–7
Angel (character): see Guardian
  Angel
angle of image: see ground of
  image
Announcer (character) 107, 108

anteposition 50, 51–3, 55,
  104n21
apodosis 56–8
appearance of printed text,
  stylistic devices related to
  64–6
Aquinas, Saint Thomas 94–5
archetype 5, 13–14, 65, 79, 99;
  in conveying religious level
  96; in conveying emotional
  level 124, 160n30
asyndeton 50, 54n6, 71–2
attack, as image code 6–7, 22,
  24–5, 44–6, 70, 93, 158–9
Augustine, Saint 135
author's interventions 21, 22,
  64, 107–14, 169–70, 171:
  see also Claudel, Paul
autonomous elements 28, 33–5

Balthazar (character) 148–50,
  155, 167, 174
baptism, as image code 96–7:
  see also water, as image code
barrier, as image code 58,
  72–3, 74, 85, 92–3, 103, 138
Barthes, Roland 175n68
Bettleheim, Bruno 125n31
Blanc, André 176n70
blindness, as image code 88–9,
  152–3
book, as image code 69–70, 119
La Bouchère (character) 82,
  83–4, 104, 165n44, 172n59

UNIVERSITY OF TORONTO ROMANCE SERIES

This book
was designed by
WILLIAM RUETER
under the direction of
ALLAN FLEMING
and was printed by
University
of Toronto
Press